The Language
of Fiction

University Press of New England

Hanover & London

Brian Shawver

The Language
of Fiction

A Writer's Stylebook

University Press of New England
www.upne.com
© 2013 University Press of New England
All rights reserved
Manufactured in the United States of America
Designed by Mindy Basinger Hill
Typeset in Quadraat

University Press of New England is a member
of the Green Press Initiative. The paper used
in this book meets their minimum requirement
for recycled paper.

Library of Congress Cataloging-in-Publication Data

Shawver, Brian.
The language of fiction: a writer's stylebook / by Brian
Shawver.
        p.   cm.
ISBN 978-1-61168-330-1 (pbk.: alk. paper) —
ISBN 978-1-61168-331-8 (ebook)
1. Fiction—Authorship—Handbooks, manuals, etc.
2. Fiction—Technique—Handbooks, manuals, etc.
I. Title.
PN3365.S53 2012
808'.042'dc23   2012034379

5   4   3   2   1

to Pamela

Contents

Introduction

When I was in college, a professor loaned me a book of Ernest Hemingway's selected letters. Because I loved Hemingway, and because I was a little startled that a professor had loaned me a book, I took it home and read it straightaway. For several hours, the letters engrossed me with their rich historical detail, their personal gossip, their casual wisdom. But at some point I hit upon a passage that cast everything else in deep shadow. It came from a note Ernest sent to F. Scott Fitzgerald in 1925, and it consisted of two sentences: "You write a swell letter. Glad somebody spells worse than I do."

I believe these words altered the course of my life, or at least my life as a writer, in two very different ways: while they led to a moment of profound revelation, they also prolonged my belief in a harmful delusion. Let's start with the happy stuff. Here's why it was wonderful to discover that these two titans of literature couldn't spell.

A writer, especially a beginning one, spends much of her time being daunted. She's daunted by the odds of getting published, by the breathless articles that claim (and have been claiming for more than a century) that fiction is a dying art form, by the rolling of the eyes she gets from her finance-major friends when she talks about her novel. But mostly she's daunted by her veneration for certain authors and their works.

Most writers became writers because one day they finished *Sense and Sensibility* or "Barn Burning" or *The House on Mango Street* and said to themselves, "Holy cow! I want to do *that*!" But doing *that*, one quickly learns, is incredibly hard. Compounding the problem is the fact that great writers make it seem like it's easy. When we read *The Lord of the Rings* we don't consider Tolkien's decades of labor, when we read James Joyce we don't think about how it took him an entire day to write three sentences. Instead, we conclude that an enormous gap exists between people like us and the mystical beings who create profound literature.

But then, if we're lucky, we learn that they were bad at spelling.

Anyone with a mild interest in Hemingway and Fitzgerald knows about their alcoholism, their irascibility, their misogyny, et cetera, so it wasn't news to me they had human foibles. But I'd always assumed that in terms of language usage they must have been perfect, that creating "Big Two-Hearted River" or *The Great Gatsby* would have required a virtually superhuman facility with every aspect of writing. The fact that I didn't have such facility, and didn't expect to get it anytime soon, daunted me tremendously. So when I learned Ernest and F. Scott didn't have total mastery either, it was like the scene in *Rocky IV* when Rocky makes Ivan Drago bleed, and his corner guy yells, "You see? He's not a machine! He's a man!"

In short, it gave me courage. It led me to the essential discovery every beginning writer must make: the writers you idolize are not goddesses and gods (except for Chaucer), they are men and women who struggle with language just as much as you do. If you don't accept that, you'll never join their ranks.

So that was the happy result of my discovery of Hemingway's remark. I was emboldened and empowered by the knowledge that the gates of literature don't deny entrance to someone just because he makes a few linguistic mistakes. Now for the bad news...

The realization that these two men had spelling problems led me to believe in one of the more insidious fallacies about writing: I came to think that spelling and its cousins (grammar, syntax, punctuation, convention) were not important aspects of the creation of art, that they were matters for copy-editors and composition teachers. Character, plot, thematic implication — these, not pedantic rules of grammar, were the tools I would employ to construct my masterpieces. I thought about correcting linguistic errors the way a young doctor might think about taking blood pressure: if you're any good, eventually you'll have people do it for you.

Utter nonsense, of course. To believe that it's somehow artistic to maintain an ignorance of prose mechanics or literary convention is simply a way to rationalize laziness. But certainly it's an easy idea to cling to, especially for beginning writers, who tend to be more interested in Grand Themes and complex plots than in pronoun-antecedent agreement. I personally grabbed onto this fallacy with both hands, as soon as I found that letter from Hemingway. If Ernest didn't care about such bagatelles as spelling and mechanics, then why should I?

What I didn't understand was that Hemingway's note to Fitzgerald exaggerated the problem (both of their spelling errors were minor), while taking a very Hemingway-esque dig at a rival. Also, forgiving oneself the occasional spelling mistake is much different from ignoring considerations of style and grammar. In truth, as I would later learn, Ernest was sort of obsessed with the way language worked, which you have to be if you rewrite a single page thirty-nine times, as he reportedly did for the ending of A Farewell to Arms. His grammatical mastery is also evident in the beginning of that book. As the critic Walter Ong has pointed out, his unexpected use of the demonstrative pronoun and the definite article in the first paragraph sharply influences the way the reader approaches the narrator and the subsequent action.

In other words, far from shrugging off the minor points of language usage, Hemingway knew that nothing else — the development of his story, the articulation of his themes, the interplay of his characters — would matter if he didn't control the nuances of grammar. The study of language and prose mechanics is not beneath a great writer's attention, it is the primary focus of it. I would have noticed this earlier if I'd been paying real attention to Hemingway's work, instead of just trying to figure out how to get to a bullfight.

The romantic myth of the writer as someone who eschews technical study in order to take a big fat bite out of life is thoroughly imbued in our culture. Aspiring writers are encouraged to believe that preparing oneself for a life of fiction writing should involve getting adventurous jobs, like Jack London did; or having a torrid and star-crossed love affair, like Mary Shelley did; or hitting the road with a few dollars and a tank of gas, like Jack Kerouac did; or suffering from profound psychological problems, like Sylvia Plath did; or getting drunk all the time (hard to choose just one example here). Even people who know better sometimes seem to think we should let aspiring writers maintain the delusion. Eventually, the argument goes, the school of hard knocks will teach them what being a writer actually means.

I wrote this book in part because I disagree with this laissez-faire approach. It's wrong to let people labor under a false idea, especially one that has been so doggedly perpetuated by the culture. I recall with a shudder how much of my time (and the time of many slush-pile readers) I wasted under the delusion that I could get by on raw talent and whatever usage rules had osmosed their way into me. This book argues that mastering language on a fundamental level is an essential part of becoming a literary artist, as necessary to focus on as character development or plot construction. I wish I had heard this thesis around the time I learned that Hemingway needed spell-check.

But more importantly, the book is meant to serve as a resource, because there aren't many other places for you to turn if you want to examine the relationship between language usage and fiction. Most creative writing books assert the importance of mastering prose mechanics, but not many give adequate advice about how to do it. I've never been in a creative writing classroom in which the instructor didn't tell students how crucial it was to know basic grammar, yet I've never been in one (including those I've taught) in which the class spent more than a few minutes talking about how to learn it. This is understandable—writers of fiction manuals have only a few hundred pages, and instructors have only sixteen weeks, to discuss the innumerable elements of their subject. Still, a destructive message is being sent: "Grammar, style, and convention are important, but not so important that we're going to talk about them."

This isn't to say that aspiring writers don't get any advice about the subject. Usually, they're told to read a comprehensive grammar manual or Strunk and White's *Elements of Style*. Unfortunately, the former tend to be long and dry (the *Allyn and Bacon Handbook* comes in at 909 pages in the sixth edition, and it's about as fun to read as the Canadian tax code), while the venerable latter is, I'm sorry to say, pretty dated. But the real problem with these books is that they aren't intended to be read and used exclusively by fiction writers. When someone tells an aspiring fiction writer to read them, the implication is that people writing novels and stories don't use language any differently from people writing vacuum cleaner manuals, or social science essays, or opinion pieces for the *Washington Post*. Suffice to say, I think that's a huge mistake.

This book will deal with matters of language as they pertain exclusively to the writer of fiction. Of course, the technical rules governing linguistics don't change depending on form and genre; a colon serves the same function in *Jane Eyre* as it does in *Cat Fancy*. But there are elements of language that a fiction writer needs to pay special attention to, just as there are some that he won't have to think about much. Ideally, we would all be able to pontificate on the subjunctive mood or the history of the hyphen. But in practical terms, it's more important for a creative writer to have mastery of the past perfect tense, for example, or the specific functions of the semi-colon. Furthermore, many elements of fictional convention and style, such as the methods for portraying dialogue or the techniques for indicating thought, will not be covered in grammar resources. Language is the water that all writers swim in, and you need to know your element as thoroughly as you can. But it's a big ocean, and mastery for a creative writer involves the knowledge of specific currents and swells. The investigation of these metaphorical currents and swells is the project of this book.

Along the way, I'll invoke a number of examples, a few of my own invention but usually ones from other writers. Most of the passages, naturally, will be taken from works of fiction. I tried to use an equal number of long and short works; while there may be subtle differences in the way novels use language as compared to stories, I don't think those differences are explicit enough to fall within the scope of this book. I also tried to favor contemporary writers over older ones, although I've cited a few nineteenth- and eighteenth-century texts (some elements of grammar haven't changed much). The only other criterion I consciously used was that the works must have been originally written in English, although I allowed for a few exceptions.

A book like this is necessarily limited by the fact that it doesn't offer the best method for improving your ability to write imaginative literature. The surest way to do that, as any experienced writer will tell you, is to read as much fiction as you can, and to write the rest of the time. As Giorgos Seferis said, "A lion is made up of the lambs he's digested, and I've been reading all my life."

As profound as that point is, it can also frustrate—and mislead—aspiring writers, because it implies that you can't write anything of value, or improve your work fundamentally, until you go into a cave for a few years and do nothing but read the classics. Is your own fiction destined to be clunky and unsophisticated until you've put the collected Faulkner and Morrison and Woolf under your belt?

The short answer is no. Reading will always empower you as a writer, but it's ridiculous to think you can't improve your work in other, more direct ways. In any human endeavor, experience will be the best teacher, but that doesn't mean it's the only one.

So while I encourage you to read widely and intelligently, I believe other methods can help you achieve the linguistic mastery every creative writer needs. Such methods include the consideration of stylistic decisions from different angles, the investigation of what is implied by literary conventions, and the analysis of how great writers have explored the vast potential of English. We'll do all these things and more throughout this book.

part one

Stylistic
Decisions

one

Which Verb Tense Should You Write In?

When a person sits down to write a novel or story, many decisions present themselves: when and where to set it, which narrative point of view to use, even what to call it (writers love to think up titles; it's much easier than actually writing). However, writers don't always consider one of the first and most significant decisions they're asked to make, which is whether to use the simple past tense or the simple present tense. Many writers select the former because that's what most books use. Others go with Door Number Two, the present tense, although they don't necessarily make that decision with any more awareness; often people do it because they like how it sounds.

So our first task will be to recognize that a verb tense should be chosen with deliberation and reflection, even if instinct will have something to do with it in the end. We'll investigate the subject by looking at the past and present tense exclusively. Some have tried the future tense, but it contains so many difficulties I don't think it's worth getting into.

THE PAST TENSE

It's something of a simplification to say you can write a work exclusively in the past tense. To do so implies that every construct will be of the "I saw the tree" variety, when in truth any work that uses past tense will also use the past perfect ("The tree had stood for years"), the past progressive ("The tree was standing in the shade"), and the past perfect progressive ("The tree had been standing since 1888"). But most of the sentences in such works will be in the simple form ("The tree stood"), so we'll stick with the term "past tense." (By the way, you don't need to know the names of the other tenses unless you plan to teach language arts in a Catholic middle school.)

If you write in the past tense, the reader will probably not think about your decision at all. When we pick up a book and see "It was a dark and stormy night," we do not have to make any mental adjustments. We've been trained to expect this formulation, because most of the narratives ever written have used it. The reason for its popularity, both historically and currently, is pretty straightforward.

Most fiction writers want their readers to engage in the "willing suspension of disbelief," as Coleridge put it. This means that readers of fiction are meant to slip into a state in which they believe in the events and people they're reading about. Readers know, of course, that Scarlett O'Hara and Tom Sawyer never existed, but for the length of the book they pretend not to know it. To encourage such a state, the writer must endow his work with verisimilitude, which means "a sense of reality." (Etymologically it means "likeness to truth," which may make you think of Stephen Colbert's "truthiness," and that's actually a close synonym.) I'll use that word (verisimilitude, not truthiness) a lot, so try to hang on to it.

To further augment the suspension of disbelief, a writer must avoid anything that reminds the reader that she is consuming a constructed series of words and scenes. Such reminders may include mistakes, like bad spelling and confusing metaphors; or stylistic eccentricities, like word repetition and Comic Sans font; or odd grammatical elements, like non-standard verb usage. If you open a novel and read, "It will be a dark and stormy night," you'll start thinking about the unusual use of the future tense. You will thus be considering the work as an artificial construction, rather than as a testimony of truth. It may be a fun intellectual exercise, but you won't believe in the story. The past tense, though stodgy and traditional, at least doesn't call attention to itself. It's the most popular form because it best protects the suspension of disbelief, which remains a cherished goal for most writers.

Along with the past tense's low profile comes an inherent authority. It is more declarative and assertive than any other tense, because it implies an immutability in what it describes. These are not images of Christmases-yet-to-come, the past tense tells us, these events already happened, and thus they cannot be changed or mitigated. Although millions of works use the past tense, whenever I think of examples, I come up with big, omniscient, nineteenth-century novels that ooze authority in their other elements, too: *Vanity Fair* ("While the present century was in its teens, and on one sunshiny morning in June, there drove up to the great iron gate . . .") and *Middlemarch* ("It was hardly a year since they had come to live at Tipton Grange . . .") and so on.

Further evidence of its authority can be seen in the fact that when we need people to believe a story we're telling, we use the past tense ("Mr. Farnsworth, I missed the client meeting because my wife went into labor . . ."). You may argue that we use this tense whenever we describe anything from the past, but that's not actually the case. Stories and anecdotes about past events are often related in the present tense ("So I'm at a bar, and I see this girl looking at me . . ."), because the style adds a sense of intensity or irony. News headlines use the present tense as well ("Scientists discover new species of badger"), because it contains a jazzy immediacy, and a headline's main job is to grab the reader's attention. But these tonal advantages come at the cost of authority. The past tense may not be flashy, but using it is a way of saying, "I assert that these things actually happened; either you believe me or you don't." In short, it's another method of establishing verisimilitude.

THE PRESENT TENSE

Conversely, there is something absurd about using the simple present tense when telling a story in written prose. Its very formulation implies a simultaneity of word and deed, yet the works themselves usually don't want us to believe in that simultaneity. For example, in Bharati Mukherjee's "The Management of Grief," when the narrator tells us, "Selfishly I break away from Kusum and run, sandals slapping against stones, to the water's edge," she is obviously not telling the truth; she couldn't be running along the beach and writing about doing so at the same time. (Well, she could, but we're not supposed to think she is.) In almost all instances of present-tense narration, such as when Barry Hannah's Ray tells us "she covers me with kisses" or when the narrator of Raymond Carver's "Where I'm Calling From" says, "I push the curtain away from the window," the author does not actually want us to believe the character is recording his actions at the moment he's performing them. Thus a present-tense work, especially those written in first person, asks the reader to adjust for an inherent artificiality.

In narratives with a third-person point of view, the contradiction is not as overt, because the narrator is not saying that he/she/it personally performed the actions. But even in these works, the verb tense stands at odds with the author's meaning. Let's look at a passage from Jhumpa Lahiri's novel *The Namesake*:

In the autumn of his sophomore year, he boards a particularly crowded train at Union Station. It is the Wednesday before Thanksgiving. He edges through the compartments, his duffel bag heavy with books for his Renaissance architecture class, for which he has to write a paper over the next five days.

Technically, the verb tense implies that the third-person narrator observes these events in real time. That is, the narrator appears to describe the protagonist, a young man named Gogol, boarding a train at the moment he does it. Then the narrator remembers to tell us it is Wednesday. Then the narrator sees — and simultaneously describes — Gogol edging through the compartments. And so on.

But of course Lahiri doesn't want us to think her narrator is staking out Gogol like some FBI agent, describing the subject's movements into a walkie-talkie. We know that's not the intention because Lahiri's novel, like most narratives, contains a sense of order. The narrator reveals a structured, coherent, and suspenseful story, and thus we get the sense that the narrator knows, at every moment, what will happen later on.

The present tense as a narrative form rarely makes sense when you think about it for very long. Part of its problem is that it doesn't cover any ground, chronologically speaking, especially compared to the past tense. I might say, "Neanderthals *roamed* southern Europe," or "I *lived* in Vermont as a baby," or "Today I *ate* lunch early," and the past tense works for all of them. The present tense has a much smaller window. It would no longer be accurate, for example, if I were to write, "I now write a sentence that includes the phrase 'smaller window.'" Yes, I recently wrote such a sentence, but that was ten seconds ago; it exists in the past. It doesn't matter how far or close — if it's already been accomplished, the past tense is the appropriate one to use. (NB: for the purposes of this chapter, I'm painting these tenses with a somewhat broad brush. Nuances and qualifications will be dealt with in chapters 6 and 15.)

But that's not the only way the present tense is removed from authenticity; there's a stylistic discrepancy going on too. I mentioned earlier that, although Mukherjee surely didn't intend such a reading, it's possible that the protagonist of her story, Mrs. Bhave, would be able to run along the beach while simultaneously writing about it. Perhaps she runs very slowly, scribbling a description on a waterproof notepad. Yet even if she were performing this odd feat of multitasking, she still wouldn't use the simple present tense; she would use the present progressive.

Think about how this works in real life. When you're on a cell phone, trying to meet up with someone, you say, "*I'm turning* left on Elm, now *I'm going* north, that's me, *I'm waving* at you." In other words, you use the present progressive. You don't say, "*I turn* left on Elm, now *I go* north, now *I wave* at you." The simple present tense is usually reserved for conditional statements ("I wear green on Thursdays," "Tim eats egg yolks when he trains") or statements that are true in a general, indefinite way ("I hate Mondays," "Dogs like ham"). When we describe limited, distinct events that are happening in the present, we say or write, "I *am wearing* a green shirt," or "Tim *is eating* an egg yolk," or "My dog *is revealing* his love of ham by drooling copiously." So fiction written in the present tense isn't just removed from reality by content, but also by style.

This dual separation from reality means that readers are more likely to notice the artificiality of the tense. If they think about it too much, it's harder for them to suspend disbelief. This point has many implications. In fact, it's the foundation for everything else that matters in terms of what you should think about if you're tempted to use the present tense.

For one thing, it's why the present tense is more popular, and probably less risky, in short fiction as opposed to novels, and in short novels as opposed to doorstops. Every time a reader picks up a present-tense narrative, she has to accept the bargain the writer presents her with: *you must try to suspend disbelief in spite of the artificiality of the verb tense, and I will try to make my use of this tense pay off.* If, as Poe suggested, we read a short story in one sitting, then we only have to make this distracting adjustment once with short fiction. Perhaps we make it seven or eight times when we read a short novel. But consider how many times you put down and pick up a book like *Moby-Dick* or *Oliver Twist* in the course of plowing through it. If Melville and Dickens had written in the present tense, those works would have asked the reader to make the bargain dozens of times. Of course, some long novels do use the present tense to good effect; Michael Chabon's *The Yiddish Policemen's Union*, Hilary Mantel's *Wolf Hall*, and Richard Ford's *Independence Day* are all over four hundred pages. But it's worth considering what a writer risks when she attempts the present tense in a long narrative.

So, if the present tense endangers suspension of disbelief—that sacred goal of most fiction writers—why use it at all?

One answer is that, paradoxical as it may sound, in some circumstances the present tense can actually augment, rather than detract from, a work's verisimilitude. We can see this in a passage from Wilkie Collins's *The Moonstone*:

> My daughter Penelope has just looked over my shoulder to see what I have done so far. She remarks that it is beautifully written, and every word of it true. But she points out one objection. She says what I have done so far isn't in the least what I was wanted to do.

In the pages that precede these lines, the narrator, a butler named Gabriel Betteredge, has used the past tense to describe events that occurred many years earlier. He's doing so, he tells us, at the insistence of the woman he serves; the narrative we have been reading, and which used the past tense, is the one he will turn in to his boss. But at a certain point, his daughter Penelope appears in his office, and at this moment Gabriel switches to the present tense (she *remarks*, she *points out*, she *says*) and stays with it until he returns to the memoir section.

Technically, Penelope's remarks are past events—we may imagine that Gabriel jotted them down right after she left—so they should be related in the past tense. But Collins thinks it would be misleading to use the same tense for such different parts of the narrative. After all, one section describes events that occurred decades earlier. Plus, the work is meant to be a historical record for his employer, so he would want the formal authority of the past tense. The other section describes remarks that are minutes old, and since the description is presumably intended for the reader's eyes only, a more casual tone seems appropriate. In short, Collins needed a way to separate these narratives, and the mechanism he used was verb tense. He violated the grammatical rule because he thought that following it might lead to even greater distraction and confusion on the reader's part.

Another way the present tense can create a heightened sense of reality appears in William Faulkner's *As I Lay Dying*. In the following passage, Darl, a member of the Bundren clan, tries to cross a swollen river with his brother:

> We submerge in turn, holding to the rope, being clutched by one another while the cold wall of the water sucks the slanting mud backward and upstream from beneath our feet and we are suspended so, groping along the cold bottom. Even the mud there is not still.

In this case, it might be useful to reverse the question — instead of asking why the present tense works, we should ask why the past tense wouldn't.

When a first-person narrator uses the past tense, the style usually implies that the words you're reading have been written down in some future moment, after the conflict has been resolved. Sometimes this is done overtly, as when Humbert Humbert admits he's writing the manuscript that we know as *Lolita* from prison, or when Robert Walton tells the story of *Frankenstein* from a ship in the Arctic. More often the narrator's situation at the time of the narrative's composition is unspecified but implied. When we read *Moby-Dick*, we may imagine that Ishmael, the only survivor of the *Pequod*'s wreck, has holed up in a rented apartment somewhere with a stack of paper and a fresh quill, even if Melville doesn't give us such a scene.

An imagined scenario like this doesn't work for *As I Lay Dying* for a simple reason: by the end Darl is in no position to write a narrative. If Faulkner had used the past tense, we would naturally wonder how Darl was able to retrospectively write about his family's travels to Jefferson, given what happens to him. (Spoiler alert: he goes crazy and is sent to an asylum.)

But it still may seem that we're left with the inherent contradiction of the present tense, the one we discussed in relation to Mukherjee's story. While it's impossible to imagine Darl writing his narrative after he's had his breakdown, it's equally hard to conceive of him writing the description of the river crossing at the moment of its occurrence.

So why does the present tense work in this case? Because throughout the novel we are not meant to assume that Darl, Jewel, Dewey Dell, Vardaman, and the rest of the present tense narrators have written the words at all; in fact, many of them are probably illiterate. Instead, Faulkner implies that we somehow experience the thoughts going through their heads at the precise moment they have them. An element of our suspension of disbelief in this work is that we assume some mystical force has gained access to their brainwaves and translates them into words. This translation is alchemic, magical, and thus it can be simultaneous. When Darl describes the way the water sucks the slanting mud, we're supposed to believe that his thoughts and the words representing them are basically the same, occurring at this exact moment, so the paradox of the present tense does not exist. To represent a character's consciousness, Faulkner asserts in this novel, it must be portrayed in all its immediacy and urgency, rather than as something that can be captured in retrospect. (We'll discuss the various methods of portraying consciousness in chapter 5.)

Another narrative that uses the present tense effectively is Margaret Atwood's dystopian novel *The Handmaid's Tale*. The protagonist is Offred, a young woman who lives in an oppressive, theocratic version of the United States. She narrates mostly in the present tense, as in the following passage:

> There's someone standing in the hall, near the door to the room where I stay. The hall is dusky, this is a man, his back to me; he's looking into the room, dark against his light. I can see now, it's the Commander, he isn't supposed to be here. He hears me coming, turns, hesitates, walks forward. Towards me. He is violating custom, what do I do now?

Unlike Mukherjee and Lahiri, Atwood apparently *does* want us to perceive that the scene is being recorded at the moment it is happening, even if we can't yet figure out how such a thing is possible. The suspense created by the passage, in which Offred sees a man lingering outside her room, is heightened by the fact that it's suspenseful for Offred, too. When she says, "It's the Commander," we discover this fact at the exact moment that she does. When she asks, "What do I do now?" she doesn't appear to know the answer any more than we do. In another passage much later, speaking to her missing daughter, she also exhibits an ignorance about later events:

> But I keep on going with this sad and hungry and sordid, this limping and mutilated story, because after all I want you to hear it, as I will yours too if I ever get the chance, if I meet you or if you escape, in the future or in heaven or in prison or underground, some other place.

Her ignorance is the same as ours, which makes her highly sympathetic.

Yet there are other moments in the novel where Offred does seem reflective and aware of what comes next. At one point she writes, "I don't want to be telling this story" before revealing a grisly scene, a clear sign that she knows what's coming. It's one of the hallmarks of her voice that at various times she appears to be entirely ignorant of her future, and at other times somewhat resigned to a known fate. In fact, Atwood creates suspense this way, by making us ask the question of how this is possible.

So how does she get away with it? For most of the novel Atwood uses a clever trick: she doesn't tell us how Offred is narrating in the present, but she does tell us one way she's *not* doing it. Early on the reader learns that Offred has no access to paper and pen, because it's illegal for people in her social role. Thus Atwood eliminates the absurd notion that the woman is jotting down her story; we have to believe she narrates it in some other way. Are her thoughts being transcribed by some futuristic monitoring system, are her brain waves being recorded by the government? For most of the book, we simply don't know. But we do know that Atwood has not insulted us by asking us to believe in a note-taking Offred, and that's enough for us to give her the benefit of the doubt.

It all works pretty well. We go along trusting the narrator to eventually make sense of it, so our suspension of disbelief remains. When the revelation of the present-tense mechanism comes (another spoiler alert), it also makes sense: it turns out that Offred has narrated her story into a tape recorder, after being delivered into the hands of a latter-day Underground Railroad. When we learn this, a few pages before the end, we retroactively understand how the present tense worked. In some cases when she expressed ignorance about what would happen, such as in the passage addressed to her daughter, she genuinely didn't know what her fate would be. In those moments when she used the present tense to describe her life in the Commander's house, as in the first cited passage, Offred used the present tense as a narrative device; it conveyed the immediacy and urgency she felt at the time. Interestingly, this is addressed in the final chapter, when a professor, two hundred years after Offred's death, explains the narrative mechanism she used:

> Obviously, it could not have been recorded during the period of time
> it recounts, since, if the author is telling the truth, no machine or tapes
> would have been available to her, nor would she have had a place of
> concealment for them. Also, there is a certain reflective quality about
> the narrative that would to my mind rule out synchronicity. It has the
> whiff of emotion recollected, if not in tranquility, at least post facto.

Atwood deliberately calls attention to the artificiality of the present tense by having a scholar question Offred's reasons for using it, just as the reader may have done.

So those are some examples in which using the present tense doesn't threaten suspension of disbelief at all, in which its use is actually more logical and verisimilar than the past tense. But there are other reasons to use it, too. The most obvious one is that the present tense can work for writers who don't expect or want the reader to believe in the story's reality.

Consider how we often use the present tense when we tell jokes: "A duck *walks* into a bar . . ." or "A priest *meets* a rabbi in a bowling alley . . ." Because the listener isn't being asked to believe in the reality of those scenarios, the paradox of using the present tense to describe an event that ostensibly happened in the past doesn't bother us. In effect, the nonsensical verb tense acknowledges the nonsensical nature of the content. In a similar vein, Italo Calvino, in the first chapter of *If on a winter's night a traveler*, writes, "You turn the book over in your hands, you scan the sentences on the back of the jacket, generic phrases that don't say a great deal . . ." Like the joke teller, Calvino isn't trying to get you to believe in the reality of his fictional world, at least not in the traditional sense (the protagonist in this novel is "you," a person searching for a genuine copy of the new Italo Calvino novel, so obviously verisimilitude isn't a priority), and the present tense underscores the unreality of it all.

The tendency to distrust the concept of suspension of disbelief, to overtly violate the traditional contract between reader and writer, is a trait of the movement we call "Postmodernism." It's an ambiguous concept, but for now we'll say that many Postmodernists saw verisimilitude as a tired old trick, one that could be compromised for the sake of style or effect or aesthetic/social/political commentary. It's no accident, then, that they ushered in our contemporary usage of the present tense. While authors have used the style for hundreds of years, in the past few decades it's become more prevalent than ever before. The trend began, more or less, with John Updike's 1960 novel *Rabbit, Run*.

Updike wasn't as radical as some of his contemporaries, but many of his works prioritize stylistic effect, which fits in with the Postmodern agenda. Updike does not use the present tense in *Rabbit, Run* for logistical purposes, like Collins or Faulkner or Atwood, but for stylistic ones. For him, the tense did not augment the reality of the content, it just helped the sound of the prose. As Updike himself said in an interview, "There are kinds of poetry, kinds of music you can strike off in the present tense." We see some of that music in the novel's finale:

This illusion trips him. His hands lift of their own and he feels the wind on his ears even before, his heels hitting heavily on the pavement at first but with an effortless gathering out of a kind of sweet panic growing lighter and quicker and quieter, he runs. Ah: runs. Runs.

This passage could have been told in the past tense without sacrificing coherence. But it simply sounds better this way. In avoiding the hard -ed endings of past tense verbs, the prose achieves a more fluid and graceful rhythm. And even when the verb forms are irregular (and thus wouldn't use –ed endings), Updike makes use of the lyricism of certain present tense sounds. Compare the thrusting, zooming "he runs. Ah: runs. Runs" to the nasal "he ran. Ah: ran. Ran."

In the years following *Rabbit, Run*, a number of major Postmodern works made use of Updike's innovation. Two in particular were Ishmael Reed's *Mumbo Jumbo* (1972) and Thomas Pynchon's *Gravity's Rainbow* (1973). Both novels disdain traditional verisimilitude (*Mumbo Jumbo* lacks anything like complex characters, while *Gravity's Rainbow*'s weirdness is too hard to sum up here), and both use the present tense as a natural supplement to their Postmodern ambitions. When you encounter a sentence like "Sprawled upon his knees is Zuzu, local doo-wack-a-doo and voo-do-dee-odo fizig" (from *Mumbo Jumbo*), verb tense is the least of your distractions. Pynchon's novel begins with the famous and inscrutable line "a screaming comes across the sky," which serves as a good indicator of how the immediacy, verve, and artifice of the present tense suit the iconoclasm of Postmodern narrative.

Postmodernism lost some steam after a couple decades, giving way to new forms of realism in the 1980s, but by then the use of the present tense had become something of a convention. What began as a technique that was emblematic of a rejection of traditional realism had become accepted as just another way to represent reality. In fact, the acceptance of the present tense as a convention may be Postmodernism's most significant legacy, now that many of its other innovations (metafiction, pastiche) have come to feel a little dated.

The upshot is that the risks posed by the paradoxical nature of the present tense are probably not as extreme as they once were, simply because of our familiarity with it. But I think it's worth noting that some of those risks remain. No matter how many times we pick up a story and read "Johnny wakes up to the smell of bacon" or "It is a cold day in Barcelona," a part of our reading brains still must make an adjustment, still must deal with the paradox of what is being asserted. A writer who uses the present tense must understand that risk, and decide whether the reward is worth it.

two

How Should You Format and Punctuate Dialogue?

Because examples in this chapter contain many quotation marks of their own, italics are used to indicate quoted or invented passages.

Most writers in English choose one of four methods to show that a character is speaking. Of these methods, using double quotation marks is far and away the most common in American prose, so I'll discuss it first. But I'll also investigate other styles, because too often beginning writers don't see them as options. Instead they go along with the double quotation mark convention out of some misguided idea that it's incorrect or inappropriate to do anything else. As our discussion will show, many published authors certainly don't believe that. Mastery means being able to exploit every element of language to create your desired effect, and nontraditional dialogue formatting, when used judiciously and thoughtfully, can be another weapon in your arsenal. However, it can also backfire, so I'll spend some time on the drawbacks of the various styles.

DOUBLE QUOTATION MARKS

To repeat: In most American fiction, writers use double quotation marks to indicate when a person is speaking. Here's a sliver of conversation from Ann Beattie's "A Vintage Thunderbird":

> "Would you think it was awful if I offered to go to bed with you?" Stephanie asked.
> "No," he said. "I think it would be very nice."

It's important to master the punctuation and formatting that go with this convention (and I mean *master*; it really should become second nature), mostly because you're likely to use it, but also because the other methods integrate its concepts. So here are five basics elements of formatting and punctuating dialogue that uses double quotation marks.

1. If a line of dialogue is followed by a dialogue tag (*he said, she commented,* etc.), then a comma should come before the final quotation mark. That's why there's a comma after the "No" in the example's second line: "No," *he said.*

Here's an exception: if the line of dialogue is a question, as is the first one in the Ann Beattie example, then you use a question mark and skip the comma. The same holds true for exclamations ("Hell yes!" *he said.*). Later on, we'll discuss some other implications of using exclamation points and question marks near or within dialogue.

2. When a dialogue tag comes *before* a line of speech, a comma should appear at the end of the tag and before the first quotation mark. In the example's first line, Beattie could have easily reversed the order of the tag and the dialogue, but if she'd done so, she would have needed a comma after the introductory tag. It would have looked like this: *Susan asked, "Would you think it was awful if I offered to go to bed with you?"*

3. Dialogue tags are often put between words spoken by a single character, as we can see in the Beattie example's last line: "No," *he said.* "I think it would be very nice." When punctuating such dialogue, it's important to pay attention to the grammar of the speech. To illustrate the point, let's look at two passages from Elizabeth Strout's *Olive Kitteridge*:

> "How can it be," said Olive, "that you grow up in Vermont and can't even drive a car?"

> "The funeral's private," Daisy told Harmon. "Just the family."

In both examples, the writer puts the dialogue tag in the middle of words spoken by a single character. There are significant differences between them, though. In the first one, a comma follows the dialogue tag *said Olive,* and the first word in Olive's second speech segment (*that*) is not capitalized. This is because the quoted segments form a monolithic grammatical element; *How can it be that you grow up in Vermont and can't even drive a car?* is a single sentence, which the author has decided to interrupt with a dialogue tag for pacing reasons.

On the other hand, the second example shows a character making two separate statements. The first part is a complete sentence: *The funeral's private*. The second part, *Just the family*, is a fragment, but it's meant to stand by itself. The dialogue tag, therefore, doesn't belong to both parts—it's commenting on the first statement exclusively, which is why it's attached to it with a comma. The period after *Harmon* and the subsequent capitalization of *Just* tell us that the remaining phrase stands alone, with no dialogue tag.

The final sentence from the Beattie example probably could have gone either way. If she had written "No," *he said*, "I think it would be very nice," we would have gotten the sense that all his words are meant to run together as one grammatical unit. Nothing wrong with that. But by putting a period after *said*, Beattie asks us to hear it differently—*No* becomes a sentence by itself. The character says it, then pauses to gather his thoughts (while the author gives us the dialogue tag), then delivers the last line.

4. You should indent whenever a new character speaks. In the second example from *Olive Kitteridge*, we know that Daisy says "*The funeral's private*" because a dialogue tag tells us so. But the remaining segment, "*Just the family*," is separated from everything by periods. So how do we know who said it? Because the lack of indentation tells us the words belong to the same person who gave us the first chunk of dialogue. Conversely, in the Beattie example, even without the *Stephanie asked* and *he said*, the indentation would make it clear that two different people were speaking.

This is a simple fact, but a significant one. Later we'll look at the nature of dialogue tags in general—why some authors choose to limit them, what they do for a reader's experience, etc.—but the more important point is that indentation, rather than *he said/she said*, is the primary way we know a new speaker has appeared.

However, some exceptions are useful to think about, one being a technical matter, and the other two stylistic. The technical rule involves what to do when a character speaks in paragraphs. In that case, indentation shows the organization of the speech, rather than signifying a new speaker. I find the convention for this to be confusing and inelegant, but it's what we're stuck with: you begin every paragraph the character speaks with quotation marks, but you don't put quotation marks at the end of the paragraphs until you get to the last one. The best way to handle this issue is to avoid having your characters give long speeches.

Again, indenting to show a new speaker is the basic rule, and if you're ever in doubt, stick with it. But writers with mastery may want to think about how to suspend the rule for effect. Consider the following example:

> "Crap, it's cold," Robert said. Lulu acted as though she hadn't heard him. He gave her a few seconds, but she merely continued to play with the buttons on her cell phone. So she hadn't forgiven him after all. Just like that time in Marseilles, except that now it truly was his fault, and they both knew it.
>
> "Don't you think?" he pressed.

The indentation of *"Don't you think?"* isn't necessary, according to our aforementioned rule, because the same character speaks both lines—a new speaker hasn't been introduced. However, the writer has chosen to indent the character's second line in order to give a sense of the enormity of the few seconds that have passed since he first spoke, the awkwardness of the silence and all it implies. The writer doesn't want *"Don't you think?"* to be read as a mere continuation of *"Crap, it's cold."* He wants to treat it as a second entity, which indeed it is—the first line is Robert's attempt at small talk, but the second one is a challenge, an engagement in a passive-aggressive battle with Lulu.

Violation of the convention can also go in the other direction, when a writer decides not to indent a line of dialogue even though a new speaker appears. The following exchange comes in the middle of a paragraph in a Joyce Carol Oates story:

> Grandmother at the stove stirring my oatmeal in a pan must have heard my thoughts for she said, "—Claire why don't you come live with me it's almost time isn't it?" and I said, "Oh yes," and Grandmother didn't seem to have heard for she repeated her question, turning now to look at me . . . and she laughed saying, "—Claire, why don't you come live with me it's time isn't it?" and again I said, "Oh yes Grandmother," nodding and blinking tears from my eyes, they were tears of infinite happiness, and relief, "—oh Grandmother, yes."

For aesthetic reasons, Oates wants this scene to hurry onward without the speed bumps of white space and indentation, so she crams the conversation into one paragraph, defying the conventions of dialogue because her verbal sensitivity tells her it's the right move. She also creates the quickened pace by making the entire paragraph one long sentence, and by eschewing commas to create run-ons (as in the line that gives the story its title: "Why

Don't You Come Live With Me It's Time"), but that's a different issue, one we'll deal with in chapter 12.

5. The last point has to do with the placement of punctuation. I've so far indicated that punctuation at the end of a segment of dialogue should go inside the quotation marks, and that guideline will stand you in good stead most of the time. However, it's only a rule in the American style, and it's only valid when we use commas and periods. Colons and semicolons always go outside the quotation marks. (For example, *The survey responses included* "Once a week"; "Sometimes, but never on Tuesdays"; "Every day"; and "Please repeat the question.") But this situation won't arise often. And in applying question marks and exclamation points, we use common sense. If a punctuation mark applies to the character, we give it to the character by placing it inside the quotation marks: "Is it Tuesday already?" *she asked,* and "You bet!" *he said.* (Notice, by the way, that the *she* and *he* following the question mark and exclamation mark are lowercase, as if commas had ended the dialogue.) But if the question or exclamation belongs to the author/narrator, we do not put it in within the quotation marks, because in those instances the mark isn't meant to inflect the character's words. *What did Antonia mean when she said,* "It's not likely"? may look strange, but it shows that the inquisitiveness belongs to the narrator, not Antonia.

Finally, you should notice that in all instances, the alternative punctuation marks replace the comma or period that would ordinarily end the dialogue. Unless someone's invented a new emoticon I'm not familiar with, you'll rarely see a period or comma directly next to a semicolon, colon, exclamation point or question mark.

SINGLE QUOTATION MARKS

This is the traditional style for authors in the United Kingdom ('I am going to thrash this man within an inch of his life,' writes P. G. Wodehouse), and by writers in the British Commonwealth states. The key word in that sentence may be "traditional," however, as many major writers in Britain (Ian McEwan, Rose Tremain) and the Anglosphere (Alice Munro, J. M. Coetzee) use the double quotes. It's also common for a British novel to contain single quotes when it's published in the UK, and double quotes when the American publisher takes over.

Most of what I said about double quotation marks holds true for single quotation marks. The difference is primarily visual, although that difference is worth considering. The single mark is less obtrusive than the double. Double marks, especially when the lines come at us quickly because of clipped language and lack of narrative description, can clutter a page. In the following passage from Hemingway's "A Clean, Well-Lighted Place," the dialogue indicators take up a large chunk of space relative to the rest of the type:

"What did he want to kill himself for?"
"How should I know."
"How did he do it?"
"He hung himself with a rope."
"Who cut him down?"
"His niece."
"Why did they do it?"
"Fear for his soul."

Even if the difference wouldn't be all that dramatic, using single quotes with a passage like this would allow you to keep the punctuation a bit more in the background.

There are some problems with the single quotation marks, though. In the American version, we use them when someone speaks within a quote, as in "I can't stand the way that woman uses the phrase 'ain't that a hoot' all the time." The British style inverts it, as in 'I can't stand the way that woman uses the phrase "ain't that a hoot" all the time.' I'd argue this looks imbalanced, since it calls more attention to the spoken nature of "ain't that a hoot" than to the rest of the words. But that could just be my American bias.

Another problem can occur when apostrophes are used at the end of a quotation. Imagine you want to give a character the sentence The chair does not belong to the teacher, it is the students'. In the American version, the final phrase would look like this: ". . . it is the students'." It's not pretty, but at least you can tell what it means. The final phrase in the British version would look like this: '. . . it is the students''. (The Brits put punctuation outside the quotation marks.) This is odd and misleading, because the two single quotation marks next to each other look like a double quotation mark, which has a different function. Chaos ensues.

However, such conundrums won't arise very often, and when they do you can rearrange the syntax to avoid ending with the apostrophe, so I wouldn't consider it a deal-breaker. Like deciding to drive on the other side of the road and to spell *color* without a *u*, the abandonment of single quotation marks may have been an American deviation that wasn't necessary.

NO PUNCTUATION MARKS AT ALL

More often than you'd think, writers simply don't use quotation marks, or any form of punctuation, to set off dialogue. Here's an example from Cormac McCarthy's *Blood Meridian*:

> The sergeant had been squatting on his heels and now he rose and spat.
> Well, he said. Is there any direction you caint see twenty mile in?
> The recruits studied the emptiness about.
> I dont believe the folks here is gone that long.
> They drank and walked back toward the jacal. Horses were being led along the narrow path.
> The captain was standing with his thumbs in his belt.
> I caint see where they've got to, said the sergeant.

Not putting quotation marks around dialogue is even less obtrusive than the British style. You get to do away with those ugly little punctuation markers entirely. McCarthy doesn't even use apostrophes in words like "dont," so clearly the all-letters-no-punctuation aspect of this method appeals to him.

There is an obvious risk here, however. After all, we don't use quotation marks because we think they're cute; they serve the purpose of alerting a reader to the fact that certain words belong to a character, rather than a narrator. Getting rid of them can lead to confusion. In the McCarthy example, you wouldn't be stupid if it took you a moment to realize that *The recruits studied the emptiness about* was not a line of speech, but the assertion of a third-person narrator. There are a couple of reasons, however, that McCarthy gets away with this style, reasons that may be instructive for all writers.

In this novel McCarthy uses a narrative prose that won't be confused with the speaking style of his characters, with one exception (a character called "The Judge," whose diction and syntax is uncannily similar to McCarthy's). When the line *The point was of hammered copper and it was cocked in its blood-soaked bindings on the shaft* gets followed by *Stout lad, ye'll make a shadetree sawbones yet*, it's not hard to figure out which is dialogue and which is narrative. The contrast between McCarthy's writing style and the characters' speaking style is so pronounced, quotation marks would almost be redundant.

Another thing McCarthy has going for him is that he doesn't comment much about what his characters look and sound like when they're speaking. He may go on for pages about dried riverbeds and desert mirages, but when he writes dialogue, he gets in and out quickly. He doesn't portray the expression Toadvine wears while saying *Kick his mouth in*, and he doesn't describe the gruffness in Glanton's voice when telling an old woman *By god you will shut up*. Thus McCarthy avoids blurring the line between narrator and character by keeping things brief, and by making the narrator largely absent when the characters speak.

This may illustrate one argument in favor of the style: it forces a discipline on the prose, by encouraging the writer to stop butting into the conversations so much. Generally speaking, writers don't need to comment on the speech of their characters as often as they do. The lack of quotation marks indicates that the writer is going to shut up and let the people in the story do the talking. The narrative presence will be so negligible that punctuation won't be required.

Another reason to drop quotation marks—a reason that might excuse any violation of convention—is because you're trying to achieve verisimilitude. Peter Carey's *True History of the Kelly Gang* is narrated by Ned Kelly, an Australian outlaw, and the book derives much of its power from Carey's realistic imitation of the character's voice. A necessary aspect of that voice is its lack of grammatical sophistication. Kelly writes 1st instead of *first*, he messes up pronouns, he mismatches subject and verb. And he renders conversation like this:

You don't know what you're talking about said he.
You are a coward she cried.

Carey's decision not to use the convention encourages us to believe, as we must if this novel is to have its full effect, that what we hold in our hands is not a carefully structured and manipulated fiction by a Booker Prize–winning author, but rather a document written by a nineteenth-century scoundrel-hero—a man who doesn't know you're supposed to put quotation marks around dialogue, and who wouldn't care if you told him.

DASHES

The fourth way to introduce a character's speech is to begin his line of dialogue with a dash. The most famous work that uses this method is James

Joyce's *Ulysses* (he also used it in "The Dead" and *Finnegans Wake*). Here's a conversation from the first chapter:

> —Will he come? The jejune Jesuit!
> Ceasing, he began to shave with care.
> —Tell me, Mulligan, Steven said quietly.
> —Yes, my love?
> —How long is Haines going to stay in this tower?

In this style, you get a big physical indicator that a character has begun speaking, but you don't get one that says he's stopped. This means that, just as in the McCarthy style of not using any quote indicators, you'll have to limit yourself in terms of dialogue tags or narrative sentences after the dialogue. Because there's no punctuation to announce when a speaker has finished, the readers' brains will hear everything in the character's voice until they've moved on to a new paragraph. Joyce manages his style using the same tactics as McCarthy, in that his characters' speech is often very different from his narrative tone, and he doesn't follow dialogue with a lot of descriptors in the same paragraph.

There's a kind of non-American feel to the dash, and in fact it seems to be more popular in Ireland than anywhere else. This may be due in part to Joyce's influence, but also because Irish writers often emphasize the mellifluousness or eccentricity of Irish speech. Dashes, which are more stark and unobtrusive than quotation marks, distract less from the poetry of the verbal language. Roddy Doyle, a writer known for his skill at capturing contemporary Irish vernacular, uses the dash regularly as a dialogue marker. Here's an excerpt from his novel *The Van*:

> —D'yeh want to be me partner, Jim? said Bimbo.
> —Wha's tha'?
> —Would yeh think abou' becomin' me partner? said Bimbo.
> He looked serious in a way that only Bimbo could look; deadly serious.
> —We'd make a great team, said Bimbo. —I was talkin' to Maggie
> about it.
> —Jaysis—said Jimmy Sr. —Eh, thanks very much, Bimbo. I don't
> know.

Another Celtic writer, Irvine Welsh, used the same method in *Trainspotting*. Though Welsh is Scottish, not Irish, he also attempts to capture a highly particular accent:

—How should ah go n see her? It's goat nowt tae dae wi me, ah sais defensively.

—Yir her friend, ur ye no?

Even if this isn't the traditional way to introduce speech, there is a logic to it. One of the purposes of the dash, as we'll see in chapter 13, is to draw attention to what follows, and presumably a writer always wants dialogue to contain a certain amount of emphasis.

OTHER METHODS

If none of these four ways of indicating speech provides the effect you want, there are alternative methods. The French convention is to use the guillemet («Bonjour» dit la femme), and German dialogue often looks like this: „Guten tag," sagte er. It's hard to imagine getting away with either method in an English-language work without seeming very pompous, but you never know. South African writer Nadine Gordimer uses dashes not just to introduce quotes but to close them off as well. Here's a conversation from her novel The Pick-Up:

—Nothing gives a white male more of a kick than humiliating a woman driver.—

—Sexual stimulation for yahoos—

—Someone else shouted something . . . like Idikaza . . . mlungu . . . What's that, 'white bitch', isn't it?—Her question to the black friend.

—Well, just about as bad. This city, man!—

You get used to it after a while, but it does look strange at first.

Another possible method is to put dialogue in italics. The major complication here is that italicizing is one of the conventions for thought, and even if you use another method for doing that (see chapter 5), a reader may still associate italics with something going on inside a character's head. But if that distraction can be overcome, there may be artistic reasons for using italics for dialogue, as is the case in some sections of Nicole Krauss's The History of Love:

It's from a novel by the late Isaac Moritz, he said.

Ha, ha, I said.

Pardon me?

No, it's not, I said.

Yes, it is, he said.
No, it's not.
I assure you it is.
I assure you it isn't.
Yes sir, it <u>is</u>.
OK, I said. It is.

The dialogue italics appear in the sections narrated by Leo Gursky, a lonely, dying old man consumed by his memories. In relating conversation in a format normally reserved for the portrayal of thought, Krauss blurs the line between what occurs in Leo's mind (where he spends most of his time) and what occurs in the real world. The italics in the above exchange call attention to Leo's interior experience of the conversation at the same moment the conversation occurs in the novel's external reality.

Daniel Defoe, the father of the modern novel, occasionally used italics for dialogue tags rather than the dialogue itself in *Moll Flanders*:

Sit down Robin, *says the old lady*, I must have some talk with you;
With all my heart, madam, *says Robin, looking very merry*; I hope it is
about a good wife, for I am at a great loss in that affair: How can that
be *says his mother*, did you not say, you resolved to have Mrs. Betty?

If it works, perhaps it does so because the novel limits its amount of dialogue. *Moll Flanders* was intended to imitate an actual confession narrative, so too much dialogue might have felt artificial—a real narrator wouldn't remember exactly what people said. In light of that, it's interesting to note that Defoe has Moll use the present tense with most of her tags. As we saw in chapter 1, the present tense carries a sense of artificiality ("a duck walks into a bar . . ."), so maybe this was Moll/Defoe's attempt to acknowledge the inexact nature of recollected speech.

three

What Words Should You Use to Present Dialogue?

As in chapter 2, italics indicate quoted or invented words and passages.

In the previous chapter we discussed how to format speech in fiction, which mostly had to do with visual markers—whether to use italics, quotation marks, and so on. But that's not the only issue you have to deal with when you use dialogue. In addition to deciding how it looks, you also have to determine how your characters' words will be given context by the narrative words that surround them (and, of equal importance, the words that don't).

This is a significant decision, because it's tied to a larger philosophical question: How much control do you want to exert over your reader's experience? A writer's language constantly answers this question, whether he's aware of it or not. Consider these two sentences:

Trees lined the road.

Stout oaks and narrow sycamores, their leaves blending in a salmagundi of greens and browns, lined the dusty, twisting road to Hampstead.

The sentences say basically the same thing, but the first is stripped bare, while the second is chock full of descriptive modifiers. In effect, the writer of the first sentence has ceded control of the image. He says, *Hey reader, it's your tree, it's your road, you get to fill in the rest of the blanks.* Conversely, the second writer takes away the reader's agency by supplying the exact image she wants him to have. The reader doesn't get to put aspens or maples in there, he doesn't get to pave the road or send it to Brooklyn. The writer rules this scene with an iron fist, and the reader acts merely as the receptacle for the images she provides.

Because of the way I've described it, you may be leaning toward the first method. We like freedom and the people who offer it to us, while we're suspicious of those who crave control. But we could also give it a different spin, by saying the first writer has abdicated too much responsibility, either out of laziness or a lack of confidence in his descriptive abilities, while the second writer has provided a vivid, detailed image. Of course, there's no way to judge this without knowing context. While some writers err on the side of exercising too much control, and while others would rather provide too few details than too many, in general most writers adjust the level of control based on how much the reader needs to know at any given moment.

I went into all this because we're now going to talk about the use (or non-use) of dialogue tags and other dialogue supplements, which always present the writer with a question of control. Because readers cannot actually hear the character's voice, you've got to decide how much you want to manage your readers' experience of it—whether you think a good deal of control is called for, or whether readers should imagine the speech for themselves. The language you use to present dialogue will be the primary way you implement your decision.

VERBS IN DIALOGUE TAGS

Dialogue tags are the narrative phrases that accompany lines of dialogue. At their simplest, they do nothing more than indicate who is speaking by attaching *he said* or *she said* to the quoted words. This method is the equivalent of writing *trees lined the road*—the writer gets the point across, but offers his readers little guidance. Or, to put it more positively, the author encourages his readers to imagine on their own how the line is spoken.

The other method, at least when we consider dialogue tags that consist only of a subject and verb, is to include a synonym or variation of *said*, some verb that gives specific guidance (or a totalitarian command, depending on how you look at it) about how readers should hear the words. *He said* becomes *he bellowed*, or *she said* becomes *she cackled*, and so on.

Opinions vary about whether you should stick exclusively with the verb *said* in dialogue tags, or whether you should mix it up by using the occasional *explained* and *replied* and *questioned* and *asserted*. No matter what you've heard, there isn't a hard-and-fast rule. As with almost every other subject in this book, grappling with the issue for yourself, coming to your own conclusions after considering the implications of both sides, is an element of linguistic mastery. So let's look at the pros and cons of each style.

To begin with the proponents of the simpler method, consider the advice Elmore Leonard gives in *Ten Rules of Writing*: "Never use a verb other than 'said' to carry dialogue." While this may be dogmatic, it has some good reasoning behind it, which has less to do with the virtues of the *he said* style than with the sins of the alternative. The first such sin is that packing your dialogue tags with too many synonyms for *said* can be distracting and even melodramatic. We can see this in Richard Connell's story "The Most Dangerous Game." Here are some of the dialogue lines from the opening scene, with the verbs in the tags italicized (I've cut out a lot of stuff, so the content won't make sense):

"What island is it?" Rainsford *asked*.
"The old charts call it 'Ship-Trap Island,'" Whitney *replied*.
"Can't see it," *remarked* Rainsford.
"You've good eyes," *said* Whitney, with a laugh.
"Nor four yards," *admitted* Rainsford.
"It will be light enough in Rio," *promised* Whitney.
"The best sport in the world," *agreed* Rainsford.
"For the hunter," *amended* Whitney.
"Don't talk rot, Whitney," *said* Rainsford.
"Perhaps the jaguar does," *observed* Whitney.
"Nonsense," *laughed* Rainsford.
"Cannibals?" *suggested* Rainsford.

The multitude of different verbs in the dialogue tags implies that the writer equates good prose with the possession of a thesaurus, and it's distracting. At some point we stop thinking about two men gazing out into the Caribbean night, and instead we see the image of Richard Connell chewing on his pencil, desperately trying to come up with a new way to say *replied* or *observed* or *amended*. As a general rule, anytime the reader starts thinking about your phrasing instead of the characters' behavior, you've made a mistake.

Another reason the overdiversification of tags (let's call it) might rankle has to do with the freedom-versus-control issue. The writer who uses alternative verbs exerts more control over his reader's experience, which sometimes is perfectly fine. The writer may be the only one who knows Judy *screeched* her line, so it's nice of him to share the information with us. However, including too many of these alternate verbs can indicate a pathological need to control the way the reader hears the dialogue. A writer who does this comes off as the literary equivalent of a micromanager. He wants us to hear every line as he hears it, he refuses to allow us to participate in the experience. And as every good reader knows, great fiction demands that we use our imaginative faculties; it doesn't just tell us to sit there quietly.

But perhaps the most troubling result of using too many alternative tag verbs is that they can come off as insulting. Dialogue tags are primarily intended to help the reader, and there's a fine line between assisting someone and patronizing him. When Connell wrote that Whitney *observed* something and Rainsford *admitted* something, perhaps he thought he was being helpful. But it's not helpful, because we can already tell what the characters' words have done. Adding these verbs to the tags implies we're too stupid to understand that Rainsford's speech constitutes an admission and Whitney's an observation. *Oh, the phrase "Can't see it" is a remark? Thanks a ton, Mr. Connell, I wouldn't have known that if you hadn't told me.* In other words, the problem is redundancy—you've given the readers information they already have, assistance they don't need.

Alternative verbs often seem redundant because so many other elements of dialogue can give clues as to how something is said. Often, punctuation obviates the need for an alternative verb. When you write *"Is that you?" she queried*, the word *queried* does something that the question mark already accomplished. The line *"Stop bothering me!" Tom yelled* is not aided by the verb *yelled*, because the exclamation mark already told us about Tom's emphatic voice.

The content of the dialogue can also render the tag verb redundant. This is another big problem in "The Most Dangerous Game." (I'm sorry to keep picking on this story, but it really could have used some editing.) When Whitney comments, *Great sport, hunting*, and Rainsford says, *The best sport in the world*, it is quite evident that Rainsford agrees with Whitney about how great hunting is. Thus, *Rainsford agreed* as a dialogue tag comes off as silly.

Finally, the context of the scene may indicate how the words in the quotes are spoken. If two characters are hiding from a vengeful mobster in a closet and one of them says, *I hope he doesn't find us*, you probably don't need to write *he whispered*. For some reason, dialogue tags that ignore the context of a scene often seem the most melodramatic, as when a besotted lover says, *I've never met anyone like you* and the tag is *she gasped*, or when a gunshot victim says, *I think St. Luke's is the closest hospital*, and the writer adds *he groaned*. In such moments, writers appear too desperate to reinforce a certain trait or condition. It's as if they don't think they've done a good enough job establishing the emotion of the scene, so they have to remind you with an emotive verb.

In other words, there's a lot to consider. Because of that, and out of fear they'll have to correct such mistakes over and over again, many creative writing teachers offer a variation of Elmore Leonard's advice. The virtue of *he said* is not its elegance or mellifluousness, it's the fact that it doesn't call attention to itself, and it's hard to make a glaring mistake with it. Thus its use results from a simple risk-reward calculation. Quite often, tags like *she implored* and *he avowed* either distract or insult the reader. And even when they are used well, they don't add all that much; a well-placed *he asserted* works only marginally better than *he said*. So why not stick with the simple form of attribution?

Because mastery involves exploiting narrow margins, that's why. A fiction writer shouldn't look for ways to play it safe, she shouldn't be shooed away from difficulty with the notion that there's a cheap way to avoid it. Instead, she has to engage with that difficulty until she can use it to her advantage, even if the advantage is slight. The payoff of most techniques is not immediately noticeable, but these things add up.

So what is that payoff? What can be gained from taking the risk of ignoring Elmore Leonard's advice? I'm afraid the approach to this question has to begin with negativity, as the approach to the previous one did—that is, we'll look at what's wrong with *he said*.

Great writers instinctively want every word and phrase of their fiction to serve more than one function. *He said*, for all of its virtues, has one job and one job only—to let the reader know who's talking. In its functionality and simplicity, it's not much different from the attribution method you see in play scripts (HAMLET: O I die, Horatio). It can thus strike us as unambitious, underemployed. When we replace *said* with a different verb, we're trying to get the dialogue tag to multitask, we're making it perform an enriching function as well as a technical one. A well-placed *Manning pronounced*, for example, not only tells the reader who's speaking, it lets him know that Manning spoke with a certain fastidiousness that might not be indicated by punctuation, content, or context. It exerts more control over the reader's experience.

An alternative verb tag can also spice up the prose. The main problem with dialogue tags in general is that they get repetitive, which explains why writers have come up so many ways of getting around them. If you decide to use only *he said*, you either are going to numb the reader to the phrase eventually, or you're going to have to go out of your way to attribute dialogue by other means (with the methods we'll discuss later). The occasional *he replied* or *she agreed*, even if they're redundant, can at least save the reader from seeing *said* for the umpteenth time, which in itself can become a distraction.

Furthermore, all those simple tags have an effect on pace and rhythm. Specifically, they often result in a staccato, rapid-fire sound that doesn't work for every narrative. It's easy enough for Elmore Leonard to follow his own advice, because he mostly writes crime thrillers, in which the monosyllabic tags match well with the clipped, tough-guy speaking style. "*Screw off,*" *Chili articulated* or "*They whacked Bibi,*" *Raymond proclaimed* wouldn't sound right. Similarly, when Raymond Carver limited himself to this style, it suited the subdued atmosphere of many of his stories and characters. But not everyone writes crime thrillers, and not everyone shares Carver's aesthetic. Sometimes an alternative verb is tonally or rhythmically appropriate. When Dickens writes, "*In their presence,*" *pursued Pumblechook*, he's extending the alliteration of the phrase, as well as using a verb that matches the grandiloquence of Pumblechook's speaking style. Or consider this line from *Amalgamation Polka* by Stephen Wright: "*Damn you,*" *muttered Potter, and, as abruptly as he appeared, he was gone.* Besides providing consonance with "Potter," the "t" sound in "muttered" contributes another hard stress to the sentence, along with "Damn you" and "abruptly" and "appeared."

Finally, and perhaps most obviously, sometimes you need your reader to understand that a character speaks in a particular fashion, and you can't think of any other way to do it. In a line like "*I love your shirt Madge,*" *Eileen scoffed*, the tag verb serves a necessary function. Without it, we wouldn't understand why Madge then bursts into tears. At such a moment, the limitations of fiction as a form have forced the reader into using an alternative tag verb. A screenwriter or a playwright can depend on actors to get across the subtext of neutral lines. But often a fiction writer can only control a character's intonation or intention through dialogue tags.

NO TAGS

We've probably all had the experience of reading a work that eschewed tags, and being frustrated at some point when we lost track of who was saying what. An extreme example of such an experience occurs to anyone who tries to tackle William Gaddis's JR, which contains pages and pages of unattributed dialogue. That example is extreme, because Gaddis doesn't really want us to know who's saying what. In most cases authors expect you to follow along, whether that's a reasonable expectation or not.

The impulse to eliminate tags comes from the desire to let dialogue fulfill its destiny to be, as David Lodge puts it, "the purest form of showing." Lodge points out that when a writer uses dialogue, "language exactly mirrors the event" being described, because that event is simply the transmission of words. When we read the phrase *How nice to see you, Madame Bovary* or *Don't cry, Celie*, we see fiction come as close to an exact simulation of reality as it can get. Narrative helper phrases like *he said* diminish the verisimilar effect.

Let's look at this effect in action. In a passage from Hemingway's "Indian Camp," the dialogue represents what it would be like to actually hear two people have this conversation:

"Why did he kill himself, Daddy?"
"I don't know, Nick. He couldn't stand things, I guess."
"Do many men kill themselves, Daddy?"
"Not very many, Nick."
"Do many women?"
"Hardly ever."
"Don't they ever?"
"Oh yes. They do sometimes."
"Daddy?"
"Yes?"
"Where did Uncle George go?"
"He'll turn up all right."
"Is dying hard, Daddy?"
"No, I think it's pretty easy, Nick. It all depends."

As we read, we may feel like we're eavesdropping on Nick and his dad. If Hemingway had thrown in writerly flourishes like *the father intoned* or *the boy queried* or even *he said*, he would only have reminded us that we are reading a story.

One risk involved with this technique, as I mentioned, is possible confusion. Nothing will distract a reader like the moment when she discovers that it was Bob who said *You're dead to me* while Brenda begged for forgiveness, rather than the other way around. One obvious solution is to do what Hemingway does in the above passage: have the characters occasionally address each other by name. This, too, has its risks, though. We don't often use people's names in our conversations with them, unless we're trying to sell them something, or unless the conversation involves hierarchical roles (*Very good, Jeeves; Why, Mommy?; I'll do that right away, Mr. President*). Therefore, if you do it too often or too clumsily, it can strike an expository note; the reader will know you're only doing it to replace dialogue tags.

Also, eschewing tags has a visual effect on the prose. Without the tags completing the lines, so to speak, the text can read almost like a play script or screenplay—that is, very quickly, cinematically. In the "Indian Camp" passage, I don't think it's a problem, because Hemingway doesn't want us to linger over the characters' gestures and expressions, he just wants us to think about what they're saying. But you may not always want your dialogue to move so quickly. Consider the following passage from Susan Glaspell's "A Jury of Her Peers," in which two farm wives discuss a woman who might have killed her husband:

> "It was an awful thing was done in this house that night, Mrs. Hale," said the sheriff's wife. "Killing a man while he slept—slipping a thing round his neck that choked the life out of him."
> Mrs. Hale's hand went out to the birdcage.
> "His neck. Choked the life out of him."
> "We don't know who killed him," whispered Mrs. Peters wildly. "We don't know."
> Mrs. Hale had not moved. "If there had been years and years of—nothing, then a bird to sing to you, it would be awful—still—after the bird was still."
> It was as if something within her not herself had spoken, and it found in Mrs. Peters something she did not know as herself.
> "I know what stillness is," she said, in a queer, monotonous voice. "When we homesteaded in Dakota, and my first baby died—after he was two years old—and me with no other then—"
> Mrs. Hale stirred.
> "How soon do you suppose they'll be through looking for evidence?"
> "I know what stillness is," repeated Mrs. Peters, in just that same way. Then she too pulled back. "The law has got to punish crime, Mrs. Hale," she said in her tight little way.

Glaspell actually doesn't use alternative tag verbs as much as she uses dialogue supplements, which we'll talk about in the next section. Still, the point remains: stripping dialogue passages of everything but the dialogue itself can work against you. In this scene, none of the narrative parts do anything in terms of plot or action; they just describe the way the characters sit and speak. Yet such dialogue supplements are necessary. They provide editorial descriptors, such as the reference to Mrs. Peters's *tight little way* of speaking, and the tag *said the sheriff's wife*, which reminds us of Mrs. Peters's social role. The movements and speech patterns of the women, as they come to terms with a terrible crime and their belief that it was justified, are crucial to the tension. The reader needs to know that Mrs. Hale touches the birdcage (which serves as a symbol of oppression), that she then sits stilly as her friend discusses the stillness of her household, that Mrs. Peters whispers one of her lines *wildly*, and so on. Here's how that passage would look without any dialogue tags or supplements:

> "It was an awful thing was done in this house that night, Mrs. Hale. Killing a man while he slept—slipping a thing round his neck that choked the life out of him."
>
> "His neck. Choked the life out of him."
>
> "We don't know who killed him. We don't know."
>
> "If there had been years and years of—nothing, then a bird to sing to you, it would be awful—still—after the bird was still."
>
> "I know what stillness is. When we homesteaded in Dakota, and my first baby died—after he was two years old—and me with no other then—"
>
> "How soon do you suppose they'll be through looking for evidence?"
>
> "I know what stillness is. The law has got to punish crime, Mrs. Hale."

This version not only reads too fast, it's disjointed and decontextualized. It doesn't accomplish nearly as much as the previous one, in which Glaspell makes her dialogue tags and their supplements do some multitasking.

DIALOGUE SUPPLEMENTS

You've probably already figured out that there's a way to handle the problem of dialogue tags besides just avoiding them. In discussing how alternative verbs can be useful, for example, I showed a sample sentence that included the tag *she scoffed*, and claimed that the verb prevents the reader from getting confused. But of course you also could have aided the reader with the tag *Eileen said ironically*, or *Eileen said with a menacing sneer*.

If we consider constructions like *he said* or *she promised* the core of a dialogue tag, additions to these phrases that exert more of the writer's control might be considered tag supplements. By that, I mean adverbs, as in *he said seriously*; modifying phrases, as in *she said, with a fleck of muffin spurting from her mouth*; and descriptive sentences that come between or after dialogue, as in *"That was a hell of a meal." Then, as if to prove it, he picked his teeth with his pinkie's fingernail.* Let's look at them in order.

In chapter 8 you'll be treated to a lengthy discussion on adverbs, which deals with the popular notion that adverbs are often redundant. I argue against that prejudice — they really do get a bum rap — but I have to admit that in dialogue tags, adverbs cause trouble. For one thing, tags that include adverbs force you into the pattern of subject-verb-modifier (*she said boisterously; the mailman said quietly; Jo asked suspiciously*), which gets boring and awkward. More worrisome is the fact that, because the words in dialogue can tell the reader so much, an adverb in a tag is likely to be unnecessary. Throwing in an adverb when the speech itself has already taken care of business results in absurdity or redundancy, as in the following examples:

"Would you like to come in for a nightcap?" Marco said insinuatingly.

"It's gonna cost ya," the cop said menacingly.

"But I'll miss you so," Letitia said lovingly.

In these lines, the adverbs appear to be trying too hard; the writer wants control over how you hear the speech, but he exerts that control clumsily. The adverb in a dialogue tag can't really be subtle, in part because we realize the sentiment either was or should have been taken care of by the dialogue itself, and in part because adverbs tend to be polysyllabic –ly words that get stuck there at the end of the tag, waving in the breeze.

A way to get the adverb's work done without placing so much pressure on one word is to attach a modifying phrase to the tag. Here are some examples to get us started:

"Let's get out of here," said the thief, glancing at the security camera.

"No more, I beg you," Angela said to the waiter, rubbing her bloated belly.

"I'll do it!" said Rich, encouraged by that afternoon's whiskey.

The nice feature of this method, as you can see, is that you don't have to include actual adverbs — the entire phrase acts as an adverb, because it modifies or describes the clause in the tag. It offers you a good deal of control, much more than does an adverb, which is limited by the definition of a single word. You can pack an adverbial phrase with as much detail as you want — make the waiter tall, make the security camera a Nikon, whatever it takes to tighten your grip on the reader's experience of the scene.

The primary danger, as far as I can tell, lies in overuse. Modifying phrases attached to dialogue tags tend to begin with verbals — words that were once verbs and have now been turned into something else (in our examples, *glancing*, *rubbing*, and *encouraged*). Because most verbals end in either *–ing* or *–ed*, and because a distinctive cadence develops when you add a phrase to a simple independent clause like *he said*, a reader will notice if you use too many of them. We can only handle so much of *he said, turning to the senorita and cackling in that distinctive way of his* before we see the prose as mannered or repetitive.

Now for the last technique: including descriptive sentences that are near the dialogue, yet that are not grammatically connected to it. Let's approach it with an example from Peter Carey's *Parrot and Olivier in America*:

> I said that if he had an interest in my comfort he could deal with the retching varlet who had been deposited in my cabin.
> "Ha-ha." He laughed. "Very good, sir." His French was poor.

Twice — once after "Ha-ha," once after "sir," Carey includes sentences that aren't technically dialogue tags, yet which exert some control over how the reader hears the speech. "He laughed" could be a dialogue tag, if you lowercased the *He* and replaced the period with a comma, but I don't think that would be as effective. In that scenario, we would hear the character laughing out the words *ha-ha*, and Carey would have made an error of redundancy — writing, *"Ha-ha," he laughed* is like writing *"Yes," she affirmed* or *"Damn," he cursed*. Instead, because *He laughed* is a separate sentence following the dialogue, we experience the events chronologically: first, the character says *ha-ha*, then the character laughs. See how this leads to an entirely different interpretation? It shows us that the character rendered his *ha-ha* with falseness; his verbal response was perfunctory and sycophantic. A second later, though, he actually does laugh, perhaps out of embarrassed discomfort, when he realizes the narrator hadn't been kidding.

This is very subtle, perhaps too subtle for a reader to even acknowledge except subconsciously (although that certainly is enough). The next sentence, *His French was poor*, is more direct in controlling how we hear the speaker. It still isn't a dialogue tag because of its grammatical separation from *Very good, sir*, but it serves the same purpose as a tag like *he said haltingly*, or *he said in bad French*. The reason for doing it this way may be entirely stylistic, at least in this example. The sentence is sharp, it matches the style of prose (short, simple sentences) that surrounds it, and — most significantly — it separates the narrator from the speaker. This narrator doesn't want to be in the same sentence as the character; his words are sequestered, completely separate from the joyless *ha-ha* and the smug *Very good, sir*. The narrator describes the speech from the outside, not participating even grammatically in the content of the dialogue.

I've chosen this example from Carey not only because it illustrates why a writer might use separate sentences to control a reader's experience of speech but also for transitional purposes. Usually dialogue tags and their accessories help us imagine the tone/pitch/volume of a character's voice, or what he does while he speaks. In the final sentence of this passage, however, Carey's dialogue supplement *His French was poor* tells us about the particular way the actual syllables are pronounced. In other words, it raises the thorny and controversial issue of how to portray an accent, something we'll delve into in chapter 4.

four

___

Should You Phonetically Represent Characters' Speech?

___

As in chapters 2 and 3, italics generally indicate quoted or invented passages. Hereafter, chapters revert to the standard practice of using quotation marks.

When a character speaks with a particularity of pronunciation, whether it's an accent or a speech impediment or some other verbal tic, a writer has a few options for communicating the sound of that speech. One common style is to render the speech in Standard English, then give instructions on how to pronounce it in the dialogue tag or supplement, as in these examples:

"You should park your car over there," Jim said in his South Boston accent.

"I wouldn't wish that on Wilma." Amy drew out the phrase for a full thirty seconds because of her stutter.

At the other end of the spectrum is the method of portraying oddities of speech in the dialogue itself. Writers who do this indicate exactly how the words sound by using phonetic spellings and constructions, like this:

"Yoo shood pahk ya cah ovah they-uh," Jim said.

"I w-w-wouldn't w-w-w-ish that on W-w-w-w-w-w-ilma," Amy said.

Although there are other methods of communicating how a character pronounces words, we'll start by looking at these two extremes.

STICKING WITH DIALOGUE SUPPLEMENTS

We can deal with this end of the spectrum rather easily, because it's not far removed from what we talked about in the last chapter. Writing something like *"Take out the trash,"* Mom *screamed* is not so different from writing *"Take out the trash,"* Mom *said in her Cajun patois.* You simply describe the accent or impediment outside of the dialogue, often but not always in the tag. The benefits are 1) you don't slow down a reader by making him translate the letters and sounds into words, 2) it doesn't take as long to craft the dialogue, and 3) it never seems silly, as bad phonetic dialogue does.

One downside is that there are only so many words that specifically describe accents. There's *drawl* and *twang* for Southerners and *brogue* for Irishmen and *burr* for Scots, but not many others. Thus you're limited to using modifying phrases with the tag *he said,* or to adding a new sentence, as Carey did in the line cited in the previous chapter: *"Very good sir." His French was poor.* That doesn't seem so tough, until you consider what a vague thing pronunciation is, especially if you're going beyond the generic—if you want your character to sound not just Canadian, for example, but Manitoban or New Brunswickian or Torontonian—and how trying to describe something elusive or vague can lead to overwriting. An author who wants you to hear an accent, but who doesn't have the right verb or noun for it, might be tempted to craft florid prose: *His voice, shaped by the hills of Andalusia, melted off his tongue like dulce de leche.* Or the author might invoke a cliché: *his Alabama accent was as thick as molasses.* Or he might throw up his hands and use a cultural reference: *He sounded like Pierce Brosnan, with a touch of Margaret Thatcher.* All of these, I hope we can see, are mistakes.

PHONETIC CONSTRUCTION OF ACCENT

Harold Bloom calls our literary period "The Ironic Age," and indeed contemporary writers like to mock, while avoiding that which might bring mockery upon them: sentimentality, coincidence, melodrama, even plain old earnestness. If the trend these days is to lean toward the end of the spectrum that involves letting dialogue tags do most of the work, perhaps it's because phonetic representation of speech is easy to make fun of. To be sure, there are other reasons to avoid this style, as we shall see, but fear of looking silly is one of the major ones, and that's rarely a good reason to avoid doing something. I'm always impressed by students who try phonetic representation, even when they fail. Plus, many excellent writers (including Chaucer, the granddaddy of ironists) have used the phonetic style.

One of the more notable examples of phonetic dialogue appears in Zora Neale Hurston's short story "Sweat." Here's a brief excerpt:

> "Some day Ah'm goin' tuh drop dead from some of yo' foolishness. 'Nother thing, where you been wid mah rig? Ah feeds dat pony. He aint fuh you to be drivin' wid no bull whip."

Students often claim that dialect in this form is too hard to understand. I think they really mean it's hard to understand quickly. Any student can sort out what the characters mean if he's patient enough: he just reads it out loud, or deciphers the speech word by word. But as students often reasonably inquire, who wants to do that? Fiction depends on the reader proceeding with relative fluidity throughout the text, and if we have to spend a few minutes decoding a short passage, we'll have a hard time engaging with the characters and action. We'll experience it as text, not speech.

This is a fair objection, but there's a counter to it, which is that the difficulty of reading phonetic dialect can be exaggerated. Sure, it looks odd when you first see it, but your mind quickly adjusts. It's not unlike reading Shakespeare; once you've put a few pages behind you, you don't struggle with it as much. A reader's brain is wonderfully adaptive.

Besides that, phonetic dialect may provide something that justifies the risk of distraction: authenticity. In this case, Hurston wanted to record the customs and speech of African-American Florida in the 1920s, and she wanted to get it right. As a trained anthropologist, she considered her fiction to be something like an ethnographical endeavor. Her micromanaging of the way we hear the characters talk represents the same dedication to accuracy that we see in a social scientist writing up fieldwork.

An equally significant aspect to this search for authenticity is the avoidance of inauthenticity. That is to say, while writers using phonetic dialogue want you to hear a line exactly as it should sound, they also want to make sure you don't insert whatever clichés of accent and dialect you would otherwise fall back on. Like benevolent dictators, these writers believe their readers would only abuse freedom if they were granted it.

Haughty as that may sound, readers do sometimes require protection from themselves. Imagine coming across the line "My darling, I have brought you the cheese from Paris," said Guillaume in his thick accent. The writer lets us hear Guillaume's words for ourselves, giving only the vague guidance that we should imagine them in French-inflected English. And what do we do with that freedom? I think many of us hear some sort of Pepé Le Pew—or Inspector Clouseau—inspired voice (*My dar-leeng, I 'ave brought you ze chiz from Paree*), possibly preceded by the nasally *hunh-hunh-hunh* laugh of Gallic caricature. Unfortunately, certain accents—the Frenchman, the Southerner, the Noo Yawker, and so on—are so engrained in our cultural imagination that it's hard for us to hear an authentic version of them if we're just told to. This is a serious problem for someone trying to write verisimilar fiction. France, after all, contains many different regions and dialects, as does the American South, as does the New York megalopolis. What if you want your reader to hear the curious twang of panhandle Florida or the slow drawl of coastal Carolina, and instead all they hear is Forrest Gump?

That's troubling enough from a purely artistic standpoint, but there are also sociopolitical implications of allowing a reader to hear an inauthentic voice. Hurston wrote her stories in part to document lives and places that would otherwise be neglected because of racial intolerance. In forcing readers to hear these voices exactly as she wanted them to, she gave them no freedom to imagine African-American caricatures instead (this was the 1920s, remember, the decade of *Amos 'n' Andy*). And if readers can't hear those caricatures, it becomes less easy to buy the stereotypes that come with them. The same can be said of any writer seeking to document a group that is susceptible to stereotype, be it a regional/national population or an ethnic/racial one or one united by a verbal disability. To see another example, go back to the excerpt from Roddy Doyle's *The Van* in chapter 2, and see how he uses phonetic dialogue to make you hear Irish accents that are far removed from the Lucky Charms leprechaun. For these writers, there's more at stake than verisimilitude—they also fight against our cultural prejudices.

Ironically, some of Hurston's contemporaries believed her use of dialect encouraged stereotypes by making the characters appear uneducated. In recent decades, as we've come to recognize the complex grammars of dialects apart from Standard English, this criticism has lost steam. But still some readers and scholars make the argument that phonetic dialect diminishes a character in the eye of the reader, by making her look foolish or inarticulate or at the very least peculiar. They certainly have a point when they're talking about badly crafted dialect. If a writer makes an Australian say "G'day, mate" or gives a Mexican the line "Ay, caramba!" he turns his own characters into caricatures (Crocodile Dundee and Speedy Gonzales, respectively). He makes both a moral and an artistic transgression.

Another problematic aspect of phonetic dialogue has to do with the crafting of vernacular speech by people who do not belong to the group being depicted. Frankly, this doesn't happen a lot, because people are afraid of coming off as racist. But a contemporary bestseller, Kathryn Stockett's *The Help*, serves as an interesting illustration of how such a technique can play out. Stockett, a white Southerner from a privileged background, wrote some chapters of her novel from the perspective of black maids in 1960s Mississippi. Because of the first-person style, she didn't have the option of describing the characters' voices in dialogue tags; she had to construct their sound and patterns in the words themselves. Predictably, she received some criticism for this decision, from those who claimed she didn't have the right to appropriate the voices of an oppressed race and class. Stockett must have known such criticism was likely; the safe choice would have been to keep the whole novel in the voice of the white narrator, so she deserves credit for risking castigation in order to write a more rounded, comprehensive book.

It's telling, though, that she didn't actually use phonetic dialogue in the way we've been speaking about it. Here's a sample of a black character's voice in the novel:

> I take the tray a devil eggs out to the dining room. Miss Leefolt setting at the head and to her left be Miss Hilly Holbrook and Miss Hilly's mama, Miss Walter, who Miss Hilly don't treat with no respect. And then on Miss Leefolt's right be Miss Skeeter.

Even the phonetically spelled words — "*a*" instead of "*of*," "*devil*" instead of "*deviled*" — are actually words themselves, with the result that the passage doesn't contain any of the apostrophes or blatant misspellings we see in most phonetic passages. Primarily the voice comes across through grammar and syntax, in the way she uses double negatives (*don't treat with no respect*), verb conjugation (*to her left be Miss Hilly Holbrook*) and regional quirks (*setting* instead of *sitting*). This style, which we'll discuss in a later section, has many benefits. But I think one of them is to mitigate the stark, sometimes exaggerated appearance of true phonetic dialogue. Phonetically, Aibileen probably pronounced the first line in the passage "*Ah tak' de tray uh devil' eggs out tuh de dinin' room*," but this version looks more aggressive in the way it underscores her accent, it's easier to interpret as a mockery of her speech. Stockett knew she was taking a chance in appropriating the voice of black characters, but in eschewing true phonetic spelling, she chose a less overt style of presenting the dialects.

Even if phonetic dialect can lead to offensiveness—or the accusation of it—we can't throw the baby out with the bathwater. Yes, there are characters whom authors ridicule by giving them stereotypical dialect (Brer Rabbit, Jim in *Tom Sawyer*, the slaves in *Gone with the Wind*). But there are also many for whom the reader feels tremendous respect and affection (Faulkner's Dilsey, Jim in *Huck Finn*, Stowe's Uncle Tom, Dickens's Oliver Twist). Carefully crafted phonetic dialect can enrich a reader's experience of the characters, while shoddy or disrespectful treatment of the same can diminish them in the reader's eyes—and any diminishment created by such an overt technique will result in a loss of respect for the writer as well.

PHONETIC REPRESENTATION OF SPEECH IMPEDIMENTS OR VERBAL TICS

You might say that my advice in the last section boiled down to this: *If you want to write phonetic dialogue to represent an accent, great, just make sure you don't screw it up, or you'll look silly and/or racist.* I'm afraid the first part of this next section doesn't offer you even that much leeway. Accents are complex and multifaceted products of vowel and consonant formations, so if you work hard to listen to the way people speak and avoid that which is false and trite, you can replicate them in writing. But when we're dealing with speech impediments and other verbal particularities, that's not always the case.

In fiction, the most common non-standard speech that doesn't involve accent is probably stuttering. And unfortunately, generations of writers have failed to come up with an effective way to phonetically represent it. Probably the most famous stutterer in literature is Billy Budd—his speech impediment is actually a plot point in the novel—and here's how Melville had him talk:

> "D-D-Damme, I don't know what you are d-d-driving at, or what you mean, but you had better g-g-go where you belong!"

Saul Bellow gave a twist on this familiar method in *Humboldt's Gift*:

> "But what were you re-re-reserving yourself for? You had the star attitude, but where was the twi-twi-twink . . ."

With apologies to these two brilliant writers, repeating the first letter or syllable of a word doesn't satisfy. It simply fails to give a sense of what people sound like when they stutter. The noise emitting from a stutterer's mouth and throat are much more complex. In fact, the sounds don't always involve letters from the Roman alphabet, so they are virtually impossible to emulate in written English. When writers try it, the result is not just false but insulting to readers and stutterers. Because of that, it may be a fool's game to try to represent a stutter phonetically. At least I've never seen it done in a convincing and verisimilar way.

Stuttering, however, is not the only speech impediment out there, and with some of them, phonetic representation may be possible for the sensitive writer. For example, Jonathan Lethem gives a first-person voice to a man with Tourette Syndrome in his novel *Motherless Brooklyn*. The narrator, Lionel Essrog, thoroughly describes his odd tics and emissions, and he uses some phonetic constructions to show what his dialogue sounds like. Usually this involves removing the space between words and putting the phrases in italics, as in "You shouldn't make fun of—*Lyrical Eggdog! Logical Assnog!*—you shouldn't make fun of me, Julia" and "*Doctorbyebye!*" Lionel also describes the physical gestures that accompany the tics, and delves into his subjective experience of shame and alienation. We get the full picture of the man's affliction, not just the parts that might result in cheap laughs. And we become convinced that phonetic portrayals like "Anyone—*Kissmefaster! Killmesooner! Cookiemonster!*—anyone the killer might target?" are the most accurate and sympathetic methods of replicating the outbursts.

The treatment of other speech impediments (such as lisp, cluttering, whatever Foghorn Leghorn has, etc.) can be approached from the perspective of the previous discussion. That is, if a manner of speech can be fully represented by our language, or if its experience can be portrayed with a combination of phonetics and description, then it makes sense to try to capture the actual experience in the dialogue. If Lethem had chosen to merely describe Lionel's Tourette's symptoms, without ever letting us see in plain English what his speech looked like, the novel would have frustrated its readers. And yet, while stuttering manifests as a verbal affliction, I believe writers must acknowledge that it's not verbal in any way that we can authentically capture with the letters and syllables of English.

I'd like to bring up one last non-standard, non-accented style of speech that writers often don't know what to do with: the speech of a drunk person. Many of the points about accent will apply here, in particular the danger of making the character appear as a stereotype. We all know the trite soundtrack of the drunkard of caricature: the slurred words, the raised volume, the hiccups. Because of that, you may want to avoid phonetics altogether, and write something like *"You better believe it, baby," he said. The bartender could barely make out his words.*

But for the sake of authenticity, and so that your reader doesn't insert the inauthentic speech of cultural cliché, you may want to do as Fitzgerald did in "Babylon, Revisited":

> "Come and dine. Sure your cousins won' mine. See you so sel'om. Or solemn."

Fitzgerald's ear for drunken speech, which he honed with extensive field-work, is pitch perfect. He captures the tendency of drunks to abbreviate sentences (*sure your cousins* instead of *I'm sure your cousins*), to drop conso-nants (*sel'om*), to misuse and get distracted by language (*Or solemn*). This line, which occurs without any dialogue accessory, is much more effective than it would have been if he'd asked a narrative tag to do all the work.

OTHER OPTIONS: LIMITED PHONETICS AND GRAMMAR / SYNTAX / DICTION

One odd fact about phonetic dialect is that writers almost always use it inconsistently. Hurston's line *"Some day Ah'm goin' tuh drop dead from some of yo' foolishness"* uses some phonetic spelling, but many of the words—*some, dead, from, of*—are spelled correctly, even though, like most English words, they're not spelled the way they're pronounced. If she had decided to use absolute and consistent phonetics, she would have written something like this: *"Sum day Ah'm gon' tuh drop ded frum sum ov yo' foolishness."* Which might be taking it a bit far—it's the kind of ultra-faithful phonetic style that makes *Wuthering Heights*'s Joseph so incomprehensible. (A sample line: *Hathecliff maks noa 'count 'o t' mother, nor ye norther; but he'll heu' his lad; und I mun tak' him—soa now ye knaw!* Thanks for clearing that up, Emily Brontë.) Because it's untenable to phonetically spell every word of dialogue, Hurston only does it to a few of the more exaggerated pronunciations, so that the reader can get a feel for the accent. Once we have that feel, we make adjust-ments in other places; we hear every word in the dialect of the speaker. It's a trick, an aural illusion.

Writers who are uncomfortable with phonetic dialect, but who acknowledge its benefits, try to extend the possibilities of this trick, in which a little phonetic representation is made to go a long way. These writers provide long stretches of dialogue in Standard English, but throw in occasional phonetic spellings to jolt the reader back into the accent. They might drop the *g* on gerunds, for instance, or turn *them* into *em*—nothing that will slow down the reader much, but enough phonetics to give a small taste of the accent, with the hopes that the reader will do the rest. Here's how it looks in two separate excerpts from Edward P. Jones's *The Known World*:

> "I be back later. Maybe I be back tomorrow. But I want you here doin right when I get back, doin good."

> "She ain't no more dead than you or me. Now hush that ruckus. Go find them children. In the next room. Go find em and see to em."

In real life, the spelling and pronunciations of many of these words would not have matched up (*tomorrow* was probably *tomorruh*, *get* was more like *git*), but Jones doesn't want the language to distract, so he gives only a few non-standard spellings, assuming you'll make up for the rest.

These examples illustrate another method of controlling the way a reader hears accent, one that doesn't have to use phonetics at all: the manipulation of syntax, grammar, and diction—the method we briefly saw in the excerpt from *The Help*. In *The Known World* passages, the faulty grammar in the first two sentences (they're both missing the auxiliary verb *will*) and the colloquial phrases of the third (*doin right* and *doin good*) contribute to the accent Jones seeks to present—in this case, an African American in nineteenth-century Virginia. We can see another example in an excerpt from Barry Hannah's *Ray*:

> "I was saying the other day, Doc, I was telling Poot Laird, 'The large bird flies and roars because it has the span. The small bird creeps and misses because it hasn't.' That's what I told Poot."
> "That doesn't sound half-bad," I said. "What was Poot's reaction?"
> "Nothing. He can't talk. A cottonmouth bit him in the tongue when he was little. Only expression he's got, is after a big supper and beer, he lifts a leg and—"
> "Poots," I guessed.
> "But strange, like somebody mumbling."

Without using phonetic spelling (he doesn't even drop the *g*'s, although certainly his characters do), Hannah lets us know that these men speak in Southern accents, specifically the odd mixture of the elegant and the colloquial that characterizes his Mississippi setting.

The mechanisms he uses are his syntax (the ordering of the parts of the sentence) and his word choice. This includes the characters' casual repetitions, which we see in the way the first speaker gives three variations of *I said* (*I was saying the other day, I was telling Poot Laird, That's what I told Poot*). He has picked up on the odd grammatical constructions, as when the speaker introduces the main clause of a sentence with "*Only expression he's got, is after a big supper and beer.*" He uses the region's word choice and general local color: *supper*, a nickname like *Poots*, cottonmouth snakes. Even personality traits contribute to how we hear the voice, as the speaker's somewhat pompous habit of communicating through adage (*the large bird flies . . .*) makes us picture the way such tidbits come out of the mouths of certain grandiose Southerners.

five

What Are Your Options for Portraying Characters' Thoughts?

T. S. Eliot's poem "The Love Song of J. Alfred Prufrock" begins with an epigraph taken from Dante's *Inferno*. In the quoted passage, a condemned friar named Guido da Montefeltro explains that he will tell Dante about his sin only because "if what I hear is true / none ever returned from this abyss alive." Of course, the friar has been misinformed about the way hell works. Not only does Dante return to the world of the living, he goes on to record the man's secret in the most famous poem of the Middle Ages, which then gets referenced in one of the most famous poems of the twentieth century. Poor Guido!

Eliot invokes this moment at the beginning of his own poem because, like Dante, he allows the reader access into the head of a man who wants to hide the shamefulness of what is going on there. Eliot writes in the first-person voice of J. Alfred Prufrock, a fearful, meticulous man. While sitting at a tea party, Prufrock composes a love poem to a woman, but the reader soon learns that he is too meek and timid to ever summon up the courage to speak with her.

We spend the entire poem inside Prufrock's consciousness. We listen to his aborted attempts to write the love song, we listen to him castigate himself for not doing it well, we listen to him get distracted and digressive. There isn't one sentiment in the poem that Prufrock would willingly share with anybody in the world — he would be mortified beyond measure if somehow his acquaintances learned what he was thinking. In short, we get the kind of access to Prufrock's mind that Dante gets to Guido's, and for the same reason: he doesn't think anyone can hear him.

I hope you see where I'm going with this. Fiction writers get to treat their characters like Guido and J. Alfred. They can reveal things that the characters would never admit publicly, sometimes even things that the characters can't admit to themselves. It's true that most literary forms try to explore human consciousness to some degree, but fiction and narrative poetry contain specific formal advantages that allow their writers to portray a character's interior with more directness and complexity.

The ability to delve into consciousness comes with risks, primarily the ones encapsulated by the "show don't tell" shibboleth. Certainly writers do well to accept the point that readers prefer activity to passivity, that the dramatization of character interests us more than the assertion of it. Good playwrights know that people avoid revealing their interior lives directly—you rarely see a line like "Gee, I'm wracked with anxiety" in a good play. Therefore they use subtle movements or subtextual dialogue to make a character reveal himself. They *show* the interior, because in contemporary performance there aren't many mechanisms for telling it.

But passivity has its uses, especially in fiction. In fact, we often must use assertion to plunge into our characters' thoughts and emotions—we must tell, rather than show. In part this is a matter of pacing; a novel or even a long story that dramatized everything and told nothing would get tedious. But we also must tell because some emotions or thoughts are too complex or vague to imply through dramatization, at least in a way that all readers would pick up on. You might think that by having a character furiously scratch his forearm, you're relating his disdain for his wife, but your reader may think it means that he's remembering his stint in Vietnam, or that he hates his job, or that he's itchy.

So once we accept the prerogative of fiction writers to at least occasionally explain what's going on in a character's head, the next step is to examine the conventions that literary tradition has placed at our disposal for doing so. Many of my students assume there's one standard method, the way double quotation marks are standard for dialogue. However, fiction hasn't settled on a single convention, at least not with the consensus it has achieved in dialogue formatting. Writers have always used a variety of methods to express characters' interiors, sometimes employing different ones within the same work. What follows is a rundown of some common techniques for indicating thought in a third-person narrative (first-person narrators, of course, can state their thoughts directly).

THOUGHTS INDICATED WITHOUT
PUNCTUATION OR ITALICS

Probably the easiest way for a third-person narrator to portray a character's interior is to use tags, similar to the kind we use in dialogue: "I'll never get that cat back, Willard thought," or "Mother would prefer the tomato aspic, she decided." But I'd caution you against using thought tags exclusively. The style can get repetitive, plus it's not always necessary. Part of writing smoothly about a character involves moving the reader from the external events to the interior world of the character with elegance. Here's how Willa Cather does it in "Paul's Case":

> It had been wonderfully simple; when they had shut him out of the theater and concert hall, when they had taken away his bone, the whole thing was virtually determined. The rest was a mere matter of opportunity. The only thing that at all surprised him was his own courage — for he realized well enough that he had always been tormented by fear, a sort of apprehensive dread.

After the first expression of external fact ("It had been wonderfully simple") Cather glides right into Paul's consciousness by pointing out his internal response to the events: "The only thing that at all surprised him . . ." From that point on, we're situated in Paul's interior, so we can be told he "realized well enough that he had always been tormented by fear" and so on. Cather doesn't use the simple construction "he thought" at all, because it's unnecessary — the other verbs in the passage let us know that Paul is thinking, not speaking, as does the content. Notice that while the style is passive rather than active, it's engaging stuff, far removed from the "he was angry" or "she was sad" kind of writing that worries show-don't-tell advocates.

Both these styles are part of the most common method of portraying interiority, which is to make cognitive/emotional assertions without using visual markers like italics or quotation marks, and without doing radical language experimentation. One style is direct, as when you write "Wallace thought" or "she supposed." The other is indirect, as when you assert a cause-and-effect relationship between the fictional world and the character's mind, as in "the sound of his voice made her feel queasy," "he was amazed by the juggler," and "he realized well enough that he had always been tormented by fear." The two styles can be used together without anyone noticing much, and they have the virtue of simplicity—the reader will easily understand the difference between what's happening in the story and what's happening in the character's mind.

THOUGHTS INDICATED BY ITALICS

Some writers of third-person narratives use italics as a way of indicating that the words belong to a character's interior. In that sense, it's similar to the quotation marks used for dialogue. The different style of type visually indicates that the reader should experience the sentence differently. Here's how Stanley Elkin does it in *A Bad Man*:

> But even taking into account these aberrant moments, robbed of the gentle consummation he had planned, he realized that he had never had so active nor so satisfactory a sex life.
>
> *It's a goddamned love nest in here.*

The italics announce a shift from the third-person voice of the narrative to the interior voice of Feldman, the protagonist. It's simple: normal type = external; italicized type = internal.

Just as writers often don't believe quotation marks suffice to indicate speech, and thus add dialogue tags to the quoted lines, so too do some authors prefer to add tags to their italics. Thus "he thought" or "he pondered" become the equivalent of "he said" or "he replied." Here's how Faulkner does it in "The Bear":

> *So I will have to see him,* he thought, without dread or even hope. *I will have to look at him.*

One might argue that italics plus thought tags are redundant in a way that quotation marks plus dialogue tags are not. Speech in fiction usually involves two or more people, thus we need the tags to differentiate the speakers. But when someone thinks, they don't do it in exchange with anyone else, so the context makes it clear to whom the thought belongs. In Faulkner's phrase "*So I will have to see him,* he thought," either the italics or the "he thought" could be removed, and the reader would still get the point. So why are they both in here?

It's hard to say for sure, since we're dealing with Faulkner. He's an author I'll invoke later in this chapter, in part because he dealt so often with the inner lives of his characters, and in part because he used various methods, often in the same work (often on the same page). But one answer may have to do with simple risk and reward.

In this case, the risk of including both italics and thought tags is that the reader will notice the redundancy and will be bothered by it. The reward is that it's absolutely clear to the reader what the boy is thinking, because the text uses two overt methods of indicating thought. Not only does it visually separate the boy's thoughts, it also does it with a content-based assertion. Sure it's redundant, but redundancy is not always a dirty word; sometimes it's more like a backup plan. And indeed, there may be places in the story where, without the tags, the reader wouldn't quite know what the italics indicate (as we'll see in chapter 14, italics can serve many roles). In any case, the payoff was evidently worth the risk for Faulkner.

Using a combination of methods to portray interiority may violate some of the dogma you'll hear on the subject. Often in creative writing classes, someone declares that it's a mistake to use italics and a thought tag together, throwing around the word "redundant" as if that settles the matter. Again, though, redundancy is not always a pejorative. Sometimes a writer might decide that the importance of keeping the character's thought separate from the prose justifies the redundancy. The decision will come from the writer's sensibilities and priorities. Faulkner was never one to worry about whether his language would distract his reader, but he depended on the reader understanding the contents of his characters' heads and hearts.

THOUGHTS INDICATED BY QUOTATION MARKS

Some authors treat a character's thoughts as if they were another form of dialogue, by surrounding them with quotation marks. Unlike with italics, you'll usually need a thought tag if you use this method. That's because quotation marks traditionally indicate speech, and anytime you want your reader to understand a convention in a nonconventional way, you must provide guidance. An example might help—look at the following exchange:

> "Hi Jim," Lisa said.
> Jim smiled broadly at her. "That's a really ugly dress," he thought.

Take away the thought tag and it reads like this:

> "Hi Jim," Lisa said.
> Jim smiled broadly at her. "That's a really ugly dress."

In the first, Jim is two-faced but polite, while in the second he's confrontational.

Quotation marks around thoughts aren't so common these days, perhaps because they indicate that the writer considers thought to be just another version of speech, one that happens to be kept bottled up rather than released by the tongue. As the Modernists pointed out (we'll get to them soon), thought does not work that way—what happens inside our heads is not the unspoken version of what comes out of our mouths. The technique of using quotation marks around thought therefore comes off as pre-Modernist, which is to say, a little quaint.

It may be surprising, then, to see a Modernist like Hemingway using this method. Here's a passage from *To Have and Have Not*:

> "Nobody is going to come out with this breeze," he thought. "They won't look for us to have started with this blowing."

Sure enough, it looks somewhat elementary. We're asked to believe that Harry Morgan thinks in grammatical sentences; he doesn't even use many contractions. It may remind us of the thought bubbles in comic books ("I've got to get Lois and Jimmy out of that building before it explodes!"), or the voice-overs deployed by screenwriters ("There must be a con like me in every prison in America," the thought-voice of Red tells us in *The Shawshank Redemption*). It's hard to accept that the words accurately depict what it was like for Harry to experience this thought.

And yet . . .

Hemingway, I believe, had certain reasons for employing the quotation marks. He used other methods in the novel, too, including the free indirect style (see below) and italics, so it may have simply been something that felt right at the time, a way to mix it up. But we also know that Hemingway was conscientious about his language in a way that Faulkner wasn't. If Faulkner feared leaving the right word out, Hemingway feared putting the wrong one in. In short, he desired simplicity, getting his point across, doing the most with the least. This style may seem unsophisticated, but that's true of a lot of Hemingway's prose. In fact, what makes him a Modernist is the fact that his work reads as so much simpler, so much more direct, so much less adorned, than everything else at the time—his Modernist experiment was to not get fancy.

And there's certainly nothing fancy about this method of thought presentation. Indeed, it's often the method that children use when they begin to write stories that involve characters' thoughts. In Hemingway's opinion, that's not necessarily bad. You walk away knowing what the author wanted you to know, which is the number one goal. My final word of caution, though, is to note that most writers don't get the benefit of the doubt that Hemingway does. Some readers will perceive the use of quotation marks around thoughts as an unsophisticated device.

FREE INDIRECT STYLE

James Joyce's "The Dead" is so frequently cited as an example of free indirect style that I worry about using it here; it seems cliché. But of course there's a reason for its overuse—it really is a good example of the technique. So here's an excerpt from the last page:

> He wondered at his riot of emotions of an hour before. From what had it proceeded? From his aunt's supper, from his own foolish speech, from the wine and dancing, the merry-making when saying good-night in the hall, the pleasure of the walk along the river in the snow. Poor Aunt Julia!

This passage begins with an expression of the thoughts of the protagonist, Gabriel, that uses the first method we discussed: "He wondered at his riot of emotions . . ." But the next three sentences don't use any filtering devices such as "he wondered" or "he thought." Instead, these lines appear as if Gabriel himself speaks them. The question "From what had it proceeded?" consumes *Gabriel*, not the authorial third-person. When we hear about "his own foolish speech," that's *Gabriel* chastising himself, not the narrator commenting on his rhetoric. And certainly the line "Poor Aunt Julia!" couldn't belong to the third-person narrator, who is relatively objective and would not weigh in with such an opinion, let alone an exclamation point.

We see here that even though "The Dead" is not a first-person narrative, in brief moments the narrative voice appropriates the language of the characters. That's pretty much the definition of free indirect style. You can think of it as analogous to Linda Blair getting infiltrated by the devil in *The Exorcist*, or the teenage girl's body getting taken over by her mother in *Freaky Friday*. The free indirect style involves a third-person narrator being inhabited, for a brief span, by the voice of a character, without the filtering device of "he thought" or "it occurred to her" or italics or anything like that.

Free indirect style often gets formatted in exactly the same way as the method we discussed in the section "Thoughts Indicated by Italics," with the key difference that the thought isn't italicized. To clarify, let's look at the example we used in that section, with only one change to it: the italics have been removed from the last line.

> But even taking into account these aberrant moments, robbed of the gentle consummation he had planned, he realized that he had never had so active nor so satisfactory a sex life.
>   It's a goddamned love nest in here.

As with the original, there's a difference in consciousness here: the first paragraph is the expression of the third-person narrator, while the second is the interior expression of the character Feldman. But in the free indirect version, we don't have the italics to show us the difference physically, which makes interpreting it more of a challenge. We have to figure it out based only on the contrast in style. We must notice that the second paragraph, with its use of a swear word, simplistic diction, and the cliché "love nest," differs from the first, which uses formal diction and complex sentence construction.

I don't mean to overstate the difficulty. Sometimes writers make it easy to spot the free indirect style, as Elkin does in the above example, and as Annie Proulx does in the opening lines of "The Blood Bay": "The winter of 1886–1887 was terrible. Every goddamn history of the high plains says so." But often free indirect style does ask us to read with an elevated attention and sensitivity. The first line of "The Dead" is "Lily, the caretaker's daughter, was literally run off her feet," which contains a word choice error. The reader has to comprehend that the error exists because the prose "belongs" to Lily, the uneducated servant girl, rather than Joyce, the master of language. A reader who doesn't understand Joyce's style might say to himself, "This writer stinks — he doesn't even know the difference between literally and figuratively." The free indirect style asks readers to judge which elements of the language belong to the author/narrator, and which elements belong to the people in the story.

The free indirect style should not be abused. If the reader constantly has to decide whom certain words and phrases belong to, and never gets any help in the form of italics or tags, the work can become wearying. But used judiciously, it can indicate the strength of a character's personality, giving the impression that her voice and sensibility are so profound and fully realized that they can't help but break through the wall of the third-person from time to time.

THE STREAM OF CONSCIOUSNESS

The methods we've looked at so far don't confine themselves to any particular movement in literature. In your reading life you'll see all kinds of writers using these techniques, and their decisions won't have much to do with whether we call them Realists or Romantics or Naturalists or whatever. Unfortunately, our tendency to attach literary movements to writers often limits our experience of them. We may call Katherine Mansfield a Modernist, but that didn't matter to her; she used whatever tropes and techniques the vast canon of literature provided her with.

In this section, however, we do have to consider literary-historical context, because we're looking at a style developed by writers of the Modernist movement. That style is called "stream of consciousness." There are varying interpretations as to what the term means, many of them flat-out wrong. For example, some people use the term for any description of a character's thoughts, thus confusing it with interior monologue. The term actually refers to an attempt to capture in language the actual thought *processes* of a person.

The literary Modernists of the 1910s and 1920s rejected traditional and dominant modes of narration, and one of the dominant writers of the late nineteenth century was Henry James. I'm tempted to discuss James at length, since his insistence on interior characterization as a necessary facet of realism is one of the reasons we're having this chapter at all. It's not that writers before James didn't use interiority, but they didn't use it as much or in quite the same way. However, to investigate stream of consciousness, we only need to know that James used an expansive form of the third-person limited, and he stuck to the first method we discussed: he asserted the thoughts of a character without any punctuation or italics, as in this passage from *Daisy Miller*:

> Winterbourne stood looking after her; and as she moved away, drawing her muslin furbelows over the gravel, said to himself that she had the *tournure* of a princess.

Throughout this and other works, James immerses his reader in the character's consciousness with phrasing like "he considered," and "it seemed to Winterbourne," and "he told himself," and so on. All in all, very much like the passage we looked at earlier from "Paul's Case."

Many Modernists believed that this method no longer cut the mustard, because it did not authentically capture what goes on inside a person's head. The critique has merit. In fact, it's the downside of all the methods we've looked at so far: they all imply that people think the way they speak, that when you see a tasty piece of cheese (for example), a ticker tape with the words "I really want to eat that cheese" runs through your brain. To test this out, look at the several ways our aforementioned conventions would indicate that a character desires cheese:

> I really want to eat that cheese, Stan thought. (thought tags)
>
> Stan stared at the brick of gouda. *Good God, it looks yummy.* (thoughts in italics)
>
> Stan stared at the gouda, thinking, *Good God, it looks yummy.* (redundant italics)
>
> Stan thought, "I really want to eat that cheese." (thoughts in quotation marks)
>
> Stan stared at the gouda. Good God, it looked yummy. (free indirect style)

Surely these assertions don't quite capture the true essence of cheese desiring. In recognition of this problem, the Modernists used nontraditional syntax, diction, and punctuation to get closer to the truth of what it's like to think. A writer utilizing the stream of consciousness to achieve the goals of the previous sentences might write something like this: "Cheese splendid tummy belly cheesecheesecheese happy yum yum."

Faulkner, with varying degrees of comfort, is considered a Modernist, and he certainly employed the stream of consciousness technique. However, I believe he's often said to be using it when he's not, and it's important to look at the difference between stream of consciousness and simple close third-person narration. For example, look back to chapter 1, at the passage from *As I Lay Dying* in which Darl attempts to cross a river, and you'll see that the text does *not* use stream of consciousness. Even though the passage shows us what's going on in Darl's head, it's narrated straightforwardly, with grammatical language. Rather than an actual transcript of the words firing across Darl's synapses, it seems more like an author's organization of those words. Thus it's not so different from the way Henry James portrayed thought.

In other novels, however, and in other places in *As I Lay Dying*, Faulkner wears his Modernist colors more overtly:

> When it runs the track shines on and off. Pa said flour and sugar and coffee costs so much. Because I am a country boy because boys in town. Bicycles. Why do flour and sugar and coffee cost so much when he is a country boy. "Wouldn't you ruther have some bananas instead?" Bananas are gone, eaten. Gone. When it runs on the track shines again.

That's more like it. In this scene, the boy Vardaman stands at the window of a toy shop, looking at a train set and thinking about what his father told him earlier. Faulkner's depiction shows us the random, disassociated nature of thought—the boy goes from considering the train to thinking about Pa's directive to worrying about bicycles and bananas and so on. It uses a fragmented, ungrammatical prose. It even reveals, in true Freudian style, some of the Oedipal implications that the young Vardaman's id might be wrestling with. You won't catch Henry James doing this.

The problem is probably evident: it's hard to follow. Even a close reader of *As I Lay Dying* may get stumped by Vardaman's thoughts at times, especially his repeated insistence that his mother is a fish (don't ask). And *As I Lay Dying* remains one of the more accessible stream of consciousness narratives. Joyce's radical experiment with the style in *Finnegans Wake* is notoriously incomprehensible. Or look at this beauty from Gertrude Stein's *Tender Buttons*:

> Sausage in between a glass.
>
> There is read butter. A loaf of it is managed. Wake a question. Eat an instant, answer.
>
> A reason for bed is this, that a decline, any decline, is poison, poison is a toe a toe extractor, this means a solemn change. Hanging.

The passage may not be true stream of consciousness, since the words don't attach to a specific character, but still Stein asserts (I think) that our thoughts are hopelessly fragmented and subjective and incoherent. Unfortunately, her portrait of this fact makes her fiction incoherent, too. A large price to pay for authenticity.

Yet the ultimate failure of the stream of consciousness isn't incomprehensibility. Its fatal flaw is that it doesn't achieve its goals of accurately representing the processes of thought. The Modernists began with the notion that people don't think in coherent sentences and phrases. But can't we take this further, and say that most of the time we don't think in words at all? If we're practicing for a speech, or trying to recall a memorized poem, we may will ourselves into seeing words and letters in our mind's eye. But experience and neuroscience tell us that most of the time our thoughts are beyond language. While we don't think, "I would like to eat that cheese," we also don't think, "Cheese splendid tummy belly happy yum yum." And if thoughts don't manifest in words, why would the stream of consciousness be more accurate than any other convention? Modernism's experiment in this regard was something of a noble failure. They certainly came up with a different way to represent consciousness, but it's a stretch to say they came up with a more accurate one.

OTHER STYLES

We've looked at the five conventions for portraying thought most commonly used in fiction, but there are other ways to go about it. In Virginia Woolf's *Mrs. Dalloway*, for example, we can see a style that might be considered a hybrid of various techniques:

> She was wearing pink gauze—was that possible? She seemed, anyway,
> all light, glowing, like some bird or airball that has flown in, attached
> itself for a moment to bramble. But nothing is so strange when one
> is in love (and what was this except being in love?) as the complete
> indifference of other people.

This novel is often held up as an example of either stream of consciousness or free indirect style. To me, it doesn't seem like either of those, except in short bursts. Instead it invokes a distinct method, one that flits from objective assertion ("she was wearing pink gauze") to free indirect ("was that possible?") to stream of consciousness ("like some bird or airball that has flown in, attached itself for a moment to bramble") to the detached authorial irony we see in Jane Austen ("nothing is so strange when one is in love . . . as the complete indifference of other people"), and it does all this with grace and fluidity. It's one of the more complex novels you'll ever read in terms of what it does with the character's interior, yet it somehow doesn't feel like it.

And, of course, the Postmodernists have tried a thing or two with the portrayal of thought. William Gaddis's *Agapē Agape*, for example, consists of "an unstructured monologue of a man living through his last days," in the words of literary critic Sven Birkerts. For nearly one hundred pages, the narrative voice rambles on without once indenting a paragraph or providing more than a handful of periods. Whether this is an autobiographical deathbed rant, a portrait of a man thinking about art and life, or a latter-day style of stream of consciousness is up for debate. In the book's introduction, Birkerts calls it a "thought fugue," which I suppose is as useful a term as any other.

Such experiments are responses to the inherent contradiction presented to a writer who tries to convey thought: he attempts to represent in words an experience that does not use words. It's true that we do this in other areas of writing—boxing matches don't contain much language, and people write about those. But thought is different, because unlike most other subjects, it seems to be inherently related to language. When we sit down at a keyboard and start typing, sometimes we see thoughts revealed that we didn't know we had but which we instantly agree with. And occasionally something might occur to us in a flash of words, or we might hear an internal voice speaking to us in grammatical English (hopefully this doesn't happen to you too often). Tantalized by the close association of thought and word, we keep searching for more accurate ways to represent the former with the latter.

After achieving a sufficient degree of linguistic mastery, you may want to engage in this experiment yourself, although I tend to think that we have hit a wall in this particular enterprise. Just as experts believe no one will ever invent another pitch in baseball, perhaps we've already explored as many ways of representing thought as we can without taxing readers' patience too much. But then again, I may be like the patent office commissioner who declared in 1899 that everything that could be invented already had been. It may be that a more truthful, or at least more verisimilar, method of representing consciousness will be literature's next great achievement.

part two

Fundamentals of Language

six

The Past Perfect

I mentioned in chapter 1 that you don't have to memorize the names of the more complicated verb tenses, but there's one exception: the past perfect. This comes up so often for the writer and reader, and has to be used with such nuance and artistry, that you might as well know what it's called.

We use the simple past tense for most events that happened at finite moments in the past. *Marty skipped home. Lucy smirked.* But so much of language is chronological—a speaker or writer relating not just what happened, but when—that we have to find ways to indicate where certain events occurred relative to other events on the time continuum. The primary way of doing this is to use the past perfect.

To understand what the past perfect is, we need to look at how it's constructed, and what it indicates. Here's the past perfect in action:

Veronica had warned Deke about her lizard, but he screamed anyway.

"Had warned" is a past perfect construction. As you can see, a writer creates it by combining a form of the verb "to have" (in this case, "had") with a past participle (in this case, "warned"). A past participle is usually the infinitive form of a verb with -*ed* stuck on the end; the infinitive "to warn" becomes "warned." That's how you make the past perfect—*had* plus a participle.

Now for what it indicates: the past perfect teams up with the simple past tense to tell us when things occurred relative to other things. In our example sentence, we have two events that occurred at two different points on the time spectrum. We don't know if Veronica warned Deke last Wednesday or five years ago, but we do know her warning occurred before he screamed. The past perfect tense ("had warned"), when juxtaposed with the simple past tense ("screamed"), tells us so. The two different forms of the past tense don't even have to be in the same sentence to indicate the time relationship of the events. It could look like this:

Veronica had warned Deke about the lizard. Nevertheless, he screamed.

We still get the idea. At some moment in the past, Veronica warned Deke. At some point *after* that moment, he screamed.

A minor but easily handled wrinkle is added when you deal with things that existed as a condition or state of being, rather than something that happened at a specific moment in time, like Veronica's warning of Deke. Let's change our example slightly:

Deke had been dealing with lizards for a long time, but he still screamed.

The verb formation here — "had been dealing" — isn't the past perfect. It's called the past perfect progressive, but the concept is more important than the name. When you discuss an ongoing series of actions or a general condition, rather than a specific action, you need to use the construct that brings in the infinitive of "to be" (in this case, "been"). It makes sense, because this phrasing invokes a state of being. For Deke, dealing with lizards was a lifestyle, something he did over an extended period of time, rather than something he did only at ten o'clock on October 11. If the sentence read, "Deke had dealt with lizards before, but he shrieked anyway," we would know that in the first phrase the writer referred to a specific instance (or instances) of dealing with lizards, not a lifestyle that involved dealing with lizards continually. If all of this seems hazy, look at some more examples. The past perfect progressive appears in the first sentences, the past perfect in the second.

PPP: Mark had been dabbling in real estate for a while before the market crashed.

PP: Mark had dabbled in real estate in 1996, long before the market crashed.

PPP: Quebec had been threatening to vote for independence for years, so the referendum came as no surprise.

PP: Quebec had threatened to vote for independence during Jean Chrétien's second year as prime minister, so the referendum came as no surprise.

Notice that in the second sentences, the ones that use the past perfect, a specific time is implied or specified (1996, and whatever year was Chrétien's second as P.M.). In the past perfect progressive sentences, giving a specific date wouldn't make sense—the opening phrases refer to ongoing and indefinite periods of time.

It's dry but straightforward. Logical, coherent laws govern the usage of the simple past tense, the past perfect tense, and the past progressive tense. So why does using them require nuance and artistry?

Well, as you may notice, two of these constructions sound clunky. To create the past perfect, you have to keep shoving the passive "had" or "have" in front of more active, useful verbs. The past perfect progressive is even worse, forcing us to insert the lame verb formations "had been" and "have been" between the subject and participle. This all slows down the narrative. We don't notice much when we're writing essays or scribbling notes to our kid's teacher, because they don't come up that often in most written communication. But they do come up in layered and complex narratives, stories that provide deep, rich analyses not only of a person's present but also of his past—how he named his first pet, when his grandparents emigrated from Armenia, where he was when the Red Sox won the World Series. That is, imaginative literature.

One way to get around inserting multiple instances of "had" and "have" is to put your narrative in the present tense. Scott Spencer's *A Ship Made of Paper* can help illustrate how this works:

> Daniel is both stunned and amused by the untruthfulness of this.
> First of all, he and Lionel were never close friends and did not spend
> their time after school in each other's company . . . The house itself was
> a meticulous and unfriendly place, and the pictures on the walls were of
> skulls and spinal cords, giving the place a kind of permanent Halloween
> ambiance—a chilling, childless Halloween. But Daniel knows better
> than to challenge their take on the past—he has tried it before when
> other inconsistencies have arisen, and it has caused hard feelings.

Spencer narrates in the present tense: "Daniel is both stunned and amused," "Daniel knows better than to challenge their take on the past," etc. But this present interaction with Daniel's parents involves the description of some elements of his childhood, which necessitates a different verb tense.

To discuss something that came before the conversation, Spencer simply goes back one step in the line of verb tenses, from the present ("Daniel *is* both stunned and amused") to the simple past ("he and Lionel *were* never close friends"). Had Spencer used the past tense for the bulk of the novel, moving back a step would have meant going to the past perfect ("he and Lionel had been . . . ," "the pictures on the walls had been . . ."). It would have necessitated, in other words, using "have" and "had" and "been" more often, in a way that would bog down the narrative, or at least make it less elegant. I doubt that's the only reason Spencer chose to write in the present, but it's certainly an advantage.

In a similar way, the present tense benefits Richard Ford's *Independence Day*, a long novel about the meanderings of Frank Bascombe, a habitually discursive middle-aged narrator. Bascombe so often veers into tangents about the near past, the distant past, the subjunctive ("If I sell you a house . . .," "If I were married to Sally . . ."), and even the future, it would be easy to get tangled up in all the helping verbs demanded by a past tense style. Ford uses the present tense as a sort of stable ground zero, from which he can more easily dip and loop into other tenses without having to use "had been" and "have been being" and "should have been having."

But, as we established in the first chapter, the present tense creates challenges that a writer may not want to deal with. So how do past tense narratives handle the inherent passivity and clunkiness of the past perfect tense? After all, you can't stop including assertions about previous times just because you don't like the language required for such devices. You can, however, decide to ignore the requirement.

What often happens in past tense narratives that rely heavily on flashback, and which thus are obliged—in a grammatical sense—to use the past perfect and the past perfect progressive, is that they simply don't do it. Instead, once it has been established that the scene takes place in a time before the events in the fiction's present, the writer decides it's no longer necessary to use the past perfect. This avoids the problem of passive syntax. I also like it because it underscores the point of grammar—these rules are not here because some pedants are going to arrest you if you misuse them, they're here because they make things easier on reader and writer alike. If the sense provided by grammar has already been established, and thus the grammatical signals are unnecessary, then the writer should be free to abandon them.

Here's a passage from John Casey's *Spartina* in which he ultimately abandons the past perfect tense, even though the events he's narrating technically call for it:

> He considered whether it would be worthwhile moving some pots to a deeper hole . . . that hole was more frequented by sport fishermen who weren't above pulling a pot if the striped bass weren't biting.
>
> Dick had caught a pair of them at it once. He'd come round the rock just in time to see them drop his pot overboard. A college kid and his girlfriend in a deluxe Boston Whaler, all white fiberglass, white vinyl rubrails, and chrome rodholders. Dick had come alongside, jumped into their boat with his six-pronged grapnel in his hand. He swung it against the kid's outboard casing, cracking the plastic.
>
> Dick said, "I see you near one of my pots again, I'll put this through your goddamn head."

The first paragraph uses the simple past tense, as does most of the rest of the novel. So when we see the past perfect verb phrase "had caught," we know we're leaving the contemporary narrative and entering the land of flashback. The scene that follows, in which Dick confronts some college kids, occurs prior to the time frame of the novel, probably a few years earlier.

For a while Casey sticks with the conventional use of the flashback verb tense: "Dick had caught," "He'd come round," "Dick had come alongside," and so on. However, Casey doesn't seem entirely comfortable with it, or at least he goes out of his way to avoid the blandness of "he had" construction. He does this by using a contraction in the second sentence ("he'd") and by using a sentence fragment that avoids verbs altogether in the fourth ("A college kid and his girlfriend . . ."). Casey's ear has told him that the "had" inhibits the intensity of what should be a vivid scene. He can't cut out "had" usage entirely, because then we won't have the grammatical clues showing us it's a flashback, but he can pull out a few tricks that allow him to limit how many times it appears.

After he's used the past perfect three times to establish that the scene takes place in a previous era, he abandons it. This happens with the sentence "He swung it against the kid's outboard casing," and again with "Dick said." In these instances, Casey uses the simple past tense, which doesn't make strict grammatical sense. Dick's swinging of the grapnel and his pulling up alongside the boat belong to roughly the same time period, one that occurs before the novel's contemporary action. So to use the past perfect tense with "he had come alongside" and the simple past in "he swung" is inconsistent. But Casey knows you don't require further reminders that the scene is a flashback, and he assumes you won't be distracted by the shift (and you weren't, were you? Did you even notice?), so he gets rid of the clunky repetitions of "had." Here's what the last part would have looked like if he'd stayed with the grammatical dogma:

> . . . Dick had come alongside, had jumped into their boat with his six-pronged grapnel in his hand. He had swung it against the kid's outboard casing, cracking the plastic.
>
> Dick had said, "I see you near one of my pots again, I'll put this through your goddamned head."

This version is less vivid and engaging, because the passive and awkward usage of "had" detracts from the stark tension of Dick's words and deeds.

This doesn't mean that you should ditch the past perfect tense whenever possible. In other passages in Spartina that depict the past, Casey uses it regularly. For one thing, it can contribute to the tone of a scene meant to be nostalgic or contemplative, as many scenes that refer to previous times are. Here's an example from later in the novel:

> Dick had wanted to spend the day raising the big skiff. He'd wanted to make a list of repairs to Spartina's wheelhouse and check the hull and go see his insurance agent. Everyone else had been working. Eddie had been out on the roads all day, the boys had been busy in Eddie's yard, and May had done a load of wash by hand and hung it out.

Casey doesn't avoid the past perfect or the past perfect progressive here, and it works. The repetition of "had" and "had been" adds a soft, slow rhythm to the prose, which matches with the leisurely pace of the passage. No grapnel hooks are being slammed into casings here, no profane threats are being leveled. It's a depiction of a quiet day's work, and the prose shouldn't be too aggressive or intense.

The use of the past perfect also reinforces something about the character's mental state. This passage isn't quite a flashback (the narrator relates what happened that morning, not decades ago) but it still refers to time that is now lost to the protagonist, and the fact that it is lost matters to him. We know that because the first phrase, "Dick had wanted . . . ," implies that he did not get his wish, that for whatever reason he could not tend to his to-do list or join in with the happy busyness of his wife and children. Thus a tone of regret appears, and gets reinforced by the additional uses of "had," a marker that signifies an event that is lost except in memory.

As with all things, one must consider effect and purpose. The more vivid, intense, or action-based a flashback or past-event narration is meant to be, the more detrimental the repetition of weak auxiliary verbs is likely to prove. But they can sometimes augment tone and rhythm, or reinforce thematic motifs.

Finally, one must consider the complexity and length of a flashback when thinking about whether to limit the use of the past perfect. Regardless of what tone you're going for, sometimes the content of your flashback simply demands so many verbal twists and turns that you'll need to simplify. This is especially true of flashbacks within flashbacks, or flashbacks that cover a long period of time or many events. To explore this, we'll look at an example of a piece that gets too ambitious in its use of pre-contemporary events, and which hurts both the reader's brain and eyes. Before we get to it, though, we need to think about the nature of the past perfect, and why it causes the problem in the first place.

I said in chapter 1 that the present tense covers everything that's happening *at* this exact moment, while the past tense covers everything that happened *before* this exact moment. As you know by now, that's not the whole story — we also have the past perfect (and a few others we're avoiding). But it still holds true that verb tense is a way of locating events in time; specific tenses put actions on a specific spot on a theoretical timeline. All we've done in this chapter is add another verb tense that helps writers and readers situate events on that timeline. When you read *Spartina*, you imagine most of the action taking place during a few weeks in the late 1980s. The events that occur within this cluster of time get narrated with the simple past tense. The ones that occur to the left of it — months or years or decades before the novel's contemporary action — get the past perfect or past perfect progressive, unless Casey abandons them for stylistic reasons.

The issue gets tricky when you realize that, in theory, everything in human history, from the Big Bang through the Punic Wars through the Nixon administration, occurs on the left of the timeline, and thus should be described using the past perfect tense. No matter what the novel, the domain of the left part of the timeline is enormous. If Casey's third-person narrator were to mention sabertooth tigers or King Hammurabi, he would be grammatically obliged to describe them using the same verb tense he applied to the scene in which Dick scares the college kids. An absurd notion.

But we only notice the absurdity through juxtaposition. If various writers tell us, "the Moabites had lived at peace for generations" or "Milt had grown up under the yoke of Soviet totalitarianism" or "the Ford F-150 had undergone a series of tests," we don't think much of it. We can even read all these sentences in the same page and probably not flinch. But if such constructions are situated too closely, the difficulty of grouping all of human history under the same verb tense becomes apparent. It also becomes hard to keep things straight. The timeline gets jumbled, because the markers are all the same. In effect, the narrator tells us that time doesn't matter. It all gets pretty heavy and disconcerting for a person who just wants to read a good yarn.

Now let's look at an example to see the problem in action. It should be clear that I made this up, since nothing like it would get published, or so one likes to think.

> She looked across the table, where Sherman sat chewing a toothpick. Jane had married him ten years ago. But she had first caught sight of him during a freshman history class at Yale. The instructor had been droning on about how Magellan had died in the Philippines. Jane hadn't listened to a word. She had been staring at Sherman's back for a half hour, when he suddenly had turned and had caught her staring.

In this case, stylistic problems and content-based problems are codependent. Stylistically, it sounds terrible because of all the past perfect and past perfect progressive constructions, which are more or less grammatically appropriate. Thus the real flaw is that the writer has constructed a passage that requires too many past perfect forms. After leaving the contemporary narrative action, which uses the simple past ("She looked across the table"), the writer then asks us to envision events that take place at several different points on a timeline: her wedding, the moment she first saw Sherman, the indefinite period of the professor's lecture, the death of Magellan in the sixteenth century, the indefinite period of Jane's staring, and the moment Sherman caught her. Sheesh.

Obviously, I exaggerated the extent of the flashbacking in this passage, but it's not so far removed from what I see in my classes. Following the imperative to flesh out their worlds and their characters, writers sometimes overdo it, try to present too much exposition. When this happens in the course of a flashback—that is, when the author tries to zap you back in time, when you're already back in time relative to the contemporary narrative — and when all this is done using a mass of ugly auxiliary verbs, then the reader will object.

The lesson, of course, is to beware of excessive flashbacking. But I don't mean to imply that the past perfect only comes up when the writer invokes a flashback or an extensive precontemporary scene. Because fiction requires its writers to create worlds and characters of tremendous breadth and depth — people with pasts as well as presents — often you'll use the past perfect in a glimpsing way. You might write, for example, "Judd had lived in Spain, so Omaha's flamenco scene delighted him," or "A coffee factory had once sat near her home, and Lettie missed the smell of the ground roast."

In such cases you won't need to worry about the past perfect's negative effects. It doesn't detract stylistically when it's used like this, because the "had" only occurs once, and the reader accepts it as a grammatical convention. Plus, you don't have the space and time to gradually wean your reader off it, the way Casey does in the *Spartina* passage. If you remove "had" from the previous paragraph's first example, you get "Judd lived in Spain, so Omaha's flamenco scene delighted him," and your readers will rightfully wonder what continent Judd is currently on. Usually when you suspend the rules of the past perfect, it will be when you've taken your readers into a specific scene that shows the novel's distant past, and you want to linger there without clunking up your prose.

seven

Pronouns

One of the interesting features of simple pronouns is that their raison d'etre is aesthetic, rather than grammatical. While most sentence elements exist in order to make prose coherent or clear, simple pronouns exist so that our writing won't be ugly. One could argue that the complex forms — relative pronouns and interrogative pronouns — serve essential functions, but the more basic kinds, like "she" and "their" and "it," are not strictly necessary. If you wanted to, you could write, "Barbara took Barbara's wallet out of Barbara's purse and Barbara gave Barbara's check to Barbara's landlord," and the reader would understand what you meant.

But that reader would also become infuriated by the awkward repetition, which is the problem that pronouns take care of. In doing so, they don't actually eliminate the need for repetition, since the writer is often obliged to repeat the pronoun itself, as in the amended sentence "Barbara took her wallet out of her purse and gave her check to her landlord." But the "her" is much less obtrusive. Like other elements that get repeated often, such as articles and conjunctions, pronouns tend to be quiet little words that don't call attention to themselves, at least compared with "Barbara" or "Seattle" or "that jerk from accounting" or whatever else they replace. The objects that pronouns replace, by the way, are called antecedents.

In addition to replacing nouns, pronouns replace possessive adjectives like "Barbara's" or "the lumberjacks'." When they do that, with words like "her" and "their," they're called possessive pronouns, which is one of three pronoun forms. The other two are subjective and objective. Subjective ones, like "he" and "she" and "we," act as the subjects of a clause, while objective pronouns, like "him" and "her" and "me," act as direct objects or objects of a preposition. Also, you can refer to pronouns by whether they're singular or plural.

But man, is this boring. And we don't even need to hear most of it, since pronouns are parts of speech that we grasp early in life. We make some missteps now and then, especially in terms of differentiating the objective and subjective, but for the most part we have them under control, because we use them so often.

However, there are some instances of pronoun use in which our lifelong experience with them doesn't help us. In this chapter, we'll look at two issues concerning pronouns that involve grammatical or aesthetic complications, especially for those who write fiction.

MY KINGDOM FOR A SINGULAR NON-GENDERED THIRD-PERSON PRONOUN

Chapter 17, "Betrayals of Language," deals with the notion that sometimes the English language's inherent limitations, rather than our own shoddiness, cause ineffective prose. We'll look at one of the more troubling limitations here, rather than in the later chapter, because it's a significant pronoun usage issue. Specifically, the problem is that the English language lacks an effective singular non-gendered third-person pronoun. The name alone may have already put you to sleep, but if you stay with me for a while, you'll see that it's a real problem, perhaps one you've had to wrangle with before.

The need for a singular non-gendered third-person pronoun typically comes up when we invoke a theoretical person, as when we say, "A fan of opera should wonder about Bordoni's health" or "Someone should tell Rich to shut up." "A fan" and "someone" are theoretical beings who have the characteristics of liking opera and being obliged to silence Rich. Because these beings are individuals rather than groups (i.e., singular), and because we don't know if they're men or women (i.e., non-gendered), we need a singular non-gendered third-person pronoun whenever we replace them. If we want to avoid the repetition of "a fan of the opera should wonder if a fan of the opera will ever see Bordoni perform again," it's time to figure out what should stand in for the second "fan of the opera."

English actually does have a couple singular non-gendered third-person pronouns, one of which is "it." But that won't work in our examples, because when humans are being replaced, we expect the replacing pronoun to acknowledge their humanity. People can get sensitive about this. In my pre-fatherhood days, whenever I learned someone was pregnant, I would ask, "What are you going to name it?" and then suffer slings and arrows from people who rejected my use of "it" for the human baby. Even with nonhuman animals, "it" or "its" can touch a nerve. If someone were to tell me, "Your dog has gunk on its tail," I might say, "His name is Gordon, and he likes gunk, thank you very much."

Fiction writers can exploit this sensitivity, as Paul Harding does in *Tinkers*. A woman in the novel fears that she doesn't love her children as much as she should, and she deals with this fear by treating them with great strictness: "When one of her children wakes with a fever and a painful cough . . . [she] yanks the covers off of the shivering child and throws its clothes at it and says, Go get dressed, unless you want a good dousing." "The shivering child" is a person, but Harding—using a narrative voice aligned with the mother—gives "its" rather than "his" as the possessive pronoun, and instead of throwing the clothes at "him," the mother throws them at "it." The use of the pronoun meant for nonhuman objects underscores the mother's emotional frigidity—she doesn't think of her children as people. In fact, Harding tells us, "she felt no more connected to them than she would to a collection of stones." So not only does Harding underscore the mother's character by using "it," he also gets around the fact that he hasn't identified whether the child is a daughter or a son.

Usually, however, you can't take the easy way out. Harding has invoked the impersonal pronoun with subtlety, but most of the time if you try it, you'll sound like the serial killer in *Silence of the Lambs* ("It puts the lotion in the basket . . ."). So we're not left with many options, at least in Modern English (feel free to try to bring back the Middle English pronoun "ou"—I hear there's a Facebook group dedicated to the cause).

The actual singular non-gendered pronoun that would work in a perfect world is "one." Unfortunately, it's come to seem stuffy and archaic. Stevens, the narrator of *Remains of the Day*, can deliver lines like "Only in this way . . . could one be sure one's skills were being employed to a desirable end" because he's an English butler in the 1950s. But as the pronoun "one" has faded from our speech, so too has it gotten left out of third-person narratives. When a modern reader sees "he visited them as one goes with curiosity to call upon remarkable persons" in Joseph Conrad's *Nostromo*, the use of "one" seems as outdated as the use of "to call upon."

The most common method of dealing with the problem when we speak is to use the plural non-gendered pronoun forms "they," "them," and "their." This is technically a mistake because the pronouns are plural, while the object they're replacing is (say it with me) singular. In a worst-case scenario, the mismatching of a singular antecedent with a plural pronoun will cause confusion. To return to the earlier example, imagine you asked a pregnant woman, "What are you going to name *them*?" You've avoided the insensitivity of "it," and the awkwardness of "him or her," and the sexism of "him." But you've also implied that the woman is having twins ("What do you know that I don't?" she growls, grabbing your lapels).

In that example, the difficulty makes itself clear. More often, though, when we use plural pronouns to stand in for singular antecedents, the problem isn't obvious. We write sentences like, "Every true Philadelphian has their favorite cheese steak place," or "If someone wears white gloves, they should avoid popsicles," and everyone knows what we mean. So the good news is that the reader is unlikely to be distracted by the error. The bad news is that it's still an error, even if some linguists now argue for its acceptance—language changes, after all. It's up to you whether the error is so significant that you should only put it in the mouths of inarticulate narrators, or whether a reasonably intelligent first-person voice might use it.

You even may decide that a third-person narrator can employ the style. It seems to me that when authors do this, they often use a narrative voice closely aligned to a character, so the error becomes attributable to free indirect style. In Claire Messud's *The Emperor's Children*, for example, the third-person narrator tells us, "Anyone who said that *they* just woke up and found *themselves* in the place *they'd* always wanted to be was lying." The "anyone" is a single theoretical figure, and thus should get a singular pronoun, but the error works here because the voice is casual and brisk in the manner of the character being discussed. With more distant or objective narrative styles, the technique could risk distraction.

The use of "you" as a third-person pronoun is the Bizzaro World equivalent of "one," in that it's informal and modern rather than stuffy and archaic. Compare the butler Stevens's "*One* has had the privilege of practicing *one's* profession" with Forrest Gump's "Life is like a box of chocolates; *you* never know what *you're* gonna get." (The line never appears in Winston Groom's novel, by the way.) The informality derives from the fact that it's an erroneous usage; "you" is a second-person pronoun, meant to refer to someone the speaker is directly talking to. Pressing it into service as a third-person pronoun is non-standard. Consider the famous tag line for the film *Alien*: "In space, no one can hear you scream." If we read it literally, we might point to our chests and say "Me? No one can hear me scream? But I don't go to space. And why would I be screaming?" Instead, of course, we interpret the "you" as a theoretical third person. The line basically means, "In space, one's screams will not be heard," which isn't quite as catchy.

Most readers will understand and accept the secondary, informal function of "you"; actual second-person address is rare in fiction, so readers won't think the author's speaking directly to them. However, because the style creates a casual, ungrammatical voice — probably even more so than the use of "they" as a singular third-person pronoun — it's best used to reinforce the style of a certain kind of first-person narrator. Forrest Gump may not actually contain the box of chocolates line, but the eponymous narrator uses the third-person "you" quite often, as do other youthful, uneducated, or generally casual narrators: Scout Finch, Holden Caulfield, Chief Bromden, etc.

There are a few other reasons to be wary of "you," such as the fact that it won't work grammatically in many situations, because it tends to refer to a vague theoretical entity that basically encompasses all of humanity. You can't ask the pregnant lady, "What are you going to name you?" because the second "you" can't stand in for an individual figure, the way "him" or "it" or even "them" can. The "you" has to be applicable to pretty much everybody, as in "you reap what you sow" and "you are what you eat," and that's not always what theoretical third-person pronouns should do. The combination of its subjectivity and its technical oddness means that third-person narrators should use it sparingly.

In this book, I've used a couple of these methods, but mostly I've stuck with what I think is the best solution for the fiction writer, at least one who uses a third-person voice or a noncasual first-person one. Whenever a theoretical person comes up, I assign that person a random gender. I try to alternate between the masculine and the feminine, so that I won't seem sexist. Until the 1960s, style books advised using the masculine pronoun for all theoretical people, which wasn't just unfair to women, but could result in some weird constructions. In Angle of Repose, Wallace Stegner has some pronoun trouble when he describes a married couple going to bed: "They undressed in the dark, kissed lightly, and lay down, each in his separate narrow cot." The "his" at the end is ludicrous, because one of these characters is Susan Ward, Oliver's wife (in this case, the people aren't theoretical or unknown, but Stegner's grammatical construction means he has to treat them like they are). So in this sentence, the masculine pronoun in "his separate narrow cot" is wrong in 50 percent of its applications. One sympathizes with Stegner, though — my technique of randomly assigning genders wouldn't work here either; "her narrow separate cot" would also be 50 percent wrong.

The obvious fix for this—obvious to us, anyway—would be to write "each in his/her separate narrow cot," the method that's taught in nonfiction prose courses. The subjective forms "he/she" or "he or she" or even "s/he" and their objective and possessive counterparts ("him/her" and "his/hers") avoid favoring one gender even for a little while. Stephen King employs this style in a quote about adverbs we'll see in chapter 8:

> With adverbs, the writer usually tells us *he or she* is afraid *he/she* isn't expressing *himself/herself* clearly, that *he/she* is not getting the point or the picture across.

This passage clearly shows the problem with the style: it's disrupting and inelegant. Remember that a pronoun should allow you to avoid awkward repetition. Well, "him/her" and "himself/herself" call attention to themselves, so when they're repeated they neutralize that purpose. In the King sentence, all those slashed-together pronouns are only marginally less distracting than the repeated use of "the writer" would have been.

King gets away with it in this phrase, which is from *On Writing*, because of the nature of that book. It's simply not as concerned about lyricism or rhythm as works of fiction are (as far as I can tell, King has never used "he/she" in any of his novels). Plus, a nonfiction work doesn't worry about suspension of disbelief—it's okay with King if you know the sentences were constructed by a guy sitting at his desk, eating M&M's and worrying about the Red Sox. But the fiction writer has to avoid calling attention to the fact of her existence. Trying to be grammatical and nonsexist at the same time is a very human, very writerly thing to be concerned about. When a reader sees "he/she," he might appreciate your attempt not to offend anyone, but the fact that he's thinking of you at all is a small failure. It's hard to imagine any fictional work using "he/she" in a nondistracting way, unless it contained a first-person narrator who was fastidious about such things.

All this means that your decision about how to deal with our language's lack of an effective non-gendered singular third-person pronoun has to be based in large part on who tells the story. If you have a first-person narrator, you have most of the options at your disposal. Charlie Citrine, narrator of Saul Bellow's *Humboldt's Gift*, uses a variation of the first method: he always assumes masculinity in theoretical figures. This doesn't comment on the narrator's chauvinism, it was just the standard style of the time (and Citrine is a writer, so he would be up on standard usage). Kazuo Ishiguro, as we saw, made his traditionalist narrator in *Remains of the Day* repeatedly use "one." Huckleberry Finn, a character at the opposite end of the spectrum in terms of formality, matches singular antecedents with plural pronouns ("if a body can get anything *they* pray for . . .") because that's what he would do, just as Scout Finch would use the informal second-person. In all these instances, the writers solve the third-person non-gendered pronoun issue in a way that harmonizes with their characters' voices.

But when you use a third-person narrator the options are more limited. Except when the narrative voice is closely aligned to a character, I believe you've got to be both grammatical and non-distracting, which means either using some of the above methods in extreme moderation, or alternating between "he" or "she," or even biting the sexism bullet and using only one gender form.

THE RELATIVE AND DEMONSTRATIVE PRONOUN

It's now time to wrestle with perhaps the most problematic and multifunctional word a fiction writer will encounter: *that*. It's one of the most commonly used words in English; most people know how to use it, more or less, but few people can tell you specifically what it is or what function it serves in its various incarnations.

A line of dialogue from John Grisham's *The Associate* can help us get started: "And I'm guessing that I'll be involved in this plan that has yet to be created." The character gives us two different instances of "that" and one of "this" (which is so similar to "that" that we'll treat it as basically the same thing), and each one of these versions of "that/this" serves a different grammatical function.

The first "that," in "I'm guessing that I'll be involved," is not a pronoun at all, it's a conjunction, meaning it connects one clause ("I'm guessing") with another ("I'll be involved in this plan"). So we don't get to dwell on it in this chapter. You should certainly still think about the issue, not just because the conjunction "that" comes with complex usage rules—at least compared to the conjunctions you learned about in the *Schoolhouse Rocks* song—but also because it can often be removed from a sentence without sacrificing clarity. "I think [that] I'll have the scotch and soda" and "Kurt said [that] he'd be there at noon" are fine without them. Being able to effectively remove such conjunctions allows you to avoid ugly repetition, as in "I would argue that that is the issue at hand" or "he believes that that man killed Lucia," and in general it can make sentences more elegant. But again, we're sticking with pronouns in this section.

The second appearance of "this/that" in the Grisham sentence comes in the phrase "I'll be involved in *this* plan," and here it serves as a demonstrative element. A demonstrative element is one of four words — "this," "that," "those," "these" — that point to or replace a noun. Unfortunately, we have to split a couple hairs before we move on, because not all demonstrative elements are pronouns — some are demonstrative adjectives. A demonstrative pronoun occurs when the word replaces a noun entirely; if you say "that looks dangerous" while pointing to a roller coaster, notice that "roller coaster" never appears in the sentence. It's been replaced by the demonstrative pronoun "that." But what if you keep the noun, as in "that roller coaster looks dangerous"? You've now used "that" as a demonstrative *adjective*, because "that" modifies "roller coaster," it doesn't replace it.

You might say the difference is negligible — "that looks dangerous" and "that roller-coaster looks dangerous" mean the same thing — and I would agree with you. Yes, the difference in terminology makes sense, because pronouns replace nouns entirely, while adjectives modify them. But I think we can get along for the rest of the chapter by referring to these things as demonstrative pronouns (I hope so, anyway, since the chapter's about pronouns).

Whether to use "this" or "that" has to do with how close or far the referenced object is from the speaker. You say, "*This* train is comfortable" if you're sitting in it, but "*That* train was my last chance to get to Nashville" if you're watching it leave the station. "These/those" are simply the plural analogues of "this/that": "*These* shoes are killing me; I wish I hadn't lost *those* Birkenstocks."

Easy enough so far, right? Demonstrative pronouns sound like complex grammatical units, but they're not so tough. Even the name helps you out — you use them when you're pointing out something, as in a demonstration. But complexities certainly do ensue when we look at the third way the word "that" can function, which is to say as a relative pronoun. If you can't handle relative pronouns, you're likely to make a mistake in terms of word usage, tone, or commas. Plus, one of the issues raised by them involves an aesthetic decision you will have to make at some point, I guarantee it.

A relative pronoun is a word that connects a modifying element (a phrase that describes, specifies, intensifies, etc.) to a noun. In the Grisham example, the speaker uses one when he refers to a "plan *that* has yet to be created." It's not just a plan, it's a plan *that has yet to be created*. The latter phrase elaborates on the word "plan," and the two are connected by the word "that" (it may seem odd to call "that" a pronoun, since it doesn't seem to stand in for a noun, but let's not worry about it for now). While a number of words can be considered relative pronouns, in this case, the speaker has to use "that" for two reasons: 1) the object being modified is not a person, and 2) the modifying phrase attached to the object is restrictive—that is, essential to the meaning of the sentence.

To explore this point, let's consider the appropriate language to use if these facts did not apply. First off, what if the speaker were referring to a person, rather than a plan? Let's say he wanted to attach a modifying phrase like "has yet to be promoted" to a noun that is a person, like "employee." The phrase "the employee *that* has yet to be promoted" contains the same problem I encountered when I referred to an unborn baby as "it"—I've taken away the humanity of a person by referring to him with the same pronoun I'd use for linoleum. It may not look as egregious here, but it shows up more starkly when you get specific, as in "I gave the rugby ball to my son Simon that likes sports." Using "that" as a relative pronoun with a person can be a vernacular eccentricity, as it is in some Irish dialects—characters in James Joyce's *Ulysses* describe "the flatulent old bitch that's dead" and "a rotter that's insincere." But in Standard English "that" as a relative pronoun is reserved for nonhumans.

To understand the second rule—use "that" when the modifying phrase is restrictive—we have to realize that a restrictive phrase is essential to the meaning of the sentence; in fact, the term is interchangeable with "essential phrase." If we call a phrase nonrestrictive or nonessential, we mean its inclusion isn't necessary for the sentence to achieve its main goal. Consider, for example, "My car, which I bought in Reno, needs new brakes." If I take out "which I bought in Reno," the sentence is a little different, but the basic meaning remains intact. The nonrestrictive phrase only serves to provide some additional information.

But in the Grisham example, "that has yet to be created" is an essential adjunct to "plan." The speaker tells us so by his use of "that"—the word indicates he would consider his sentence irrevocably altered if you didn't catch the "has yet to be created" part. And he's right; his whole point in saying the line is to underscore the fact that the plan doesn't exist and thus it's foolish and jerky to make him be a part of it. But what if he didn't feel this way? What if he wanted to show that it didn't matter to him how complete the plan was, that he was only using the phrase nonessentially in order to give more detail of the plan in question? Well, he'd change "that" to "which," and he'd throw a comma in front of it, as in "this plan, which has yet to be created." You've already seen this in action — in the previous paragraph's sample sentence, "which I bought in Reno" is unnecessary because it doesn't have anything to do with the car needing brakes. But the use of "which," rather than "that," also advertised its nonrestrictive nature.

We've now solved one of the more troubling elements of pronoun usage for writers: when to use "that" and when to use "which." It's a simple point: you use "that" to connect an object to a phrase that you consider essential to the sentence's meaning. "I fell asleep on a rock that turned out to be a whale" is very different from "I fell asleep on a rock." But in the sentence "I fell asleep on a rock, which was unpleasant" the "which was unpleasant" is not essential. I want to reiterate that writers of all skill levels mess this up, so it's worth taking a few seconds to check your grammar whenever you find yourself using relative pronouns. If you use "which," ask yourself if the information that follows is unessential; if you took it out, would the sentence have the same meaning? If so, great. If not, change the "which" to "that" and drop the comma.

Naturally, there's a cruel exception to all this that will come up from time to time. If the relative pronoun you want to use is the object of a preposition, you need to use "which," even if it's an essential phrase. Here's what it looks like in Thomas Hardy's *Mayor of Casterbridge*:

> The sloping pathways by which spectators had ascended to their seats were pathways yet.

Pathways are not people, and the modifying phrase "by which spectators had ascended to their seats" is restrictive/essential. So it meets our two requirements for using "that." However, because the relative pronoun is an object of a preposition — it has "by" in front of it, and "by" is a preposition — you have to go with "which." It sounds strange when I describe it, but basic examples — "the house in which I grew up," "the throne on which he sits" — show how it works.

The second hill to climb in regard to relative pronouns takes us back to the two points about the Grisham sentence. I explained that the word "that" is necessary because the object referred to is not a person, and because the modifying phrase is essential. I then went on to tell you what to do if your modifying phrase is nonrestrictive. But I never told you what to do if the object is a person and you don't want to strip him of his human dignity, or impersonate a Joycean Irishman, by using "that."

This issue raises concerns that are aesthetic as well as mechanical, because you have to now reckon with a tough irony: too much grammatical correctness can actually be something that fiction writers *avoid*. But first, the technical answer to the above problem, which you probably already know: in the example phrase "the employee that has never been promoted," we should replace the dehumanizing "that" with the personal relative pronoun "who." The employee *who* has never been promoted, the king *who* sits on the throne, the man *who* knew too much—we use it instinctively. Notice, too, that it doesn't matter whether the phrase is restrictive or not. "Lila, who comes from Nice, makes an excellent crepe" uses "who" to introduce a nonrestrictive phrase, while "the girl who comes from Nice should be separated from the Parisian woman" uses "who" to introduce a restrictive one. The only difference is that the nonrestrictive clause needs to be surrounded by commas (for reasons we'll devour in chapter 13).

Native speakers of English don't usually have much trouble with such matters. Many of us know instinctively that we shouldn't write, "My attorney, *that* hails from Spain, has a big family," or "The knife *who* has a serrated edge shouldn't be used for dicing." And in many situations we can omit the relative pronoun altogether. The rule is that the omission only works with a restrictive clause, and only when the clause is independent, but it's not so important to memorize the technical usage. We don't need a grammar rule to know that the lack of a relative pronoun in "she's the kind of girl you take home to Mom" works okay, but that "I saw a girl looked exactly like a shark" needs a "who" before "looked."

The personal relative pronoun issue that truly confounds many writers concerns the usage of "who" and "whom." I believe the word "whom" is so misunderstood and feared by people that it's actually leaving our language. We're so uncertain about when to say it that we never say it. Even many English teachers won't mark a student's paper when "who" is used instead of "whom," either because they consider it a pedantic or upper-level grammatical point (an odd argument, since it's essentially the same mistake as confusing "he" and "him") or else they're not confident enough in their own ability to use it. This has serious consequences for the fiction writer, as we shall see.

"Whom" is the objective form of the subjective pronoun "who," just as "him" is the objective form of the subjective pronoun "he." Because "who" is a relative or interrogative pronoun rather than a simple one, it's more difficult to know when it should be subjective and when it should be objective. (It's not always a slam dunk with simple pronouns, either; the common phrase "between you and I" uses the objective form of the first-person pronoun, when the objective "me" is called for.) Most of the time, people go with the subjective "who" because using "whom" seems like a lose-lose scenario. If a person says "whom" correctly, she may come off as pompous, and if she uses it incorrectly, she sounds like she was trying to be pompous but instead came off as ignorant. Plus, no one gets upset if you use "who" when you should have used "whom."

But let's pretend for a moment that correct grammatical usage matters. So how do you figure out when the relative pronoun "whom" is appropriate? You ask what role it serves in the relative clause. Our previous sentence, "She's the kind of girl you take home to Mom," omits the relative pronoun, but if we had one it would be either "who" or "whom." So let's figure out which one. The relative clause—the thing that modifies "girl"—is "you take home to Mom." If you consider that phrase by itself, you realize it's missing something: "her." In effect, you're trying to say that "you take *her* home to Mom" is a trait belonging to the noun "girl." "Her" is an objective pronoun. So in replacing it, you have to use the objective relative pronoun: "whom." "She's the kind of girl *whom* you take home to Mom."

"Who" and "whom" also function as interrogative pronouns, which means they're involved with the asking of questions. You use the same process to figure them out, though: you try to decide if the word they replace is subjective or objective. Unfortunately, interrogative constructions with "who/whom" don't often have antecedents (because the question itself tends to ask what the antecedent is), so it helps to stick in a theoretical one. Let's do it with the first line of John Barth's novella "Lost in the Funhouse": "For whom is the funhouse fun?" If Barth had wondered if he'd incorrectly used "whom," he could have replaced the objective "whom" with the subjective "she," and rearranged the syntax to read "The funhouse is fun for she." The resulting awkwardness would have told him that the pronoun being replaced was in fact objective—"The funhouse is fun for *her*"—and thus he would know he'd been right the first time.

This is a lot of work, of course. If you ask someone, "Do you know who is going to host the Emmys this year?" you don't have time to fiddle with syntax and replace "who" with a theoretical subjective pronoun just to see if it works (it does). For this reason, and for the previously stated ones, we've come to accept "who" as the primary personal relative and interrogative pronoun. Even grammar sticklers use clues when they say "whom"—often they look for a nearby preposition, as in *With* whom are you going to prom?" because that tells them the pronoun functions as an object of a preposition.

Our general suspicion of "whom" has seeped its way into art. I think it's absolutely delightful that the Clash sing, "Exactly whom I'm supposed to be" in one of their songs, but in the world of pop music you could consider the band's proper usage of the relative pronoun atypical. In fact, it might even be distracting, since "whom" is often regarded as pedantic and pompous, a maneuver meant to show your mastery of grammar. As silly as that is, I'm afraid it's a hard notion to fight against. Thus, any artist—a British rock star or a literary novelist—has to consider whether sticking to the proper grammatical form fits with the tone she wants to establish. Obviously, this largely depends on point of view. If you're using the first-person, you have to decide whether your narrator would use "whom" with rigid consistency (like Ishiguro's Stevens), or would use it sporadically in an attempt to sound intelligent (like P. G. Wodehouse's Bertie Wooster), or would never even think about trying it (like Ring Lardner's Whitey).

Whether to use "whom" in a third-person narrative is a thornier subject. To some degree, it depends on the style you've selected, because third-person narrators come in all shapes and sizes. We would be shocked if a formal, articulate narrator like the kind used by Henry James or George Eliot ever mixed up the objective and subjective pronouns, but when more casual third-person narrators are invoked, we're not surprised that they sometimes eschew "whom" even when it's called for. For example, in "Female Troubles," Antonya Nelson begins an interior portrait of the story's protagonist by asking, "Who did he love?" Grammatically speaking, it should read, "Whom did he love?" But most people won't notice or care, while many readers would be distracted if the narrator were to become so grammatically precise—some would say persnickety—while trying to reveal the thoughts of the decidedly unpretentious character. It would have a distancing effect—the narrator would show itself to be adept with the technicalities of language, but removed from the chaotic, raw confusion of the protagonist.

eight

Adverbs

As an exercise, I sometimes ask my students to write a paragraph that comprises intentionally awful prose. They usually wind up with something like this: "A single tear trickling mournfully down his chiseled features, he languidly and sorrowfully dropped his head on her gorgeously heaving bosom."

This sentence is bad for several reasons, but it derives much of its wicked power from an artless use of modifiers. The core of the sentence, after all, is "he dropped his head"—nothing too offensive about that. But when you modify the core elements with awkward participial phrases ("A single tear trickling . . ."), melodramatic adverbs ("mournfully," "gorgeously"), and cliché adjectives ("chiseled," "heaving"), you're in the ugly sentence business. The lesson these students have learned is an old one: using modifiers, especially adverbs, often leads to awkward prose. In this chapter and the one that follows, we'll examine this sometimes useful, sometimes misleading advice.

We can broadly define a modifier as anything in a sentence that isn't grammatically necessary, but that expands or specifies or in some way *modifies* the core components. Those core components are the subject and the verb. As long as these two things complete a thought, you've got a sentence, but usually you'll want your prose to do more than the bare minimum. Modifiers allow writers to add nuance and sophistication to the sentence's core.

Three other points about the nature and function of modifiers before we move on:

1) Although this chapter deals with adverbs, modifiers come in a number of other forms. You can modify with a prepositional phrase ("the bear *in the woods*"), a subordinating conjunction ("the bear eats *after killing*"), adjectives ("a *pensive* bear"), infinitive phrases ("wearing cologne is the best way *to attract bears*"), and on and on.

2) A modifier can alter the core components in a number of ways. It can intensify ("if you *really* want to hear about it,") expand ("it is a truth *universally* acknowledged"), describe ("Chicago, that *somber* city"), specify ("*happy* families are all alike"), and on and on.

3) In addition to modifying the core components, modifiers often modify each other. When you say, "I grew up in an extremely ornate castle," the adverb "extremely" modifies "ornate," which is itself an adjective that modifies the noun "castle," which is itself part of a prepositional phrase that modifies the core sentence "I grew up." You can pile modifier upon modifier as much as your common sense dictates.

That might seem like a lot to think about for a grammatically unnecessary sentence element, but modifiers are enormously useful, and worthy of our attention. Plus, if we stuck only to the core elements, we'd sound like cavemen.

With this framework in place, we'll now look at one particular modifier, the adverb. In grammar handbooks, the adverb often gets lumped in with its modifier cousin, the adjective. But I'm not going to talk about adjectives, because they're not as problematic or complex as adverbs are. An adjective modifies a noun: "lucky," "humorous," "gargantuan," "stern," "hot," etc. Most people understand that using too many of them in a row is a little silly, which is about the only advice I have to offer on their usage.

The adverb is a different story. It has many more functions than the adjective, yet it's more limited in terms of what it looks and sounds like, which has implications for prose rhythm. Furthermore, of the eight parts of speech, it tends to be the most vilified, and therefore the one that most requires further investigation.

DEFINITION AND FUNCTION

You can skip this section if you feel confident about how much attention you paid in fifth-grade language arts. Otherwise, here goes . . .

An adverb is a modifier that can alter a verb, an adjective, another adverb, or an entire clause. Below you'll find some samples sentences in which the adverb has been italicized. An explanation for why the word is an adverb follows in parentheses:

She laughed *merrily* ("merrily" modifies the verb "laughed")

The *extremely* tall woman laughed ("extremely" modifies the adjective "tall")

The woman laughed *very* loudly ("very" modifies the adverb "loudly")

Surprisingly, the woman laughed ("surprisingly" modifies the entire clause)

Adverbs usually end in –ly. Not all of them do — "fast," "very," and "still," for example. And not all words that end in –ly are adverbs; "lovely" and "silly" are adjectives, "folly" and "jelly" are nouns. But it's a good rule of thumb, and we'll pick up on its implications later.

NOW FOR THE HATRED

In writing handbooks and classrooms, the typical advice about adverbs boils down to "don't use them, unless you're meeting the demands of terrorists." Elmore Leonard tells us that to use an adverb "in almost any way" is "a mortal sin." In *On Writing*, Stephen King says, "The road to hell is paved with adverbs." William Zinsser's seminal book *On Writing Well* declares that "most adverbs are unnecessary." Even Strunk and White, who defend the adverb in some places, say that "you'd probably be better off without it." All of this can be comforting to hear. Since everyone agrees adverbs will make your prose terrible, then you can just avoid them.

Of course, it's not that simple. While there may be reasons for fiction writers to tread cautiously around modification, the animosity toward adverbs strikes me as dogmatic and simplistic. I also believe that when people make the argument that adverbs damage prose, they often use assumptions about the English language that don't hold up to inspection. In the following sections, we'll delve into some of the reasons commonly offered for why adverbs should be avoided, and we'll examine the strengths and weaknesses of the logic behind them.

TIMIDITY AND REDUNDANCY

Stephen King can serve as the spokesman for the first charge against adverbs. In *On Writing*, he tells us that adverbs

seem to have been created with the timid writer in mind . . . With
adverbs, the writer usually tells us he or she is afraid he/she isn't
expressing himself/herself clearly, that he/she is not getting the point or
the picture across.

(You may notice, if you want to be snarky, that his second sentence contains
two adverbs.)

The main charge here is redundancy, which King interprets as an indicator of timidity. He believes that because most adverbs are redundant,
their usage shows a lack of confidence in the writer. After all, if you repeat
something, it often means you suspect you didn't get it right the first time.
Constructed as a syllogism, the argument looks like this:

Premise 1: Redundancy usually indicates timidity.

Premise 2: Most adverbs are redundant.

Conclusion: Most adverbs usually indicate timidity.

The rules of deductive reasoning tell us that if both premises are true, then
the conclusion must also be true. And it certainly looks hard to argue with
the first premise; repeating something does tend to show that you're worried you didn't say it right the first time. But the logic may fall apart in the
second premise, the assertion that most adverbs are redundant.

At some point in your education, someone probably told you that if you
choose your verbs and adjectives well enough, you won't need a modifier for
them. This teacher—or handbook author—might have used any number of
examples to illustrate the point. For instance, William Zinsser writes that
the phrase "a radio blares loudly" is redundant because the word " 'blare'
connotes loudness." True enough. Following this lead, you can probably
think up a long list of verbs, such as "guzzle" and "slam" and "gasp," that
don't just tell us what happened, but with what intensity it happened. You
also might consider all those highly specific adjectives, like "unique" and
"antepenultimate" and "inchoate," that abhor further modification.

This notion of the self-sufficiency of verbs and adjectives leads to a
related charge against adverbs: even when they're not redundant, they're
unnecessary, as long as you have a sufficient vocabulary. It's easy to see that
"the radio blares loudly" is redundant, because if you cut out the adverb,
the sentence doesn't change. But what about "the radio plays loudly"? In

this case, loudness is not inherent in the verb "plays," thus no redundancy. Yet the writer can still avoid the adverb, because she can find a verb that means "to play loudly," i.e., "blare." So even if adverbs aren't always redundant—the argument goes—they are at best unnecessary.

Zinsser warns us about other pairings, such as "effortlessly easy," "totally flabbergasted," and "he tightly clenched his teeth"—redundant constructions that may scare us away from adverbs. Until, that is, we realize these examples are cherry-picked; we won't see them all that often, except when someone's trying to scare us away from adverbs. Zinsser has constructed these phrases to imply that English verbs and adjectives are so specific we never have to modify them. Premise #2 rests upon this assumption, and it's a false one. In fact, the majority of words in our language do *not* connote very many shades of degree or intensity.

The premise's falsehood should be evident from experience. If you've written more than a page in your life, you've been in many situations in which you couldn't express your full meaning without an adverb or adverbial phrase. Sure, "he slammed the door angrily" is redundant. But what if I want to attribute anger to the act of clipping toenails, or washing a car, or playing the harpsichord? What if I want to signify that my protagonist isn't merely agile, but agile in a way that is surprising or suspicious or frightening? What adjective indicates that?

If you're still not convinced, test it for yourself. Take a randomly generated list of verbs—say, the first ones you find on pages 50, 100, and 150 of the nearest dictionary. Then, try to create a sentence in which a person or thing performs these actions with fear, speed, and joy, respectively. When I did this with my American Heritage Dictionary, I found myself with the phrases "she ascertained the information fearfully," and "he quickly boiled an egg," and "the monks chanted joyfully." In none of these cases could I have found a verb that obviated the need for the adverb. Will it happen occasionally? Of course. But not often.

So why do we accept an assumption that is so obviously not true? I think it has to do with a linguistic inferiority complex. We hear that we wouldn't need adverbs if we had a larger vocabulary, so our first reaction is not to question the assertion, but rather to chide ourselves, and maybe get a word-a-day calendar. In effect, our use of adverbs is portrayed as a moral problem—notice that King and Leonard use the language of damnation ("the road to hell," "mortal sin") when they condemn them. True, if all adverbs could be avoided by finding a better verb or adjective, then their use might indicate either laziness or a limited vocabulary, both of which are grievous sins for a writer. But that's simply not the case. Furthermore, even when you can replace adverb combinations with a single verb or adjective, you may not want to. You could substitute "an extremely weak hamster" with "an etiolated hamster," or "he walked slowly" with "he perambulated," but is that always a good idea?

I need to pull back a bit from the vehemence of this pro-adverb screed, because I don't want to lay it on too thickly. As we'll see in the rest of the chapter, there are legitimate reasons to be suspicious of adverbs, and adverb redundancy doesn't appear exclusively in examples set up by grammarians — you see it more than you'd like to in student and even professional fiction. I recently read a story that contained the phrase "beautifully good-looking," at which point I had to stop grading and watch a hockey game.

That phrase, of course, has redundancy problems of the type I've discussed — the adverb is superfluous because the adjective already contains the meaning the adverb seeks to add. But there's another type of adverb redundancy that anti-adverbites sometimes warn you about, and I think they're on more solid ground with this one.

Adverbs can be made redundant by context and character much more easily than they can be made redundant by language. In linguistic terms, it's impossible to convey the concept "Sam gutted the fish angrily" without using a modifier, because we don't have a verb that means "to gut fish with anger" (I bet the Germans do). However, the reader can understand with what emotion Sam gutted the fish if the writer has provided enough context — if, for example, Sam gutted the fish right after being kicked out of law school, or if the fish had murdered Sam's favorite lizard. A reader who understands Sam's emotional state does not need the adverb "angrily"; our knowledge of the character makes it unnecessary.

Sometimes we don't even have to know all that much about the character, because the situation itself, no matter who's involved, will indicate how a person responds. A writer who gives us "surprisingly, Gerald announced he was a woman" seems afraid that the announcement is not as surprising as it should be, so she's provided an adverb telling us to be surprised. The writer of "Dr. Jensen pointed the gun at her maliciously" apparently worries that his readers don't consider pointing a gun to be a malicious act. Either way, the writers are guilty of timidity; they need to have more faith in themselves and their readers.

Of course, I've now done what I've accused Zinsser of doing, by constructing the type of overt redundancy you won't see very often, and I would ask you to be aware of that—most of the time, adverbs do *not* underscore something the reader already knows. I simply want to point out that it's possible, and in fact it's more likely, for adverbs to be redundant in this way. Therefore, the real question to ask when using an adverb is not "is there a verb or adjective that obviates the need for the modifier?" Usually there won't be. The better question is, "Has the content of the scene already established the emotion, intensity, or quality that the adverb seeks to provide?"

LESS IS MORE

Besides the flawed notion that adverbs are usually redundant, another assumption colors our feelings about this sad little modifier—and, in fact, our thoughts about literary style in general—and has done so for almost a hundred years. The assumption is this: all things being equal, you should express an idea with fewer words rather than more.

This idea relates to the law of parsimony, sometimes called "Ockham's Razor," which is useful in the sciences. (NB: a scientist friend of mine claims that nonscientists always misuse the term, so I'll tread lightly.) William of Ockham declared that "it is futile to do with more things that which can be done with fewer," and indeed this seems to be a good concept to hold to when trying to explain the world around us. If I look outside and my lawn appears to be damp, it's possible that a truck full of Sprite crashed in my yard. But the explanation that requires fewer mental gymnastics, and which is thus more likely to be true, is that it rained.

The acceptance of a literary version of the law of parsimony lies at the heart of the argument that you should replace a verb/adverb combo with a more precise verb. The phrase "the radio blared" is only better than "the radio played loudly" if you think that when two phrases are identical in terms of meaning, you should choose the one with fewer words. Even the redundancy argument depends on the acceptance of Ockham's Razor. If you think about it, the only problem with the phrase "the radio blared loudly" is that it uses an extra word when it doesn't have to; thus, we should only avoid it if fewer words are better than more.

The application of the less-is-better philosophy to literature is largely a twentieth-century notion. Sure, Shakespeare tells us "brevity is the soul of wit," but we should remember the line belongs to the blowhard Polonius (who says it while using eleven lines to get across the basic point "Hamlet is crazy"), and that it appears in Shakespeare's longest play. Neoclassical writers loved the efficiency of couplets, but not to the exclusion of more expansive forms. In any case, concision as a preferred literary style isn't an ancient principle; our contemporary taste for succinct prose is something of a Modernist construction. In spite of prolix Modernists like Faulkner and Joyce, the true progenitor of twentieth-century prose style was Hemingway. As novelist Adam Haslett puts it, when Hemingway usurped Henry James, "the terse, declarative sentence in all its masculine hardness routed the passive involutions of a higher, denser style." Such prose was endorsed by Strunk and White ("Vigorous writing is concise") and reinforced by later minimalists like Raymond Carver, Mary Robison, and Denis Johnson. Zinsser sums up the preferences of the century when he turns his attention to modifiers and tells us to "avoid unnecessary adverbs."

But I have to say, I've never known what to do with this advice, or with Strunk and White's "omit needless words," a phrase that makes many writers positively giddy. These maxims remind me of how my mom would say, "Is that really necessary?" whenever I would tease my sister or stick a grape up my nose. I always wanted to respond, "Well of course not, but since when is necessity the only reason for doing something?"

Almost everything in fiction is unnecessary, or "needless," from a grammatical standpoint. "Feet hurt" is the only necessary element of the sentence "Mitchell's feet hurt so badly he has to excuse himself from the party." But necessity is not the same as clarity or elegance. So perhaps what givers of this advice mean by "necessary" is "that which is required to get across what you mean."

But that doesn't help either. If you write, "she spoke quietly," or "there was a very strong reek," presumably you have said what you meant. You didn't mean "she whispered" — there's a subtle differing between whispering and speaking quietly — and you didn't want to give the unintensified "there was a strong reek." The adverbs are therefore necessary, if by "necessary" you mean "that which is required to get across my specific point," yet Strunk, White, Zinsser, et al. would warn you away from the adverbs in these examples.

For many contemporary critics, writers, and readers, "unnecessary" really means anything that falls on the short end of a risk-reward calculation, where the risk is that you flirt with wordiness, and the reward is that your sentence becomes somewhat more specific. The question then becomes, does the modifier help the phrase more than the addition of another sentence element hurts it?

You can think of it as a calculation: pretend that every word you add to a story costs a dollar, and you have to examine everything to make sure it's worth the price. As in life, how you feel about laying out cash depends on your tastes and inclinations. Like a cut-rate contractor, you could stick to the bare minimum, getting rid of anything that ornaments or modifies and paying only for the absolute necessities (load-bearing walls, verbs). While you will have completed the project cheaply, the result might be shoddy and uninteresting. Conversely, you could be the Donald Trump of stylists, sparing no expense and packing the place with titanium-plated urinals (I'm not sure what the analogous language element would be in this metaphor—possibly Latin quotations), but you may wind up with something gaudy and distracting.

These are the two extremes. Most of us wind up somewhere other than the far ends of the stylistic spectrum, although contemporary writers, for literary-historical reasons, tend to gravitate toward the spare, terse style of Hemingway more than toward the prolix, ornamented prose that dominated the nineteenth century. Where you fall on that spectrum is up to you, but your decision shouldn't be influenced by the myth that certain types of modification—or expansiveness in general—are inherently bad. The decision also relates to other elements of language, in particular diction, which we'll look at in chapter 10.

SOUND AND RHYTHM

In the last section we explored the standard logic used to warn writers away from adverbs, that is, the idea that they're redundant, or can be avoided if you find a more effective verb and adjective, and the idea that we should always prefer concision to wordiness. Although I sought to poke holes in some aspects of that logic, I don't want you to take the section as a full-on endorsement of adverbs. The fact that the standard argument may be bogus doesn't lead to the conclusion that adverbs always help. In fact, they do tend to cause trouble for fiction writers, more so than other parts of speech. We already looked at one reason for this, when we explored how they can be made redundant by content and context. Another reason is much simpler: adverbs tend to sound worse than other parts of speech when they're overused.

Before we get into the nuts and bolts of this point, I want to introduce a sentence that can transition us from the last section to this one, because it illustrates something about the main ideas of each. It's the famous opening from Stephen Crane's *Red Badge of Courage*:

> The cold passed reluctantly from the earth, and the retiring fogs revealed an army stretched out on the hills, resting.

I think even anti-adverbites would let "reluctantly" remain here. No English verb means "to pass reluctantly," so the adverb isn't superfluous. Furthermore, if you get rid of it for the sake of economy, you've lost something—"the cold passed from the earth" doesn't connote the necessary tone of languidness, which is reinforced in the second clause and which will be a significant element of the entire chapter. Finally, Crane plays a somewhat complex literary game with the adverb. Reluctance is a trait we usually attribute to animate objects, so the adverb personifies the cold; it gives human agency to a phenomenon of nature. This is highly ironic, because Crane, as a naturalist, continually reinforced the idea that nature is indifferent, apathetic, mechanical—that it doesn't care about us because it can't.

And even if the adverb didn't earn its keep by carrying all this thematic and imagistic weight, you'd still want to keep it simply because it sounds good. Again, without the adverb, the first clause reads, "the cold passed from the earth." Every word contains a single syllable, and half of them are bit players like articles and prepositions. It's not a bad phrase, just not all that lyrical or compelling. So in the midst of these banal monosyllables, Crane sticks in a four-syllable word that is somewhat onomatopoeic (the word escapes from one's mouth with reluctance), sounds pretty (a great combination of soft l's and hard t's), and provides a syntactic balance by bifurcating the opening clause (three words/syllables to the left, three to the right). That's a hell of a day's work for one word.

Unfortunately, this usage is perhaps the exception that proves the rule. I've started with it because I want to maintain, in spite of this section's main points, that adverbs can be used with brilliance and power. I don't think any part of speech can do more than what Crane's "reluctantly" does here, so please think about it the next time you hear someone belittle the adverb as a second-class citizen when compared to nouns and verbs.

Yet it's no accident that when my students create examples of bad writing, they lay on the adverbs—"mournfully" and "sorrowfully" in this chapter's opening paragraph clearly damage the prose. They do so, in large part, by adding an awkward rhythm with their repetitive constructions. Most adverbs are born when –ly gets added to an adjective ("tireless" becomes "tirelessly") or a participle ("pleading" becomes "pleadingly"). And this means — not to get too technical on you — that if you use a lot of them, your prose will have a lot of –ly sounds.

Repetition is a tricky device, as we'll see in chapter 17. Sometimes it creates striking lyricism, and sometimes it sounds clunky. When repetition works, as in Joyce's "he heard the snow falling faintly through the universe, and faintly falling, like the descent of their last end," the repeated sounds act like a theme in a fugue, or a motif in a painting. When repetition doesn't work, as in "he *languidly* and *sorrowfully* dropped his head on her *gorgeously* heaving bosom," the repeated elements act like hurdles in a steeplechase, impediments that make the reader break stride.

When you're being lyrical and when you're being clunky is to some degree a matter of taste and time. In the mid-nineteenth century, audiences admired linguistic habits that contemporary writers can't get away with. One of them was the repetitive use of –ly adverbs. In Harriet Beecher Stowe's *Uncle Tom's Cabin*, for example, you get phrases like these (italics mine):

> "Poor creature!" said Mrs. Bird *compassionately*, as the woman *slowly* unclosed her large, dark eyes, and looked *vacantly* at her.

> She strained him *suddenly* and *tightly* in her arms, and *slowly* one tear after another fell.

Regardless of whether the adverbs help the content (Zinsser would have a fit about the redundant "compassionately," with good reason), a modern reader probably finds this –ly repetition damaging to the sound of the prose. Apologists for Stowe's style point out that she worked in the discourse of sentimentalism, in which such prose was encouraged, but that's a contextual argument; it doesn't assert that the style itself is pleasing. Ours may be a twentieth-/twenty-first-century prejudice, but it's not one we can easily shake off. To verify this, consider how you experience a revised version of the Stowe sentences in which we replace her –ly words with adverbs that don't end with that letter combination:

> "Poor creature!" said Mrs. Bird *often*, as the woman *almost* unclosed her large, dark eyes, and *still* looked at her.

She strained him *now* and *hard* in her arms, and *then* one tear after another fell.

Sure, they don't make any sense, but they work better from a rhythm standpoint, at least to contemporary ears and eyes.

If you want an example that contains actual coherence, compare "Rufus frequently ran intensely and speedily" with "Rufus often ran hard and fast." In both cases, the modifiers help to clarify the writer's intent—she wants you to know that on many occasions Rufus ran in a particular way. Stripping the sentence bare, as anti-adverbites might advise, would leave you with "Rufus ran," and that's not what the author meant. Yet in the first version, the specificity added by the adverbs isn't worth the damage they cause to the sound of the sentence. The reader won't even be able to pay attention to the content, because the ugliness will distract him. Luckily, this writer can have her cake and eat it too, by modifying the sentence with adverbs that don't invoke the –ly repetition. That won't always be a way out, though, because most adverbs do end that way. You can only use "often" and "fast" so many times.

A final complaint in the sound category has to do with another thing Strunk and White disliked about adverbs: because they can be created by adding an –ly to virtually any participle or adjective, an adverbophile writer might produce odd and distracting new words. Yes, originality is prized in fiction, but so, too, is the avoidance of distraction. To present a reader with "the telephone superannuatedly contained a rotary dialer," or "the scientists revolutionarily proved the theory" is to ask him to think about your word choice, not your content. It's probably best to not use an adverb unless you've seen it a few times.

In sum, one key prejudice against adverbs springs from the fact that, when used too often, they create an awkward sound, or at least one that contemporary readers don't like. When we read writers from pre-Modernist times, we make many adjustments for their style—we forgive them for their adverb tolerance the same way we forgive them for wearing funny hats and believing in Lamarckian evolution. Not even Stephen King would argue that Melville and Hawthorne and Stowe were timid writers, yet today's readers would not accept someone who imitated their style, at least in terms of how they embraced –ly modifiers.

So that's the strongest case against adverbs, in my opinion. Not that they're inherently redundant, not that we can always avoid them by finding more precise verbs or adjectives, not that writers should always try to use fewer words—those assertions aren't objectively true. The real reason to avoid adverbs is that they run the risk of disrupting a sentence's eloquence, because of the way most of them are constructed. That alone may be a good enough reason; sound and rhythm matter immensely in fiction. Still, it's unfortunate that such a useful linguistic tool should carry a risk that other parts of speech don't. At the very least, I think we should acknowledge that our disdain for adverbs has less to do with what function they serve than with what they look and sound like. How superficial of us.

A FINAL THOUGHT

For teachers of creative writing, the problem with instilling a fear of adverbs in students is that the bright ones will notice how many excellent writers disagree. No matter how much the instructor cherry-picks examples of dreadful modification, eventually one of the more astute young writers in the class will come across adverb usage that works brilliantly, like Joseph O'Neill's "we courted in the style preferred by the English: alcoholically," or Sam Lipsyte's "the beginning of aggressively marketed nachos," or Crane's aforementioned "reluctantly," and she'll be confused. She may even run to the teacher with copies of *Netherland* or *The Ask* or *The Red Badge of Courage* in hand and say, "They did it, so why'd you tell us not to?"

The true answer is that the teacher wanted to save himself from having to read a lot of bad writing. If he didn't warn students against adverbs, he'd be up to his neck in phrases like "she glowered menacingly" and "Arthur cried despondently" and "the dog sneezed extremely alarmingly." No shame in that—a teacher should try to prevent students from doing bad work. But a teacher should also do whatever he can to encourage good work, even mastery, and in this case our theoretical instructor has limited the students' ability to achieve it. Basically, he's told them to accept a falsehood—adverbs are redundant, adverbs always imply timidity—because it's easier and less time-consuming than explaining the delicate art of modification.

This may be a good way to protect the sanity of a creative writing instructor, but it most definitely is not the way to help anyone master a fiction writer's language. In a quote that writers love to invoke, the Roman playwright Terence tells us, "I am a human being; nothing human is alien to me." We can amend that for our purposes, and say, "I am a writer; nothing in language is off limits to me."

nine

Participial Phrases That Modify

It's time to examine another modifier that bedevils fiction writers. This one doesn't get as much critical heat as adverbs do, but it can do a great deal of damage if you don't have it under control. I'm referring to the modifying participial phrase.

If I've already used more grammatical jargon than you're comfortable with, I would ask you to hang on for a little bit longer, with the assurance that it will make sense when you see examples. A modifying participial phrase is just a phrase that 1) begins with a participle, and 2) modifies a subject, verb, or an entire sentence.

Of course, to understand this definition you have to know what participles are (you promised to hang on for a while, remember?). A participle results from taking a verb and attaching an –ed or –ing to the end. In the sentences "I am seething" and "I have labored," the participles are "seething" (that's a present participle, if you want extra credit) and "labored" (a past participle). They don't always look like this, because past participles sometimes take irregular forms ("I have lost," "the spear was *thrown*"), but usually they do.

Participles are versatile. In "I am seething" and "I have labored," they serve as verbs, aided by the helping verbs "am" and "have." But they can also act as nouns, as in "Partying rules!" and "Golfing relaxes me" (in this form, they're called gerunds — sorry, couldn't resist sneaking that one in). And they can serve as adjectives, as in "the *demented* professor" or "the *laughing* cow."

Again, a modifying participial phrase is a set of words that begins with a participle, and that modifies a subject, verb, or sentence. Go ahead and make your own. Find a participle, use it to begin a phrase, and attach that phrase to a sentence. You'll wind up with constructions like this:

Lassoing a huge bull, Evelyn feared for her life.

Disappointed in his team's performance, Scott cancelled his season tickets.

Hearing Bob Druten play guitar, I marveled at his talent.

Each of these sentences begins with a phrase, and at the head of each phrase is a participle: "lassoing," "disappointed," and "hearing." And each one of these phrases modifies its sentence's core components. Voila, they are modifying participial phrases.

A few final notes about syntax before we continue: I've put these modifying phrases at the beginning of these sentences, but they don't have to be there. You could say, "I worried for the fate of the planet, hearing the weather forecast." However, writers tend to place them earlier, for reasons we'll get into. Also, while I said that these phrases begin with participles, that's not always true. Because participles are verb-like, they can be modified themselves with adverbs, meaning you can start participial phrases with something like "nervously lassoing" or "starkly disappointed." But that doesn't change much about them. Finally, you don't necessarily need the "phrase" part of "participial phrase" to modify with a participle. A sentence can begin with a single participle that modifies the rest of the sentence, as in "Disappointed, Scott cancelled his season tickets." In this chapter, we're dealing with phrases, but the concepts remain when a single participle acts as a modifier.

Okay, so those are the fundamentals we need. Now let's look at the problematic nature of participial phrases. I won't dwell much on a philosophical defense of this grammatical element, the way I did with adverbs. Instead, we'll look at three things that can go wrong—or at least three things to consider—when writers use and misuse modifying participial phrases.

THE ILLOGICAL MODIFYING PARTICIPIAL PHRASE

A modifying participial phrase is a modifying phrase, not a verb phrase. I know I said this already, but it's easy to forget because they look so much like verb phrases. Participles began life as verbs, but then mutated (the infinitive verb "to lasso" became "lassoing," "to disappoint" became "disappointed," etc.). And treating participles like verbs, and modifying participial phrases like verb phrases, causes one particular headache for the fiction writer: it screws up your sense of time.

Fiction is inherently narrative, meaning it always contains a chronology. We read a story assuming the events progress in standard chronological fashion. True, some texts specifically indicate otherwise, like Martin Amis's *Time's Arrow*, which has a reverse chronology, and many narratives will jump around in time with flashbacks and frame set-ups. Still, when we read a specific scene or passage, we tend to believe that the events in paragraph one occurred before paragraph two, and that the action of sentence fifty-five preceded the action of sentence fifty-six, unless the narrative tells us otherwise.

We carry this logic even to the level of the sentence. Look at a very basic one like "I walked the dogs, and I mowed the lawn." This is a compound sentence, in that it contains two independent clauses connected by a conjunction. Nothing fancy here. Also, because "and" is a coordinating conjunction, rather than a subordinating one, we know that the clauses are equal; neither the walking of the dogs nor the mowing of the lawn is emphasized more than the other. (Incidentally, the equality of clauses implied by this kind of sentence is called parataxis.)

But when you read the sentence, you actually do presume a difference between the clauses: you believe that one happened before the other. When you imagine the sentence's action, you see the character walking the dogs *before* he gets out the mower, in spite of the fact that the words don't tell you to see it this way. After all, it's not "I walked the dogs, *then* I mowed the lawn."

None of this is problematic yet. The writer of the sentence probably saw things that way himself. It's pretty basic logic: if something comes first in a sentence, it comes first in the story. The only exception is when a writer directly tells you otherwise. In "Before I walked the dogs, I mowed the lawn," the dog walking comes first in the sentence, but the "before" tells us to imagine that it occurred later. Without that kind of clue, we will equate physical placement of an action on the page with temporal placement of the event in our mind's eye.

The problem lies in the fact that not all clues about temporality are as obvious to us as words like "before" and "after," and placing first things first gets us in trouble if we don't notice the clues. Such an error occurs quite often when we use modifying participial phrases. Consider the first example we used in the previous section: "Lassoing a huge bull, Evelyn feared for her life." Given the mind's tendency to conflate order of occurrence in the sentence with order of occurrence in real life, you might think this sentence tells us that Evelyn first lassoed a bull, then she feared for her life.

But that's not correct, according to the grammar of the sentence. If it read, "Evelyn lassoed the bull, and she feared for her life," it might be okay to see the clauses as chronological, since "lassoed" and "feared" are both verbs. But remember, modifying participial phrases are not verbs. They exist to modify something, not to make a noun do something. The phrase "lassoing a huge bull" does not actually tell us what Evelyn did at a particular moment in time, the way "she lassoed a bull" does. Instead, it describes Evelyn's state of being at the moment when she feared for her life. It functions as an adverb, not a verb.

Many absurdities or impossibilities can result when writers act as if a participial phrase performs an action. It happens a lot when speech is mentioned, as in "Laughing uncontrollably, Ramona said, 'You're a hoot!'" or "Sneezing like a yak, the blind man apologized." In both cases, the participial phrases describe a condition that prohibits the sentence's subject from speaking. You can't form words when you're sneezing or laughing uncontrollably. Yet the writers indicate that these people, who are verbally incapacitated, and who will be in this state until the sentence ends, speak coherent phrases.

Other examples are easy to think up — "Walking to the store, the boy paid the cashier in nickels," "Driving to the beach for the weekend, Jill and Max built sandcastles." Trust me, these instances aren't tortuously constructed to prove the point. The error is extremely common, because it's easy to toss out sentences like these without thinking about the fact that the introductory elements, which look so much like verbs, actually function as modifiers.

MISPLACEMENT

For some reason, the phrase "dangling participle" gets a lot of press. It's just one of those grammar terms people latch on to, usually without understanding what it is, but suspecting that they do it frequently, and that English majors judge them for it.

The paranoia may be somewhat justified, since the error can result in ridiculous sentences like "Walking over the hill, the refrigerator came into view." Dangling participles can also result in less overtly silly constructions, like "Travelling in Greece, the Parthenon looked impressive." We know what this means, of course — when the writer travelled to Greece, she admired the Parthenon. But the grammar doesn't hold up to inspection. "Travelling in Greece" is a participial phrase, so it must modify something.

Yet when we look around, we don't find anything to which it logically attaches. The reasonable thing would be for the sentence to have a name or a pronoun, so that "travelling in Greece" could refer to "Jimbo" or "Mrs. Honeyfeather" or "I," but the sentence contains nothing like that. "The Parthenon" is the only noun, and I hear it doesn't travel much these days. Thus the participial phrase is "dangling" — it twists in the wind, looking for something to modify.

Again, it's a problem. It makes the reader imagine a refrigerator with legs, or a Parthenon with a backpack and a *Lonely Planet* guidebook. But I actually think a related mistake poses a more serious and common threat. I'm referring to the error known as the misplaced modifying participial phrase (you can see why the name hasn't caught on the way "dangling participle" has). The general problem is actually the "misplaced modifier," but for now we'll limit ourselves to participial phrases. At the end of the section we'll look at examples of misplaced modifiers that aren't participial phrases, just because we know how to have a good time.

To figure out this one, let's try to fix the dangling participle in the example. I mentioned that the independent clause needs a name or a pronoun, so let's add one: "Travelling in Greece, the Parthenon seemed impressive to Jimbo." This looks better, but there's still a problem. Sure, we've included a noun for the phrase to stick to, but it *doesn't* stick to it, because participial phrases tend to attach themselves to the closest noun, especially when the closest noun is the sentence's *subject* (the noun that performs the action). In this case, "Jimbo," the noun that I want the participial phrase to attach to, is far away from the phrase, plus it's a mere object of preposition. The modifying participial phrase refuses to affiliate with such a meager and distant sentence element.

Usually, we don't have to think much about this, because modifying participial phrases often come at the beginning of sentences, and in English syntax the subject is often the first noun of the independent clause — therefore it's usually close to the modifying phrase. See for yourself:

Grimacing like a maniac, Steve smacked Dr. Thornburg.

Crouched below the desk, Buster taunted his mother.

Both of these sentences have independent clauses that contain two nouns — Steve and Dr. Thornburg, Buster and his mother. Yet there's no confusion as to which of these people is grimacing like a maniac and which is crouched below the desk. You don't have to figure out which one is a subject and which is a direct object, you just have to attach the modifier to the first noun you see. In that way, you can imagine participial phrases as loose vacuum hoses, wildly flailing until they stick to the first noun in sight. If the noun closest to your introductory participial phrase isn't the one you want the phrase to modify, you've misplaced it.

This method for connecting modifying participial phrases and nouns gets a little muddled when we consider participial phrases that *don't* come at the beginning of a sentence, as in "Sylvia ran down the street, bellowing like an idiot." In this instance, we can't hold too firmly to our attach-a-modifier-to-the-closest-noun dictum, because if we did, we'd think the street, not Sylvia, was bellowing like an idiot, and that's not what happens when we read it—we don't have trouble understanding what this sentence tells us, do we? Often (but not always), a modifying phrase at the end of a sentence can be further from the noun it modifies without causing confusion. This is because the meaning of the core sentence has already appeared by the time you get to the modifying phrase. Having read the main clause, the reader knows what the subject is and what the verb does; there's not much mystery left.

Let me expand on that. In the example above, the first element we encounter is the independent clause "Sylvia ran down the street." Whatever else the sentence throws at us can now be easily slotted by our brains, because we know the gist of what it wants to say. If the words after the main part consist of a phrase, like "which was paved with asphalt," we know to attach it to "street." If it's an adverb like "swiftly" or "awkwardly," we give it to the verb "ran." And if it's "bellowing like an idiot," we know it belongs to the subject of the sentence, "Sylvia." Our brains are good at this, as long as we've already received the sentence's core components.

In constructions where we get a modifying element *before* we arrive at the subject and verb, we aren't as nimble. As a survival mechanism, we attach the element to the closest thing that will take it. If "Paved with asphalt" or "Undergoing construction" appears before "Sylvia ran down the street," we see the modification of "street" even before we know a street exists in the sentence. Lacking any awareness of a street, we will attach the modifiers to the nearest noun, and we will assume that Sylvia has been coated in tar or is in the process of having cosmetic surgery. In short, it's easier to do the work of modification in retrospect; when we've already seen the sentence's nouns, we can decide which of them can receive the modifier.

As I mentioned before, "misplaced modifier" is a general term. It doesn't just have to do with misplaced modifying participial phrases, although that's the kind we've looked at, since they're the most problematic for all writers. Whenever grammar books discuss misplaced modifiers, they use examples like "Hanging on the wall, I saw the picture," and "Lying on the ocean floor for two centuries, divers found the shipwreck."

To be responsible grammarians, however, we should also note that problems can arise when other modifiers are misplaced. In a passage of historical backdrop, for example, we might find "An important trading post, Walter Briggs founded the town in 1818." The opening phrase "an important trading post" is not a modifying participial phrase, it's an appositive, but still we can see the confusion the misplacement causes. The town, not Walter, is the trading post, but because "Walter" serves as the subject of the sentence, our brains attach the modifying appositive phrase "an important trading post" to him.

Another common non-participial modifier is the prepositional phrase, which is a phrase that begins with a preposition. It's misused here: "With unusual acumen, the Cyclops was tricked by Odysseus." You would fix this by rearranging the syntax so that Odysseus's name, rather than the Cyclops's, stands in proximity to the phrase that's meant to modify him: "With unusual acumen, Odysseus tricked the Cyclops." As you may remember, the Cyclops doesn't show much acumen in the *Odyssey*, while Odysseus does. He's also the kind of guy who'd be upset about not getting proper credit.

REPETITION OF THE PARTICIPIAL PHRASE

This is the type of error I like to deal with in class, because it allows me to illustrate the importance of reading your work out loud. I also like it because the nature of the mistake is so obvious — once it's pointed out — that I don't have to explain it much. This may surprise you, but I really don't like to drone on about grammar if I don't have to. Although my wife would disagree.

The pattern in my classes is predictable. I read an excerpt from a particular student's work, and after I've come to the third sentence, I begin to hear exhalations of epiphany. A few more students catch on once I've read the fourth introductory phrase. By the time I've finished the passage, everyone in the class, including the author of the passage, is nodding with that half-opened-mouth expression that says "Well, I see what's wrong with it *now*."

They didn't see it before because they didn't read it out loud, which some people just won't do, no matter how many times you recommend it. It's understandable — if you have a family or roommates, reading out every word in a text might cause someone to stage an intervention. But it does help, if you can manage it.

Anyway, the error that becomes apparent with orality is the repetition of the participial phrase as a way of beginning sentences. Like this:

> Spotting the vampire, Lucas crouched below the darkened stairwell.
> Smiling with great wickedness, the beast turned to face its victim.
> Praying that his cell phone wouldn't go off, Lucas began to tiptoe in the direction of the glimmering sword. His heart pounding, he reached it.

You can spot it here because it's exaggerated, plus I told you about the problem ahead of time. But it's amazing how readily this pattern will sneak its way into fiction.

It happens, I think, because writers are told from an early age to vary their sentence structure. By that, teachers mean you should stop using so many simple-sentence constructions ("Dick kissed Jane. Spot ate a bug."). Certainly this is good advice. If you write in this style in high school, you'll seem childish and unsophisticated, and if you do it as an adult, it'll look like you're imitating Carver or Hemingway. Breaking up the rhythm can involve adding more sentence styles — compound, complex, compound-complex — to your arsenal, or it can mean modifying simple sentences ("While vacationing in Venice, Spot ate a bug.").

But any style of sentence sounds bad when you repeat it too much. Using participial phrases can break up the rhythm of a passage in a pleasing way, while also providing useful information. Yet these constructions call attention to themselves, and so should be used sparingly. I'm not saying you should limit yourself to a specific number per paragraph, just that you need to think about the way your prose sounds.

A related issue is putting too many participial phrases in a single sentence. The maneuver can work on some occasions, like when you want to underscore or dramatize the buildup to the core component: "Yearning for salvation, burdened with guilt, wondering if all those years of sin and destruction had done lasting damage, Sanford confessed." The sentence works because it almost exaggerates the extent of its modification by piling up all the phrases at the front. It also needs the modifying participial phrases to achieve its successful rhythm. Read it out loud, and you find yourself stressing the first syllable of each participle (YEARN-ing for salvation, BUR-dened with guilt, WON-dering if . . .) which creates an ebb-and-flow cadence that contrasts with its flat, anticlimactic main clause: "Sanford confessed."

In this case, the writer's ear has allowed him to use three participial phrases in a single sentence. Without this stylistic control, the writer's use of several modifying phrases in a small space might look like this: "Yearning for salvation, Sanford, burdened with guilt, confessed, wondering if all those years of sin and destruction had done lasting damage." Blech. While the first one celebrated its overmodification, this one seems embarrassed about it. It awkwardly disperses the modifiers, as if that will make us not notice. Instead, we recognize that the writer has been so insistent on packing in certain bits of information, he's sacrificed the elegance of the prose. At times writers will have to make trade-offs between style and content. But the sacrifice shouldn't come at too high a cost.

This is not to say that you'll never be able to have participial phrases flank the subject-verb in an elegant or at least neutral way. Ralph Ellison does it in "Flying Home," when he writes, "Twisting upon his elbows, he saw where dust had powdered the plane's fuselage, feeling the lump form in his throat that was always there when he thought of flight." Ellison wants to get across two points about the character: that he moved on his elbows, and that he felt a lump in his throat. He separates these two points presumably because they refer to different facets of the character (one is a physical action, the other an emotional state). In between lies the core of the sentence, and I think the reader isn't too distracted by participial phrases used as bookends.

As a side note, this sentence can serve as another example of the point about misplaced modifiers we discussed in the last section. Notice that the first participial phrase, "Twisting upon his elbows," has to be close to the subject "he" for it to make sense to us. The final participial phrase, "feeling the lump," is far away from the word it's meant to modify — if we go with the closest-noun rule, we would have to believe that the fuselage feels a lump in its throat. But when a participial phrase comes at the end, our brains more easily skip past the nearest nouns ("fuselage," "dust,") to attach it to the right object. Again, this is because when we've already seen a sentence's main components, we know what element will reasonably receive any last-minute modification.

ten

Diction

Although this kind of thing is hard to count, English is generally considered the language with the most vocabulary words. Some people argue that Finnish is bigger, because the way it pairs words with numbers allows for an infinite vocabulary, but that's a bit of an accounting trick; the vast majority of those theoretical words have never been spoken. Nice try, Finland.

English is so massive because it has borrowed extensively from other languages, and because early in its history it merged with Norman French in something like a hostile takeover. While all languages incorporate words from other tongues, few of them have done it as voraciously as English, and few of them began as an amalgamation of two distinct languages.

This gives English-speaking writers an advantage in terms of the potential precision, lyricism, and nuance of our prose; you usually have a few options whenever you say something. While in one situation you might want to write, "Get that damn ape off the couch," in another the appropriate language might be "Remove that accursed primate from the sofa," or "Eliminate the simian presence from the chesterfield." You've expressed the same idea each time, but English's variety and depth have given you many different ways to say it.

All of this has to do with diction, which refers to a writer's choice of words. That definition reminds us that we do make a series of choices, on a word-by-word basis, when we write. It may not always seem like it—we don't pause before every word and weigh its pros and cons; usually the sentences just spill out of us. But fiction writers do have general goals for the tenor and tone of their work, and they achieve these goals primarily with the words they choose.

To explore this issue, we need to look at the historical origins of English, not just because those origins explain certain features of our mother tongue, but because people continue to invoke historical terms and associations when describing the language of fiction. Specifically, the terms

"Anglo-Saxon" and "Latinate" are often used—and misused—when contemporary writers and readers consider diction.

ANGLO-SAXON AND LATINATE DICTION

During an episode of the TV show *The West Wing*, President Bartlet suggests to a high school teacher that she should make her students read *Beowulf* "in the original Middle English." I've been infuriated by this since 2002. Did no one at NBC have the Internet? The error, of course, is that *Beowulf* wasn't written in Middle English, it was written in Old English. If you ask high school students to open up a copy of *Beowulf* in its original language, they'll see this:

Hwæt! We Gardena   in geardagum,
þeodcyninga,   þrym gefrunon,
hu ða æþelingas   ellen fremedon.
Oft Scyld Scefing   sceaþena þreatum
Monegum Maegþum   Meodosetla ofteah

Great advice, President Bartlet!

Old English, also known as Anglo-Saxon, is unintelligible unless you've studied it extensively (whereas Middle English, the language of Chaucer, only takes a few weeks to get used to). It is, however, the foundation of the language we currently speak. You can find a lot of familiar words throughout *Beowulf*, especially once you learn that both of those odd letters in the above passage (þ and ð) are pronounced "th." *Deað* means *death*, for example, and *þeof* means *thief*, and *wif* means *wife*, and so on.

To modern English speakers, Anglo-Saxon sounds guttural and harsh; when people hear it, they often say it sounds like German. That's because it *is* a form of German—its original speakers, the Angles and Saxons and Jutes, were Germanic tribes. They settled in England in the fifth century and made themselves at home. "England" itself comes from "Engla-lond," or "land of the Angles," and the county names "Essex" and "Sussex" are versions of "East Saxons" and "South Saxons." (The poor Jutes got left out of all the naming.)

So why doesn't contemporary English sound more like German? Because in 1066, Norman French invaders came to England and stayed, installing their own language as the one for the nobility and the government—this is the hostile takeover I mentioned. Their language, a version of Old French, was Latinate; like Spanish and Portuguese, it had its roots in the language of the Romans. It looks like this:

A lui lais jo mes honurs e mes fieus.
Guardez le ben, ja nel verrai des oilz.»
Carles respunt: «trop avez tendre coer.
Puisquel comant, aler vus en estoet.»

This isn't much like our language either—it's obviously closer to Modern French—although you can see budding Modern English words in "honurs" (honors) and "guardez" (guard).

So why doesn't contemporary English sound more like French? Because although the Anglo-Saxons were defeated by the Normans, they weren't annihilated, and even William the Conqueror couldn't command people to stop using the only language they knew. So Anglo-Saxon stuck around, used primarily by people who had no power—the farmers, the laborers, the merchants. Thus the Old English words that have stayed with us tend to be vulgar, in the original sense of "pertaining to the common people."

While this is all interesting in its own right, we've gone over it because of the contemporary importance of the terms "Anglo-Saxon" and "Latinate" in regard to diction. Specifically, when people say that a prose style is Anglo-Saxon, they mean the words tend to be short; harsh sounding or guttural; common, in the sense that you knew them before you left grade school; and even coarse (if someone says, "Hank muttered a harsh Anglo-Saxonism," he means "Hank said the F-word"). Conversely, prose described as Latinate involves words that are longer, and thus more complex in their tonal qualities; more obscure, in the sense that you may have learned them in high school or beyond; and fancy seeming, possibly even pretentious.

To drive home the point, books and teachers often provide charts of Modern English synonyms that have different origins, like this:

Old English / Anglo-Saxon	Latinate / Norman
Fire	Conflagration
Holy	Consecrated
Home	Habitation

Sure enough, the ones on the left would have been recognized by the people of early medieval England, while the ones on the right are forms of words brought over by William the Conqueror in 1066, and clearly they differ in terms of tone and connotation. (Side note: Latinate words have entered English through other means as well—Christianizing monks, nineteenth-century scientists, Dick Cavett, etc. What matters is their Latinate origins, not who introduced them.)

At this point, we need to acknowledge that using these terms to talk about diction the way we do involves some rather lazy associations. For one thing, the words used by the Anglo-Saxons weren't always shorter than Latin-based ones. Old English has lots of long words, like my favorite, "leor-nungcnihtas" (it means "learning knights," and refers to Christ's disciples). There's also nothing inherently unsophisticated about them—"fire" isn't any cruder than "conflagration." Conversely, the idea that Latinate words are always long, sophisticated and mellifluous is contradicted by so many words of Latin origin that I don't even need to give examples (well, if you insist—how about "pus" and "mucus" and "carcass"?).

Unfortunately, thinking of Anglo-Saxon words as coarse and simple reinforces a stereotype of the people themselves. It makes us imagine them as grunting barbarians, who paused in their raping and pillaging just long enough to mutter a cuss word, when in fact they produced exquisite art and literature, developed complex social systems, and invented pancakes. Moreover, conceiving of Latinate words as fancy and elegant and a little bit prissy does a disservice to the Norman French (who were very tough folks; they beat the Anglo-Saxons, after all), and at the same time probably gives them too much credit for refinement.

But we have to grudgingly accept these stereotypes, because there are some reasons for them. While Old English originally contained words as long and sophisticated as anything in Old French, when it became the language of the hoi polloi, it lost many words related to art, culture, religion, and government; scholars estimate that 80 percent of the language's words have dropped out of use. Today, only about a fifth of our words have Anglo-Saxon origins, yet among this sliver are the majority of the ones we use most often ("the," "of," "and," "to") as well as many that you might call uncouth ("fart," "snot," "turd," even "uncouth" itself). And when you come across a long, fancy word in English, especially one with an affix—"insuperable," "perpendicularity," "nonflagitiously"—it's likely to be of Latin origin.

In any case, we're stuck with the stereotypes for now, and we may as well use them to point out some interesting things that arise from a writer's decision to use short, uncomplicated words as opposed to ones that are more complex in length and pronunciation. Therefore, as I use the terms "Anglo-

Saxon" and "Latinate" from now on, please understand that I'm making a claim about a word's basic characteristics, rather than its technical origins.

GOOD OLD ANGLO-SAXON

If that last section made you feel bad about how we stereotype the Anglo-Saxons, I've got some good news for you: Anglo-Saxon diction, rather than Latinate, is the preferred style for most writers and critics today. In fact, it's hard to find anyone who argues that Latinate should be favored as a rule, outside of ninth graders trying to win essay contests or deconstruction-ist grad students. You will, however, find many people who proclaim Old English diction inherently better, such as Strunk and White, who wrote, "Anglo-Saxon is a livelier tongue than Latin, so use Anglo-Saxon words."

That strikes me as a heck of a thing to say. How is it true? What does "livelier" mean here? How could anyone support such a claim? A similar take comes from Robert Claiborne:

> If our native [i.e., Anglo-Saxon] words are syntactically powerful beyond their numbers, they are also powerful in another way: taken as a group, they stir the feelings in a way that the borrowings do not . . . [Latinate] words are chiefly the ceremonial or celebratory garments and bejeweled ornaments that adorn and embellish our language.

I think Claiborne and Strunk/White paint with too broad a brush when championing Old English diction — the latter passage even smacks of lin-guistic xenophobia, with its claim that "native" words are honest and pure and vibrant, while the foreigners, though exotic, are not quite up to snuff. Still, we should recognize that Anglo-Saxon diction appeals to writers, especially those of the contemporary period, for specific reasons.

One key benefit of Old English words is that the reader tends to integrate them more quickly. By that I mean most readers won't just understand an Anglo-Saxon word, they'll apply its meaning without thinking about it much — the process of integrating a word like "fire" requires less work than integrating one like "conflagration," even if you know the dictionary defini-tion of both. This quality was especially appealing to certain writers of the Modernist period. As we saw in chapter 8, Modernists rejected the perceived disingenuousness and artificiality of nineteenth-century prose — all those modifiers and euphemisms and Latinate words that muddled up the writer's meaning. The poet William Carlos Williams, in a famous phrase, claimed he wrote the kind of language that came "from the mouths of Polish mothers," i.e., the simple, democratic language of the immigrants, the working poor, the hoi polloi.

This is not to say that all Modernists rejected Latinate diction or ornate language. In fact, Modernist fiction introduced a tension or dialectic between lyricism — language that is pretty, mellifluous, attentive to its sound — and prose minimalism — language that is stripped bare, that seeks to communicate its content without asking the reader to appreciate, or even think about, the way it sounds. (Consider how this hearkens back to our discussion in the "Less is More?" section of chapter 8.) The writer most often trotted out as an exemplification of the former tendency is Faulkner, who wrote phrases like "he seems to hover, shadowy, almost substanceless, a little behind and a little above all the other straightforward and logical even though (to him) incomprehensible ultimatums and affirmations and defiances and challenges and repudiations, with an air of sardonic and indolent detachment." Hemingway usually gets tapped to represent the minimalists. ("We went out. That was Jack. He could say what he wanted to when he wanted to say it.") Obviously, Latinate diction is generally affiliated with lyricism (although not always, as we'll see), and Anglo-Saxon with prose minimalism.

The minimalists, those who believe language should communicate but otherwise stay out of the way, seem to have a point. As we've discussed elsewhere, anything that makes a reader focus too much on language can be a distraction. We've mostly talked about that fact in terms of how errors distract readers, but it also holds true in regard to lyrical language. If you write a phrase of such poetical grace that the reader stops thinking about the character and starts thinking about your way with onomatopoeia, the effect is the same as if you'd spelled something wrong: distraction. Anglo-Saxon prose almost never distracts, in part because it rarely contains words you haven't heard before, and it tends not to be as aurally or visually complex.

Because Anglo-Saxon diction allows readers to integrate what's being said more efficiently, it's no surprise that most thrillers and crime novels use it; they mostly want readers to experience suspense. But even with literary fiction, one might argue that the writer's main job is to investigate matters of character, action, and theme, not to exploit the lyrical possibilities of language. If you want to do that, perhaps you should write poetry.

This, anyway, seems to be the dominant attitude of twentieth-century advice about diction. At first glance it appears to accord with the general attitude of Strunk, White, Zinsser, et al. — keep things direct, short, and accessible. Don't get fancy. Anglo-Saxon diction is livelier and grittier because everyone understands what it means, and it doesn't pretend to be what it's not.

However, it's important to avoid the dualism that gets encouraged by this tension, the equation *Anglo-Saxon = non-lyrical, functional.* Perhaps some writers use Anglo-Saxon diction because they don't want you to focus on their language too much. But other writers employ the rhythms and cadences of Old English diction as a way of crafting a different kind of lyricism; in short, they argue that lyricism isn't synonymous with Latinate, that our "native" words can also create poetic prose.

How so? Let's look at that notoriously Anglo-Saxon writer, Hemingway, for a sample of Old English prose that *doesn't* get out of the reader's way. In the following passage, the language calls more attention to its sound and patterns than does the prose of more Latinate works.

> His father had frost in his beard in cold weather and in hot weather
> he sweated very much. He liked to work in the sun on the farm because
> he did not have to and he loved manual work, which Nick did not.
> Nick loved his father but hated the smell of him and once when he had
> to wear a suit of his father's underwear that had gotten too small for
> his father it made him feel sick and he took it off and put it under two
> stones in the creek and said that he had lost it. He had told his father
> how it was when his father had made him put it on but his father
> had said it was freshly washed.

It's hard not to notice how he repeats the word "father," especially since "Fathers and Sons" is the story's title. The wealth of monosyllabic and disyllabic words also becomes noticeable after a while — when the three-syllable "underwear" shows up, it's quite a surprise.

But what really adds a lyrical rhythm to the paragraph is the way Hemingway exploits these repetitions in combination with the use of our language's most common words: the articles and prepositions. The repetition of the phrases "in his beard" and "in cold weather" and "and in hot weather" in the first sentence, and "in the sun" and "on the farm" in the second establishes a pattern of layering sentences with simple prepositional phrases. This becomes quite musical after a while — not the baroque or ornamental music that arises from long, Latinate words, but a monophonic, almost chanting rhythm.

We also see lyricism sprouting from the way certain writers employ unlikely Old English verbs and nouns. In *Housekeeping*, Marilynne Robinson uses the phrase "every fruit and bird was plumb with the warp in the earth," which sounds like pure Anglo-Saxon, yet its word choice (especially "plumb" and "warp") seems as original and exotic as anything you could say with Latinate diction. A bit later, Robinson writes "the earth will brim" to describe a flood, and the odd employment of "brim" as a verb makes the image indelible.

It's a point that needs to be understood by writers: Anglo-Saxon prose—and minimalism in general—doesn't prohibit lyricism, just as Latinate prose doesn't guarantee it. When a writer uses both unobtrusive words and bare, simple sentences, a different kind of lyricism can develop. This explains why it's been so popular in the last hundred years or so, as writers have reacted against the grandiose style that you see in writers like James Fenimore Cooper and Sarah Orne Jewett. But we don't want to paint the Latinate with too broad a brush either. It's true that in the wrong hands it can seem sentimental and florid, but in the right ones, Latinate diction contains advantages that aren't always celebrated. So now we'll look at that style.

LATINATE DICTION

Sometimes I think Latinate diction is in the same boat as adverbs, in the sense that it's out of favor in our contemporary literary climate, and for basically the same reason: lots of Modernists and Postmodernists considered it dishonest.

And as with adverbs, we shouldn't denounce Latinate diction wholesale, in part because the negative characterizations don't apply to all such words, and also because they can't be avoided. In theory you could write an entire book using only Anglo-Saxon words, but it wouldn't be easy, and it would come off as forced. The art of employing Latinate diction involves navigating its pitfalls while exploiting its possibilities.

In his essay "Mr. Difficult," the novelist Jonathan Franzen talks about the tension every writer faces between the need to craft complex, challenging, even difficult fiction, and the desire to avoid pretension and appeal to a wide audience. While he discusses the issue in terms of content, he also touches on diction, by describing a woman who considers him "a pompous snob" and who provides proof in the following way:

She began by listing thirty fancy words and phrases from my novel, words like "diurnality" and "antipodes," phrases like "electro-pointillist Santa Claus faces." She then posed the dreadful question: "Who is it you are writing for? It surely could not be the average person who enjoys a good read."

In effect, the woman complains that he's using Latinate diction only because he wants to show off his big vocabulary. A Franzen defender might argue that while it's a writer's job to communicate, it's also a reader's job to be able to receive that communication at a certain level.

The issue can be controversial. I always have students who claim that if a reader doesn't understand a word in a text, that's his fault for not having a sufficient vocabulary; plus, he can always go to the dictionary. These students also point out that reading is the primary way we build vocabulary, that if we stuck to texts with familiar words, we'd still be on Dr. Seuss. Their adversaries claim that if it's a writer's job to communicate to a wide audience, then she has to exercise common sense. Not a lot of people know what "diurnality" means, so if you use it, you have to accept that you're not going to communicate as well as you could. Sure, the readers can go to their dictionaries, but how many of them are going to? And if they do, hasn't the act of looking up the word pulled them out of the fictive dream?

I'd caution you not to dig in too rigidly to either of these extremes. If you believe adamantly in the second position, you could restrict yourself to Anglo-Saxon diction and thus feel comfortable that most readers, even the lazy ones, will understand most of your words. But to do this is to squander your inherited gift as an English speaker. You won't make use of the huge variety and potential of our language. It would be like having Alex Rodriguez on your roster and making him the designated hitter (meaning you wouldn't be taking advantage of his defensive skills — I honestly couldn't think of a non-sports-related metaphor).

But Franzen's critic has a point. Sometimes the inclusion of Latinate diction is done more for the writer's gratification than the reader's, which can come off as a misplacement of priorities. For example, when you read the sentence "There was an endless round of institutions, municipal and eleemosynary" in O. Henry's "The Cop and the Anthem," you may suspect that the entire sentence (maybe even the entire story) was constructed so that the author would have the chance to use "eleemosynary." A clear example of the tail wagging the dog.

As awkward as Latinate diction can sound in a sentence like this, it's easy to see where the impulse comes from. Writers love words, in particular the discovery of new ones (which tend to be Latinate), and when we're smitten with a new word we're tempted to share it with readers. But when I see a writer contorting his prose just to cram in "pulchritude" or "demurrage," I'm reminded of how my two-year-old son recently wore his bike helmet to Sunday school; he didn't care that it wasn't appropriate for the occasion, he just wanted to show off his new helmet.

Making Latinate language work for you, as with so many things, is a matter of verbal sensitivity, of thinking about how the careful reader will experience your language. Let's look at an example of how this works. What follows is the passage from *The Corrections* in which Franzen uses one of his "pompous" words, "diurnality":

> Life as she knew it ended with her squeeze through the half-open door. Diurnality yielded to a raw continuum of hours. She found Alfred naked with his back to the door on a layer of bedsheets spread on sections of morning paper from St. Jude.

Most of the language here is Anglo-Saxon and easily integrated by the reader. Only the words "continuum" and "diurnality" present a challenge. So it's this one short sentence that might offend: "Diurnality yielded to a raw continuum of hours."

If you were to translate this into purely Anglo-Saxon diction, you'd get "the shifting of day and night yielded to a raw, unbroken string of hours." Not too awful, but it has almost twice as many words as the original, because it needs more modification (the adjective "unbroken" and the prepositional modifier "of day and night"). Franzen's use of two words that are so precise they don't need modifiers reminds us of what many people throughout the ages have loved about Latin: it's extremely economical. In actual Latin, that mostly has to do with inflections, but it's still true that our Latinate words tend to be more specific and nuanced in meaning than their Anglo-Saxon counterparts. "Conflagration" may not be inherently more sophisticated than "fire," but it does more work. To really get the equivalent using Anglo-Saxon diction you'd have to say "a raging fire" or "a large and vicious fire."

So we see something of a catch-22 for writers seeking to distance themselves from the twin crimes of the pre-Modernists: the cure for one of these crimes can lead to the other. We know that the Modernists and their descendants (us) often feel uncomfortable with the way Hawthorne, Melville, Stowe, et al. used those modifiers and extra words. But perhaps the best way to make language concise and stripped of modification is to commit the other crime all those pre-Modernists were guilty of: Latinate vocabulary. Strunk and White's "omit needless words" collides head-on with their commandment to "use Anglo-Saxon words."

It's a tough conflict to resolve. After all, economy isn't everything; "diurnality" may save you a couple words, but that won't matter to the reader if he doesn't know what it means. Then again, when a word like that contributes to tone and rhythm, you may want to take the risk. That's what Franzen does. The risk is worth it to him because the Latinate sentence lends a lyrical flourish to the paragraph. The sentences surrounding it are fairly long, in part because they include many Anglo-Saxon pronouns and modifiers, so the inclusion of a short, economical sentence breaks up the paragraph nicely—a jolt of precision and concision in the midst of a monosyllabic, Anglo-Saxon blitz. The sentence does on a paragraph level what the Latinate word "reluctantly" does on a sentence level in Crane's "the cold passed reluctantly from the earth."

The issue doesn't just have to do with style and readability, however. In his essay "Politics and the English Language," George Orwell levels a more serious charge against Latinate diction, by claiming that it encourages obfuscation and dishonesty. Here's how he makes his point:

> I am going to translate a passage of good English into modern English of the worst sort.
>
> Here is a well-known verse from *Ecclesiastes*:
>
>> I returned and saw under the sun, that the race is not to the swift,
>> nor the battle to the strong, neither yet bread to the wise, nor yet riches
>> to men of understanding, nor yet favour to men of skill; but time and
>> chance happeneth to them all.

Here it is in modern English [i.e., the Latinate diction Orwell believed his contemporaries overused]:

> Objective considerations of contemporary phenomena compel the conclusion
> that success or failure in competitive activities exhibits no tendency to be
> commensurate with innate capacity, but that a considerable element of the
> unpredictable must invariably be taken into account.

In terms of style, he argues that the passage actually *loses* economy and elegance in its Latinate version, because while it contains fewer words (38 to 49, by my count), it has more syllables. But his real complaint is that the Latinate diction has turned powerful, concrete assertions into bland, imprecise drivel. The second passage doesn't say anything meaningful, because its language doesn't allow it to. Orwell believes this to be an almost necessary outcome of Latinate diction; by its nature, it results in abstraction, which is a moral problem as well as an aesthetic one. This isn't merely clunky writing, he claims, it also allows the writer to avoid—and to hide from her readers—the true meaning of her words.

Anyone who's read an insurance policy or a car rental contract knows what Orwell means. Corporate and political entities use Latinate diction and complex syntax because they don't really want you to understand what you're signing on for. Thus, "Financial encumbrances incur should chartering party neglect obligations" appears instead of "If you don't do this, you'll have to give us tons of money." The argument is valid and important, especially when we consider how some politicians and corporations hide their nefariousness with word choice.

But I've always wondered if the argument provides a backhanded compliment for Anglo-Saxon diction, because it basically celebrates its simplicity. It's like praising a stupid person by saying how great it is that you can understand what he's saying. That may be true, but of course we should have other goals beyond clarity. And while Latinate language can be unclear and dishonest, it can also be concrete, specific, and lyrical. Let's finish up by looking at a decidedly Latinate passage from Jane Austen's *Mansfield Park*:

> There seems something more speakingly incomprehensible in the powers, the failures, the inequalities of memory, than in any other of our intelligences. The memory is sometimes so retentive, so serviceable, so obedient; at others, so bewildered and so weak; and at others again, so tyrranic, so beyond control! We are, to be sure, a miracle every way; but our powers of recollecting and of forgetting do seem peculiarly past finding out.

Not too shabby. I'd even go so far as to call it lively and stirring.

THE FINAL POINT

As much as it can help us to talk about dialectics and tensions — Anglo-Saxon versus Latinate, lyricism versus minimalism, the pompous elite versus the unlettered hoi polloi — good writers and readers use these extremes to understand concepts, not to plant their flag at one end of the spectrum. The true pleasure of writing, in regard to diction, will be found in experimenting with your own style, and considering how you want to put your word choice into practice. You'll find that effective prose usually involves a blend of the simple/common and the lengthy/complex, a movement among "high style" and "low style" and everything in between. The critic James Wood declares this movement to be the very hallmark of literary fiction: "rich and daring prose avails itself of harmony and dissonance by being able to move in and out of place," he writes, while inferior writing is marked by "the absence of different registers." Thus we see T. C. Boyle's narrator in "Greasy Lake" moving from passive, repetitive monosyllables ("We were nineteen. We were bad.") to lyrical high diction ("savor the incongruous full-throated roar of rock and roll against the primeval susurrus") on the same page; or Junot Diaz shifting from the self-consciously Latinate ("the bureau was successfully acquired and lashed haphazardly to the roof of the automobile") to the casual and colloquial ("without really thinking about it, he'd not seen Lydia since that night the news turned bad"). The art of it lies in figuring out which proportions and ratios suit your purposes, and what scenes and subjects call for what register. It's yet another complexity the art of fiction throws at you, but it comes with the happy fact that the world's largest, most diverse language is at your disposal.

part three

Nuances
of Punctuation

eleven

Fragments

I generally advise my students to disable Microsoft's grammar-check function when they write fiction. It's not an anti-technology state-ment—I'm all for anything that gives you a linguistic advantage, such as the spell-check and the thesaurus features. My problem with grammar-check is that it's often incorrect. It seems like any time I deploy "that" as a conjunction instead of a demonstrative pronoun, or when I use "feast" as a verb instead of a noun, up comes the squiggly green line, telling me to fix an error that never was.

I must add that Microsoft isn't always to blame. Often when I disagree with the little green line, I actually *have* made a mistake, and the only rea-son I'm not grateful to Bill Gates and his minions is that I *meant* to. After all, as a fiction writer, I'm allowed to ignore a technical rule for the sake of effect. Grammar-check doesn't know when I'm doing this, nor should it—it's calibrated for standard usage, the style we employ when writing cover letters or expository essays. So I just turn it off.

You shouldn't take such an act lightly, however. The freedom to selec-tively ignore the rules of grammar confers upon the fiction writer a grave responsibility to know these rules as well as anyone. This is because of the caveat that comes with the writer's prerogative: you can violate whatever language rule you want, as long as the reader understands that you know you're violating it.

This could be one those "if you take nothing else away from this book" adages. It relates to the core problem I discussed in the introduction, how beginning writers often believe that creative writing doesn't involve think-ing about such mundane matters as grammar and punctuation. This at-titude might be encouraged when the young writer notices that Toni Mor-rison doesn't follow certain rules of capitalization, or that Virginia Woolf doesn't always respect standard comma placement. If the masters don't know their grammar rules, then why should we?

Of course the answer to that is simple. The masters *do* know their grammar rules, and in fact they know them so well they can exploit them for effect. It's not as if Morrison wrote "The Thing to fear was the Thing that made her beautiful" because she thought "thing" was a proper noun, or that *Mrs. Dalloway* would contain more commas if Virginia Woolf had had access to Microsoft. When great writers violate the rules of grammar, they do so out of artistry, not ignorance, and the reader never supposes they spliced a comma or wrote a fragment simply because they messed up. Once you truly understand the mechanics of language, it's time to think about how you can play with those mechanics to create certain effects.

In that spirit, this part of the book will begin by looking at instances in which writers deliberately misuse punctuation for artistic purposes. This chapter will examine how periods can be misused to create sentence fragments, and the next chapter will look at intentional comma misplacement. After that, we'll go back to looking at the standard methods of punctuation. But I hope you'll keep in mind that a masterful writer always thinks about punctuation in a conceptual sense, so that she can employ it in non-Microsoft-approved ways that add aesthetic value to her prose.

USES OF FRAGMENTS

A sentence fragment, sometimes called an incomplete sentence, is a phrase that pretends to be a sentence when it doesn't have the qualifications. We already saw in chapter 8 that to make a sentence, you usually need just two things—a subject and a verb (and when the subject is implied, as in "Run!," you don't even need that many). Furthermore, these two things have to express a complete thought. "When I listen to Mel Tormé" contains a subject ("I") and a verb ("listen"), but it doesn't finish a thought. This phrase happens to be a dependent clause, because it *depends* on something that comes before or after it (such as "I *dance* when I listen to Mel Tormé," or "When I listen to Mel Tormé *my cares disappear*"), but not all fragments are dependent clauses. For a group of words to be considered a clause, it must contain a subject and a verb, whereas the only requirement for being a fragment is to *not* be an actual sentence. All real sentences are *independent* clauses; they don't need any help to complete their meaning.

So basically, a group of words may contain a lot of other elements, but if it doesn't contain a subject and a verb, and if it doesn't express a complete thought, it's a fragment, not a sentence. Microsoft will almost always underline such constructions, because technically speaking you shouldn't put a period at the end of something that doesn't do the full work of a sentence.

Sentence fragments are a major concern in composition classes, where they look something like this: "The federal government is deeply in debt. Which is a problem." The fragment in this example ("Which is a problem.") results from putting in a period where it's not appropriate. Periods, after all, sever the relationship between phrases. Any given period asserts that the group of words to the left and to the right of it can exist separately. In our example, this isn't true—the words to the right of the period after "debt" don't complete a thought by themselves, so they connect with the first phrase, which is an independent clause. In this case, a comma will make that connection successfully: "The federal government is deeply in debt, which is a problem." When someone tries to sound authoritative, as when one discusses the deficit, a misplaced period comes off as an obvious and harmful error.

In fiction, however, where the reader accepts—indeed, expects—artistry and novelty and the manipulation of rules, the error can create a strong effect, in part because it's inherently dramatic, but also because fragments emphasize content. Look at how the character Carl Spackler in the film *Caddyshack* uses a fragment to end his long story about trying to get a tip from the Dalai Lama:

> So we finish the eighteenth and he's gonna stiff me. And I say, "Hey, Lama, hey, how about a little something, you know, for the effort, you know." And he says, "Oh, uh, there won't be any money. But when you die, on your deathbed, you will receive total consciousness." So I got that goin' for me. Which is nice.

In delivering the monologue, Bill Murray pauses for a few beats after "goin' for me," which tells us we should hear the final word group as a separate sentence. If he had paused only briefly, thus implying a comma rather than a period, we would hear "So I got that goin' for me, which is nice." That version would be grammatically correct but not as effective, because the funnier part ("which is nice") would be attached as a subordinate clause and thus de-emphasized—we would focus more on the independent clause "So I got that goin for me." By giving those last three words their own sentence, Murray tells us to pay extra attention to them.

But why is that line worthy of emphasis? What's the reward that comes with the risk of being ungrammatical? In this case, the phrase "Which is nice" points out the ridiculousness of the character, and stressing that ridiculousness makes it funny. The endearing and delusional Spackler believes he needs to rhetorically emphasize a phrase that is unnecessary—do we really need to be told that it's "nice" to know you'll have total consciousness on your deathbed? Of course not, and the fact that Spackler thinks so invokes dramatic irony. That is, we understand something that the character does not, and humor arises from the gap in understanding. (I know it's annoying when English professors explain why things are funny, but that's never stopped us.)

Cultural texts, especially visual advertisements, often use fragments as indicators of emphasis. Billboards, movie posters, and the like can only use a limited number of words, so the words must pack a punch. The original poster for *Die Hard*, for example, gives us "Twelve Terrorists. One Cop." while the tag line for *Gone in Sixty Seconds* is "Ice Cold. Hot Wired." In these instances, the copywriters have eschewed subjects and verbs and just thrown up some unattached nouns and modifiers. They don't want to communicate anything but an immediate image or sensation, so coherent sentence construction is unnecessary.

Fiction writers can use fragments in a similar way. That is, the writer might decide that grammatical integrity matters less than sensory impact, so he strips the sentence of everything that doesn't actively contribute to the image or action. Because the technique is both easy to read and inherently dramatic, it's a favorite style for writers in genres like thrillers and crime novels. In an essay in the *New York Times* magazine, Colin Harrison both discusses and imitates the style:

> The commercial thriller writer works hard to make speed. Short
> sentences help. So do bodies. That are dead. And discovered in certain
> places. Often the dead people were carrying secret papers. Often there's
> a blonde in the hotel lobby. The man who finds the body often finds
> the blonde. Or the blond finds the man. Because she's looking for the
> papers, too.

Harrison uses four fragments here in order to show what they do in terms of creating suspense. He likely wouldn't use any of them if he weren't parodying a thriller writer; "Short sentences help, as do dead bodies that are discovered in certain places" is more the style of a *New York Times* magazine essayist. But the abruptness makes his point. Phrases like "That are dead" and "Because she's looking for the papers, too" show how genre writers use incomplete sentences to lurch the reader onward, to spring surprises upon him with broken-up fragments of meaning.

We can find the technique in literary fiction as well, as in the opening of Charles Dickens' *Bleak House*.

> London. Michaelmas Term lately over, and the Lord Chancellor sitting in Lincoln's Inn Hall. Implacable November weather. As much mud in the streets as if the waters had but newly retired from the face of the earth, and it would not be wonderful to meet a Megalosaurus, forty feet long or so, waddling like an elephantine lizard up Holborn Hill. Smoke lowering down from chimney-pots, making a soft black drizzle, with flakes of soot in it as big as full-grown snow- flakes — gone into mourning, one might imagine, for the death of the sun. Dogs, undistinguishable in mire. Horses, scarcely better; splashed to their very blinkers. Foot passengers, jostling one another's umbrellas in a general infection of ill-temper, and losing their foot-hold at street-corners, where tens of thousands of other foot passengers have been slipping and sliding since the day broke (if the day ever broke), adding new deposits to the crust upon crust of mud, sticking at those points tenaciously to the pavement, and accumulating at compound interest.

Every "sentence" in this passage is actually a sentence fragment; nothing here contains the subject-verb arrangement requisite for sentencehood. The ones that have subjects and verbs, like "it would not be . . ." are dependent clauses. And it doesn't stop with this passage — the string of fragments goes on for nearly four hundred words.

Besides just proving that he could manage it, Dickens seems to have another reason for beginning the novel this way. If you try to convert the fragments in the first paragraphs into actual sentences, you'll be left with something like this (additions italicized): "*It was* London. *It was* Michaelmas. Term *was* lately over, and the Lord Chancellor *sat* in Lincoln's Inn hall. *There was* implacable November weather. *There was* as much mud in the streets . . ." In other words, if Dickens had used proper grammar, he would have been stuck with an abundance of weak, bland constructions — "it was," "there were," and so on.

Of course, he could have rearranged the syntax to remove the passive verbs: "During Michaelmas term in London, the Lord Chancellor sat in Lincoln's Inn hall, removed from the implacable November weather which had brought as much mud to the streets . . ." But this is an entirely different style, presumably one Dickens didn't think worked as well. So he arrived at a more elegant solution—instead of trying to find synonyms for the passive words, he simply dropped them. He knew the fragments would still communicate what he wanted them to, and that the reader would focus on the images ("dogs, indistinguishable in mire," "horses splashed to their very blinkers."). It's not so different from the *Die Hard* copywriter deciding that the phrase "There were twelve terrorists and one cop" wouldn't provide the same emphasis as "Twelve Terrorists. One Cop."

But it goes beyond just wanting to be emphatic, I think. You'll notice that in Dickens's fragments, he doesn't always just flash up an image. In fact, he often comes close to writing actual sentences, and only avoids them by using participles instead of verbs. For example, when he shows us the fragmented image "Foot passengers, jostling one another's umbrellas," he could have replaced "jostling" with "jostled" to create a proper sentence, without losing any vividness. So why didn't he? Perhaps he had just settled into the style and liked the feel of it—after all, many authors use sentence fragments to create an economical, crisp tone. Or . . .

Maybe Dickens had discovered that the continued use of fragments creates an interesting and useful paradox: stripping the non-active elements from the language ("it was," "there were," etc.) actually *freezes* the action to some degree. In this case, the fragments make us see an ugly, angry, urban scene as a tableau, rather than as a moving picture: the Lord Chancellor sits motionless on his bench, the dogs stand still and miserable in their coats of mud, the smoke hovers eternally. Verbs, after all, imply movement, while nouns and modifiers just sit there until a verb makes them do something. In beginning his novel without any verbs, Dickens makes us experience the scene as a still life, before jolting it into motion with actual sentences.

A final reason to use fragments (although you may think of others) is to imitate the clipped, truncated style of a journal writer, or perhaps someone recording events for an audience that doesn't care about style, such as a captain writing a ship's log. This may not seem like a very common occurrence, but you see a surprising number of novels written as diary entries or logs, and almost all of them liberally use fragments. To cite a quick example, William Boyd narrates *Any Human Heart* via the journal entries of a man named Logan Mountstuart, and he includes many passages like this: "La Fucina. A perfect Fucina day. Just the three of us—though we don't see much of Cesare this year." It makes sense, as far as verisimilitude goes. If the only audience for your words is yourself, you only care about getting across your point. Why bother inserting pronouns and passive verbs just to make the prose grammatical?

So that would be my response to Microsoft's green line, should it, in its personified form, ever ask me why I get upset when it appears under my fragments. Fragments, I would say, are useful things. They can focus the reader's attention on the object or sensation, and they avoid diluting the image with passive verbs. They can contribute to an economical, no-nonsense style. Used repeatedly, they can create an overall sensation of stopped motion. They can imitate a narrator who's writing a journal or a log. And they can be inherently dramatic.

THE DANGERS OF THE FRAGMENT

Upon hearing this last point, the personified green line would pounce. "Aha!" it would say, twirling its mustache, "Drama! Yes, drama is an important feature. But tell me, Monsieur" — for some reason, the green line is French — "zis drama, is it not very close to . . . melodrama?" Indeed it is, I would have to confess.

To put it simply, melodrama is the quality of being a bit over-the-top. It can be hard to differentiate between something that is melodramatic and something that is dramatic, and in fact we don't always split that hair. When we call someone a "drama queen," we mean they behave in a melodramatic fashion. In 2011, as trade rumors centered around the NBA forward Carmelo Anthony, whose nickname is "Melo," sportswriters used infinite varieties of the pun "Melo-drama." The term worked because the story contained a lot of "drama," in the colloquial sense of people getting riled up about something trivial, which is to say that they were being melodramatic.

But in narrative we do have to differentiate, and the differentiation is especially important for our purposes, because the line between drama and melodrama often comes down to language.

If something in a work of fiction causes a powerful and genuine emotional response in the reader, it's generally due to the harmony of character, situation, and language. When Jane Austen gives us the wonderful line "Elinor was then at liberty to think and be wretched," we are moved to pity because 1) we've come to love and respect Elinor (character), 2) we didn't anticipate the plot twist that provoked her grief (situation), and 3) the phrasing "to think and be wretched" is graceful, understated, and surprising (language). In any genuinely dramatic moment in literature, you'll find a similar alignment of these three forces.

When one of the elements tries too hard to create emotion or drama, melodrama ensues. If a writer trots out an orphan with leukemia who loves puppies, then his use of character is overt and clumsy. If the cop-hero finds out that the elusive bank robber is the same guy who killed his partner, then the situation has been manipulated to create drama. But we're mostly concerned about the way language transgresses.

When language creates melodrama, it's usually the result of a misuse of one of the techniques that can create genuine drama, which is why we have to be so careful and precise during highly charged scenes. Two such methods involve italics and exclamation points, which we'll talk about in a later chapter. You can also use understatement and hypotaxis (understating a dramatic clause by making it subordinate: "I was eating tacos when Lance shot me"). Yet another of these techniques, as you may have guessed, is the use of sentence fragments.

The very thing that makes fragments useful to us in many situations—their ability to focus the reader on one image or sensation or point—might lead us into melodrama. In effect, fragments can make us focus too much, so that it becomes embarrassingly obvious what the author wants us to pay attention to. Melodrama comes out of the reader's perception of the author's neediness, his fervent desire to make the reader feel a particular emotion. There's nothing wrong with having that desire; all writers should. The problem comes when the writer's neediness makes him try too hard. This happens when the writer uses a fragment in a clumsy manner. Like a guy who gives a girl a diamond ring on the second date, a writer who has lost control of his fragments shows his desires too artlessly.

Thus, the green line may serve a purpose when it underlines a fragment, even one we've made intentionally. Instead of thinking about its appearance as a signal that we've made a mistake, perhaps we should be more generous. Maybe the squiggly line simply says, "Monsieur, I understand ze fragment may be used for dramatic purposes. Still, perhaps ze gentleman would like to consider if, in zis case, ze dramatic effect is worth it. *N'est ce pas?*"

Indeed, *c'est vrai*, most of the time you should pause and think about why you've used a fragment, and what the potential dangers are. Still, I don't think I'll turn my grammar-check back on, mostly because I don't really know how.

PARAGRAPH FRAGMENTS

Now that we've looked at the uses of fragments, and ended with a warning about how they sometimes cross the line between drama and melodrama, let's take a slight detour. I have to confess the next subject doesn't quite fit under "nuances of punctuation"—in this case, punctuation isn't at issue the way it is with sentence fragments, where the location of the period causes the error. But I'd like to discuss it now because it fits with the general theme of fragments, and also because I don't know where else to put it.

The method I'm talking about might be called the "paragraph fragment." It's the technique of using a single sentence as an entire paragraph in order to create drama. Since paragraphs usually last longer than one sentence, it may seem that a very brief one is a fragment or shard of an actual one (see how I'm trying to squeeze in the theme?). Paragraph fragments can strike the reader as a legitimate and powerful means of calling attention to a sentence. But sometimes—a lot of times—they come off as melodramatic.

Let's take as an example a paragraph from Faulkner's "A Rose for Emily." On the story's last page we see, sandwiched between two long paragraphs, the separately indented line "The man himself lay in the bed." The sentence gives some important information about the character while supplying a grisly plot twist.

The story itself feels a bit gothic, and thus Faulkner may have considered himself at liberty to use a technique that, in its emphatic nature, gets associated with genre pieces like horror and thriller narratives. Or perhaps he just really wanted you to pay attention to that line, and he suspected this would be the best way to do it. I tend to give credence to that idea. Faulkner must have known that some of his passages get a bit self-indulgent, and that readers don't always pay full attention when they get halfway through one of his five-hundred-word paragraphs. To make sure the reader focuses at this key moment, he uses indentation. It works—the news comes as quite a surprise, and it's nice to receive it without the clutter and distraction of other sentences. In any case, I've never heard anyone complain about this aspect of "A Rose for Emily."

Nevertheless, the technique is frequently dismissed as heavy-handed, for the same reason sentence fragments are. In the seminal *Art of Fiction*, John Gardner condemns "superdramatic one-sentence paragraphs . . . of the kind favored by porno and thriller writers" because they result in forced emotion. While Gardner has an extremely low tolerance for sentimentality, you can see what he means; paragraph fragments attempt to emphasize something in a fairly obvious, often clumsy way. Thus they regularly appear in genres whose writers prioritize narrative expediency over aesthetic principles. The thriller writer James Patterson, for example, uses paragraph fragments so much that it's become a signature of his style. Here's a passage from his novel *Now You See Her*:

> The fact, of course, was that there was no Kevin Bloom. I wish there were more times than not, believe me. I could have really used a romantic Irish playwright in my hectic life.
>
> The truth was, there wasn't even a Nina Bloom.
>
> I made me up too.
>
> I had my reasons. They were good ones.
>
> The worst kind. The kind where forever after, you always make sure your phone number is unlisted and never ever, ever stop looking over your shoulder.
>
> It started on spring break, of all things. In the spring of 1992 in Key West, Florida, I guess you could say a foolish girl went wild.
>
> And stayed wild.
>
> That foolish girl was me.
>
> My name was Jeanine.

Patterson doesn't use the fragments with much subtlety here; he indents pretty much any time he wants a sentence to resonate. In fact, he uses so many paragraph fragments that there might be a point of diminishing returns; they lose their dramatic impact when used in such numbers. Because Patterson is unapologetic about his lack of literary pretensions, he probably doesn't care about any of that. Plus, as he has learned to his bank account's benefit, it's easy to read this kind of prose. On virtually every page of every one of his novels, you'll see paragraph fragments, not only because they add emphasis, but because he knows his readers don't like long blocks of text.

Of course, subjectivity comes into play in deciding such matters. Patterson's fragments are pretty obviously pulp fiction-y, but often it's harder to decide whether or not a paragraph fragment deserves its emphasis. In the following passage from Rose Tremain's *Restoration*, a long paragraph shows the narrator reminiscing while at the funeral of a friend, then a one-sentence paragraph completes the chapter:

> . . . at the graveside I found myself remembering how, at Cambridge,
> some cunning thieves calling themselves "Anglers" had tried to steal it
> and all Pearce's possessions from him. They worked with a long pole,
> on the end of what was a hook made of wire, and such a pole had been
> thrust through Pearce's open window one night while he slept. He had
> woken up to see a chair moving in a glimmer of moonlight three feet off
> the floor and floating out through the window. "It was only," he told me,
> "when the pole came back into the room and I saw it move towards my
> ladle that I understood there were villains at work and not ghosts. And so
> I cried out angrily, and my shouting frightened them and they ran away."
> He laughed when he had told me this story and then he said: "Perhaps it
> is always easier to frighten away the living than it is to frighten away the
> dead? What do you think, Merivel?"
>
> But I cannot remember what I answered.

This last line calls attention to itself, surrounded as it is by a thick block of text on top and a half-page of white space at the bottom. One reason it may not seem melodramatic, though, is that the content of the line doesn't strike us as overly dramatic or sentimental—at first glance, most of its impact comes from the simple fact that it's indented. However, that indentation prompts us to think about the line separately, and in doing so we ponder its significance in a way that is necessary for our appreciation of the anecdote. Merivel's failure to know the answer to Pearce's question takes on added importance as he stands at the man's grave. For Merivel will never be able to "frighten away the dead" figure of Pearce; the man's goodness and generosity will stay with Merivel like a curse, ultimately prompting him to become a better person himself. The reader is prepared for this, and understands some of it at the time, because Tremain has indicated the importance of the otherwise inconspicuous line by separating it.

If that one works to create genuine emotion, maybe we should close by looking at an example that could be considered more divisive:

> Billy's daughter Barbara came in later that day. She was all doped up,
> had the same glassy-eyed look that Edgar Derby wore just before he was
> shot in Dresden. Doctors had given her pills so she could continue to
> function, even though her father was broken and her mother was dead.
>
> So it goes.

You may recognize the famous refrain "so it goes" from Kurt Vonnegut's *Slaughterhouse-Five*, in which he uses the phrase dozens of times to express a weary acceptance of tragedy and inhumanity. It's not always used as a paragraph fragment, but when it is, some may object to it on the grounds of melodrama or sentimentality. Here's why:

Even when packed into a normal paragraph, the phrase is emotionally loaded. It often follows the mention of some terrible death, and thus its weary acceptance of man's awfulness may seem like an emotion worn overtly on the sleeve. True, it's understated in the sense of what the words actually denote; "so it goes" is a version of that modern shibboleth of stoicism, "it is what it is." But even that understatement might seem overly dramatic, because we're so clearly meant to understand that it's understatement. Plus, if it were genuine understatement, it wouldn't use indentation to call attention to itself.

In any case, when you take a phrase already teetering on the brink of sentimentality, and set it apart as a separate paragraph to remind the reader of its profundity, you might have crossed the line. That's the danger of the paragraph fragment—sometimes it doesn't just call attention to something, it does so in a way that makes a reader think you're trying too hard to achieve that emphasis.

Then again, sometimes it serves as a dramatic device in a work of enormous emotional power and resonance, like *Slaughterhouse-Five*. No one said this would be easy.

twelve

Comma Splices, Run-ons, and Semicolons

In this chapter, much of what I'm going to say will relate to the caveat I mentioned a few pages ago: you can only violate a rule of grammar and usage if the reader understands you're violating it on purpose. This is as close as we get to a truism in creative writing, and I think it's a valuable idea to keep hold of (although even it has some exceptions). Not so often discussed is a pair of questions that the caveat gives rise to: How will a reader know I'm making the mistake out of artistry rather than ignorance? And how will I know that my reader will know?

The first question may seem to depend on the subjective intelligence and/or generosity of the individual reader. But that's true of almost anything, so it's not a helpful point. Plus, we actually can submit a response that is accurate in a general sense, for most readers. After all, when creative writing instructors grade, and when agents evaluate an aspiring writer's control of language, they make the decision all the time. Pens hovering cautiously over a draft, they look for any number of clues that indicate whether the writer has comma spliced with purpose and style, or whether he didn't know it was a mistake.

So here's the answer (warning: it's not very profound): the main way to determine whether the writer has made a mistake consciously or accidentally is to evaluate the rest of the writer's language. If she's made few errors elsewhere, she'll get the benefit of the doubt. If she spelled her name wrong in the query letter or the paper's heading, if she seems to think colons serve the function of semicolons and vice versa, we assume the other errors are not artistic flourishes. I told you it wasn't very profound. But that doesn't mean you shouldn't think about it.

This goes some way toward answering the question of how you'll know your reader will interpret your mistakes in the right spirit. If you feel confident that your grammar is stellar in every other respect, you can probably tell yourself that any tweaking of a rule for stylistic purposes will be read as such. But that "probably" becomes uncomfortable as the stakes get higher. When you submit a novel to an agent, for example, I'd recommend erring on the side of not erring. If an instructor of Fiction 101 thinks your sentence fragment shows a lack of mastery or focus, you might lose a point or two. An agent might see it as a reason to close your file and start checking e-mail.

So really I'm offering a caveat-within-a-caveat-within-a-caveat. Yes, a writer should only violate a rule if he knows he's violating it. But also, a writer should only do so when he feels confident that most readers will understand the intentional nature of the error. *And,* the writer should not overestimate his reader's eagerness to make the distinction.

With that out of the way, we can get to the nitty-gritty. In the first sections of this chapter, we'll focus on two punctuation-based mistakes, the comma splice and the run-on sentence. I've chosen these two in part because, well, they're mistakes, and good writers like to know when they're making them. But in the case of comma splices in particular, we also want to investigate how they can be exploited for effect — if I had to guess, I'd say the comma splice is the most common error writers make on purpose. Later in the chapter we'll look at the characteristics of the semicolon, which relates to the opening topics in that it can be used to fix comma splices and run-ons. It also performs other functions that will come in handy for the fiction writer.

COMMA SPLICES

This is one of those grammar concepts people like to invoke as an example of grammar concepts that no one can understand. The other one is the dangling participle. As in, "I'm a finance major, what do I care about comma splices and dangling participles!? I'll be signing your paychecks someday, egghead, so watch it!" The good news is, comma splices are actually easy to understand. The bad news is, people do have a hard time remembering what exactly they are.

I don't know why. To "splice" means to join two elements together, and when a writer uses a comma splice, she's using a comma to do just that. You simply have to remember what those two elements are, and that a comma technically should not join them.

The two elements are independent clauses, phrases that could be sentences if they wanted to: "Allan smells funny," "You are incorrect," "I think the skunk got loose," "It's not a duck," whatever. When you join two of them together using only a comma, it looks like this: "Allan smells funny, I think the skunk got loose" or "You are incorrect, it's not a duck." That's a comma splice. The error derives from the fact that commas aren't strong enough to join two things as heavy as independent clauses.

To fix the error, therefore, we have to add connective strength to the comma. One of way of doing so is to add a muscle to it, by putting a dot on top and turning it into a semicolon. A cheesy metaphor, perhaps, but my students appreciate it, or at least they humor me in a convincing way. In any case, "Allan smells funny; I think the skunk got loose" solves the technical problem. I'll talk more about this and other functions of the semicolon later.

Another method of strengthening the comma is to add a conjunction, either a coordinating one like "and," "so," or "but," or a subordinating one like "because," "unless," or "while." When you do this, you should leave in the comma and add the conjunction after it: "Allan smells funny, *so* I think the skunk got loose," "You are incorrect, *unless* it's not a duck." And that's it, as far as the erroneous nature of the comma splice goes. Now for the nuance.

Comma splices are used so frequently and so eloquently by so many writers that they may not seem like a problem, unless the two independent clauses being joined have no business being together. Even Microsoft's green line inconsistently identifies a comma splice as an error. So if you feel that two clauses belong together, but you worry that a semicolon would slow the pace too much or a conjunction would sound wrong, go ahead and splice those suckers with a scrawny little comma. The caveats mentioned in the beginning of the chapter still apply, but comma splices add a slight wrinkle. The way to tell if a writer has used one on purpose is not just to look at the rest of the grammar, but to see if the rhythmic effect works. Comma splices are generally used because they create a particular cadence, one that occurs when you don't want to stop your sentence, but you also don't want to mar the style with the conjunctions or adverbs that would make the sentence technically correct.

For examples, let's look at the ones invoked in Strunk and White's *Elements of Style*. While they warn against splices generally, they allow for exceptions when "the clauses are very short and alike in form, or when the tone of the sentence is easy and conversational." Their instance for the first case is "Man proposes, God disposes." Sure enough, that pairing would lose some of its musical power if you fixed the splice. That's because, in its original form, both independent clauses have the same meter. "Man proposes" is trochaic dimeter ("trochaic" means it consists of two-syllable groups in which the first syllable is stressed and the second is unstressed, and "dimeter" means there are two such syllable groups: MAN pro-POSE-es), and so is "God disposes" (GOD dis-POSE-es). Correct the technical mistake — "Man proposes, while God disposes" — and you lose the metrical symmetry.

As an example of how informality of tone can give one the permission to splice with commas, Strunk and White show us "Here today, gone tomorrow." (They ignore the fact that neither of these two word groups is actually an independent clause; perhaps we should, too.) That line contains a balance in terms of content as well as sound — the first word in each phrase refers to a location, while the second refers to a time — and you don't want to disrupt it with an extra word. But you also don't want to ruin the casual tone, which would happen if you added a semicolon. In "Here today; gone tomorrow" the overly precise punctuation mark seems too uptight for the folksy, colloquial sentence.

If fixing a splice can ruin a casual tone, it stands to reason that putting one in on purpose can create, or at least reinforce, such a tone. Writers often use the comma splice to underscore a character's informality, as when the narrator of Alice Munro's "How I Met My Husband" writes, "I was shy of strangers and the work was hard, they didn't make it nice for you," or the protagonist of "Cathedral" says, "The blind man had right away located his foods, he knew just where everything was on his plate." With informal first-person narratives, we often get the sense that the characters are speaking to us, rather than writing to us. And aurally, the splicing comma tells us the speaker slows down only a little bit, the way people do in real life when they join independent clauses. We don't use semicolons when we speak.

Another example of acceptable comma splicing provided by Strunk and White is the intriguing sentence "The gates swung apart, the bridge fell, the portcullis was drawn up." I've always found this an odd one for them to include, because it doesn't fit either of the categories they've set up as reasons to accept a splice. The clauses aren't that short or structurally similar (at least when compared with the other examples), and the tone isn't informal. Yet they're right, this sentence works better with the splices. It may just be a case of the writer's ear and instinct telling him to prefer it over the alternatives, which are these:

The gates swung apart; the bridge fell; the portcullis was drawn up.

The gates swung apart, the bridge fell, and the portcullis was drawn up.

The punctuation in the first example disrupts the rhythm by giving the sentence a stuttering quality. Together the clauses present a dramatic, rushing scene, and we don't want to stop every few words to clear the hurdle of a semicolon. Plus, the semicolons starkly separate the events, while I think the reader should see them as fluidly progressing into each other, or perhaps occurring simultaneously.

The second sentence doesn't have those problems, but something does go wrong with the "and." Basically, it tidies things up too much. The sentence describes chaos and frenzy, and the chaotic nature of the grammar mistake contributes to that tone. Putting the "and" in front of the final independent clause orders things, so that we now read the clauses more chronologically—we put a mental 1, 2, and 3 in front of each event. In the version without the "and," the three clauses are equals, so we may see them happening all at once, or in a different order, or perhaps we don't care. To add a conjunction before the final clause may be the responsible thing to do, but this sentence doesn't call for responsibility, it calls for a dash of wildness.

RUN-ON SENTENCES

Our next item on the agenda, the run-on sentence, should be easy to dispense with. The only obstacle is the fact that it's not what the majority of people think it is, i.e., any sentence that goes on for too long. The confusion is understandable, given the error's name. If we call it a "run-on," shouldn't we mean the sentence "runs on" for too long?

Alas, no. Run-ons have nothing to do with length. True, they often are longer than other sentences, but not always, and not necessarily. "Run don't walk" is a run-on, as is "The dog drank he was thirsty."

The work we did in the previous section should help us deal with the run-on. A few pages ago, we learned that a comma is too weak to join two independent clauses. And if a comma is too weak, then imagine the disaster that ensues when you try to join clauses using absolutely nothing. Think about it this way: "The dog drank" is an independent clause. So is "he was thirsty." Therefore, "The dog drank, he was thirsty" is a comma splice. "The dog drank he was thirsty" is a run-on sentence.

Perhaps another analogy will help. Let's imagine a comma splice as the result of a carpenter who used wood glue (a comma) to connect two heavy boards (independent clauses) that should have been joined with a nail (a semicolon, or a comma-plus-conjunction). To continue that analogy, a run-on sentence would be the result of a carpenter who just held the boards next to each other and then let go, hoping they'd magically stick together.

A run-on is more obviously flawed than a comma splice, and therefore it's harder to convince a reader you did it on purpose. In student work, I rarely see run-ons that result from artistic choice. Most of the time, they're just mistakes.

It does happen, however, that writers will use the technique for aesthetic purposes. When they do, they are often working within an experimental or innovative tradition. In particular, the Modernists used run-ons with some frequency, the most famous example being Molly Bloom's soliloquy at the end of Joyce's *Ulysses*. Here's one section of it, chosen at random:

> his father made his money over selling the horses for the cavalry
> well he could buy me a nice present up in Belfast after what I gave
> him they've lovely linen up there or one of those nice kimono things
> I must buy a mothball like I had before to keep in the drawer with
> them it would be exciting going around with him shopping buying
> those things in a new city

This isn't a run-on because it's long; it's a run-on because it doesn't put periods where the content says they should go. If you were to "fix" this passage, in the sense of turning it into Standard English by adding punctuation, it might look like this (I apologize in advance to any Joyceans out there, who will surely be offended):

> His father made his money over selling the horses for the cavalry.
> Well, he could buy me a nice present up in Belfast after what I gave
> him. They've lovely linen up there, or one of those nice kimono things.
> I must buy a mothball like I had before to keep in the drawer with
> them. It would be exciting going around with him, shopping, buying
> those things in a new city.

We understand this version more easily because we've grown accustomed to the little black marks telling us when to pause and stop. When the writer doesn't use them, we have to work extra hard. But I think we can also see that the amended version loses something essential.

As we saw in chapter 5, writers using the stream of consciousness technique seek to represent the experience of thinking, and that's what Joyce is up to when he shows the tangential connections Molly makes. She thinks about a wealthy past lover, which makes her think about the clothes she could have bought with the money he gave her, which makes her think that she needs to go buy a mothball for her dresser, and then she leaps back to thinking about what her life might have been like had she stayed with the old lover. To intensify our immersion in Molly's mind, Joyce removes as much structure and artifice as he can, until all we're left with are the words that represent her thoughts. It would be hard to sink into Molly's core being in a visceral way if we were always obeying the traffic signs of punctuation, the process of which is, after all, a societal convention, not something innate in our brains. By eliminating periods, Joyce creates a run-on, but he also encourages us to read these forty-plus pages in an exhilarating, tumultuous rush that resembles Molly's internal experience.

I probably don't need to add a "however" paragraph to this, but I'm going to. However lyrical and interesting you find the Molly Bloom speech, or William Gaddis's *Agapē Agape* (an entire novel that is a run-on), or the notoriously long sentence in Faulkner's *Absalom, Absalom!*, you should keep in mind that even short run-ons are difficult to handle in a non-gimmicky way. Like comma-spliced sentences, they are errors that can be used for rhythmic or tonal purposes. But unlike splices, they do not fly under the radar—most readers will spot them as flawed constructions, so if you use them you're betting that the distraction will be worth the payoff.

SEMICOLONS

We've already discussed the primary function of semicolons. In a nutshell, they can combine independent clauses, so that you don't have to resort to comma splices or run-ons. The catch is that the semicolon must indicate a content-based relationship between the two clauses. Without that relationship-indicating quality, a semicolon wouldn't be any different from a period. In "The Datsun is acting up again; I should check the transmission fluid," the semicolon combines clauses that have a clear relationship. But "The Datsun is acting up again; I sure do like Van Halen" leaves the reader wondering why the writer didn't separate the clauses entirely.

It's not as simple a point as it may seem. Deciding to use a semicolon rather than a period can be subjective, because most adjacent clauses relate to each other in some way. Who's to say which neighboring sentences should be connected and which should not?

The fiction writer can make complex use of this ambiguity, by showing that she wants certain sentences to be read in tandem, even if they don't seem to be clearly linked. The final line of Angela Carter's "Werewolf" does this, with "Now the child lived in her grandmother's house; she prospered." Out of context, the clauses don't appear to be closely related, so we might expect a period between them. But in joining them with a semicolon, Carter suggests that the first fact somehow caused the second fact. That is, living in the grandmother's house may have had something to do with the girl's prospering. This matters because the previous paragraph reveals the grandmother to be a werewolf who is killed by villagers (thus the vacant house). The ominous idea that by moving into the house the granddaughter took on some of her grandmother's powers, and used them to prosper, is a possible implication of Carter's punctuation.

The second main function of the semicolon is to act as "Special Policeman in the event of comma fights," in the words of Lynne Truss. She means that semicolons can step in and establish order when a sentence's comma usage might cause problems. A passage from George Eliot's *Silas Marner* shows us this function:

> This view of Marner's personality was not without another ground than his pale face and unexampled eyes; for Jem Rodney, the mole-catcher, averred that, one evening as he was returning homeward, he saw Silas Marner leaning against a stile with a heavy bag on his back, instead of resting the bag on the stile as a man in his senses would have done; and that, on coming up to him, he saw that Marner's eyes were set like a dead man's, and he spoke to him, and shook him, and his limbs were stiff, and his hands clutched the bag as if they'd been made of iron; but just as he had made up his mind that the weaver was dead, he came all right again, like, as you may say, in the winking of an eye, and said "Good night," and walked off.

In this extremely long sentence, Eliot employs more than a dozen commas, an abundance that could cause disorder. So she puts in three semicolons to separate the sentence's four main elements: the point that the narrator will now give us an example of Silas's personality, the story of Jem Rodney seeing Silas doing something strange, the story of Silas appearing to be dead, and the story of his resurrection. This is how semicolons can regulate sentences that have become confusing because of length and/or comma profusion.

These semicolons don't function in the same way as the ones we talked about earlier. That is, they don't lend their muscle to connect independent clauses that are otherwise stand-alone entities ("Man proposes; God disposes"). Instead, they connect clauses already joined by conjunctions — Eliot's second, third, and fourth clauses begin with "for," "and," and "but." Normally, sentences joined by conjunctions only need a comma to complete the connection. In fact, if Eliot had used commas instead of those semicolons, she would have been on safe ground, grammatically speaking. But she decided to bring in semicolons at specific points to keep order. If she hadn't, we may not have been able to keep the clauses straight, because the passage contains so many other commas doing so many other things. Like a mayor who fears a riot but who is also wary of seeming autocratic, the writer has to carefully consider the pros and cons of bringing in a regulatory force. And some might argue that if your sentence is so confusing as to require semicolons, you should rewrite it.

As fiction writers, we should certainly master the two primary uses of the semicolon, perhaps by reading those last few paragraphs over and over again. But it's also important to think about semicolons in a somewhat conceptual way, and to understand one of the most significant rules that governs them.

We often imagine semicolons as being situated between commas and periods on the spectrum of punctuation. While a comma indicates a brief pause, and a period represents a major pause, the semicolon exists somewhere in the middle, a role that its appearance indicates — it looks like a period jumped on top of a comma. But there are some problems with that conception. In actuality, the length of the semicolon's pause varies. Sometimes it's pretty much the same as the pause involved with a period, while in other situations it's fractionally longer than the pause of a comma.

Consider the sentence "The river seems high; however, I don't believe it will flood the town." If you read this out loud, you should pause for a while after "high," because you have to show that the clause beginning with "however" is separated from the first one — if the pause weren't longish, you would attach the "however" to "the river seems high." The semicolon indicates a longer break in this instance.

But in other situations you shouldn't pause for very long when you see semicolons, like in the *Silas Marner* example, where they basically act like commas. This also happens when semicolons are used to keep order in a long list in which the items contain their own commas: "We gambled in Reno, Nevada; Joliet, Illinois; and Monaco." In a sense, using a semicolon in a list is arbitrary. We don't need anything inherent in the function of a semicolon, we just need a punctuation mark that can say to the reader "I know I look like something else, but please try to think of me as a comma." When reading such sentences out loud, you may pause a millisecond longer when you arrive at a semicolon, but it won't be as long as the pause you give prior to a conjunctive adverb like "however."

And, of course, sometimes they are what they're perceived to be—a pause whose length is halfway between that of a period and that of a comma. We often fall back on this pause length when a writer uses a semi-colon for no clear grammatical reason—when, in fact, she misuses it. In *Transit of Venus*, Shirley Hazzard includes a semicolon in the line "The tableau was brief; but even the boy remembered it." Because the two clauses are joined with the conjunction "but," all that's needed to complete the connection is a comma, not a semicolon. Yet Hazzard wants us to chew over each half of this sentence for a bit longer than a comma would allow us to. It's as if she doesn't want us to take the first part too lightly. But she also doesn't want the full stop ("The tableau was brief. But even the boy remembered it."), perhaps because the line already consists of its own paragraph, and to make it more dramatic would be risky (for reasons we explored in chapter 11). So she finds a happy middle ground, a punctuation mark that may be technically out of place, but which makes us linger for exactly the right length of time.

The final point has to do with a familiar refrain: in our era, many writers are suspicious of this punctuation mark. One possible reason relates to the issue we tackled in the who/whom discussion in chapter 7. Like those relative pronouns, semicolons have a whiff of . . . I don't want to say pretentiousness, but perhaps something like that. It's not that fiction writers try to dumb down their prose, of course. But they do have an aversion to anything that will distract a reader from the content (you may have heard this before), and certain elements of grammar and punctuation, simply by dint of being somewhat rare, or involving obscure rules, or even just looking funny, call the reader's attention to their usage.

As we've seen, straightforward guidelines govern semicolons. But they can come off as overly precise or obscure, the kind of thing that reminds readers too much of their experiences in eighth-grade language arts class.

Such associations have to do with our times and tastes. While many contemporary writers shy away from punctuation that will make their prose seem fastidious, in previous eras the precise employment of grammar and convention was encouraged in all forms of writing. In 1926 the playwright George Bernard Shaw criticized a draft of T. E. Lawrence's *Seven Pillars of Wisdom* by telling Lawrence, "You practically do not use semicolons at all. This is a symptom of mental defectiveness, probably induced by camp life."

thirteen

Dashes, Parentheses, and Nonessential Commas

This subject is near and dear to my heart, because I use a lot of dashes. I remember reading the galley copy of my first novel, *The Cuban Prospect*, and being mortified by the amount of dashes. It's the kind of thing you don't notice until you see it in print, when it's too late to change anything. I've now accepted dash usage as part of my style, and I try to use it for the purposes of good rather than evil.

The first issue to address is that the dash is not a hyphen. A hyphen is the single horizontal line you see in terms like "high-pitched" and "thirty-two." It's easy to use, and while some people get worked up over the difference between phrases like "extra-marital sex" and "extra marital sex" (think about it), such intriguing complications don't come up very often.

A dash is a longer horizontal line, the mark that gets created when you type two hyphens next to each other. In creative writing, the dash tends to be a protean thing, put to various uses that your composition instructor wouldn't approve of. For example, it's often used for rhythmic or visual effect, which is perhaps what Emily Dickinson was up to in stanzas like this:

And were You — saved —
And I — condemned to be
Where You were not —
That self — were hell to Me —

(Incidentally, if you ever meet a Dickinson scholar who wants to share his explanation for why Emily used the dash so much, run away.) So dashes are versatile, but for now we'll focus on their most common function, which will let us kill two other grammatical birds: parentheses and nonessential commas.

All three of these punctuation marks are generally used for the same purpose. To illustrate this fact (and to prolong the suspense of what that purpose might be), let's examine three different versions of a sentence from Ron Hansen's novel *Exiles*:

> Even in his editorial notes in the collected *Poems* of 1918 — which he titled identically to his own first book — Bridges could not forgive his friend's licenses.

> Even in his editorial notes in the collected *Poems* of 1918, which he titled identically to his own first book, Bridges could not forgive his friend's licenses.

> Even in his editorial notes in the collected *Poems* of 1918 (which he titled identically to his own first book), Bridges could not forgive his friend's licenses.

So which version do you think appeared in the novel? What would you base your guess on? Does one style seem more grammatically legitimate?

I won't keep you in suspense: Hansen used the version with the dashes. But you had no way of knowing that, because without context, you can't objectively say one style is better than the others. The reason for this, again, is that these three sets of punctuation perform the same function. Specifically, they set apart a sentence's nonessential elements.

You may argue that lots of sentence elements in creative writing are not exactly essential, and you'd be right (just look at Faulkner, for goodness' sake). But in grammatical terms, a nonessential element is a modifying phrase or an appositive. They can be cut out of a sentence without sacrificing basic meaning, which is how they get their name.

In the Hansen example, the nonessential phrase "which he titled identically to his own first book" is a modifying element. It provides some extra information about the book *Poems*. If the sentence did not include it, we would still be able to muddle through. But if the sentence were to lose other elements, such as "Bridges could not" or "friend's," it would not convey the meaning the author wants us to have. It would be incoherent, misleading, or ungrammatical.

Appositive phrases, the other kind of nonessential element, rename or redefine a noun. The following examples are basically the same sentence, but each uses a different punctuation marker to set off the appositive phrase.

Tank, Lisa's boyfriend, is Swiss.

Tank—Lisa's boyfriend—is Swiss.

Tank (Lisa's boyfriend) is Swiss.

These sentences all want us to know that Tank is Swiss; this nugget of information is the sentences' raison d'etre. Along the way, they have decided to throw in Tank's role as Lisa's paramour. Doing so redefines and renames Tank, which is nice, but hardly necessary in a grammatical sense. If these sentences were hot-air balloons that needed to jettison weight, "Lisa's boyfriend" would be the first thing tossed over the side.

So that, in a very small nutshell, is what dashes, parentheses, and non-essential commas have in common: they all surround and set apart information that the sentence doesn't really need. But of course that's not all there is to it.

Beyond their technical functions, all three of these markers allow writers to subtly manipulate tone and rhythm—in short, they are tremendously useful in controlling prose style. Look at how Philip Roth, a true savant of the nonessential punctuation marker, uses them to create variety and lyricism in this long sentence from *Portnoy's Complaint*:

Or just standing nice and calm—nothing trembling, everything serene—standing there in the sunshine (as though in the middle of an empty field, or passing the time on the street corner), standing without a care in the world in the sunshine, like my king of kings, the Lord my God, The Duke Himself (Snider, Doctor, the name may come up again), standing there as loose and as easy, as happy as I will ever be, just waiting by myself under a high fly ball (*a towering fly ball, I hear Red Barber say, as he watches from behind his microphone—hit out toward Portnoy; Alex under it, under it*), just waiting there for the ball to fall into the glove I raise to it, and yup, there it is, *plock*, the third out of the inning (*and Alex gathers it in for out number three, and folks, here's old C.D. for P. Lorillard and Company*), and in one motion, while old Connie brings us a message from Old Golds, I start in toward the bench, holding the ball now with the five fingers of my bare left hand, and when I get to the infield—having come down hard with one foot on the bag at second base—I shoot it gently, with just a flick of the wrist, at the opposing team's shortstop . . .

The nonessential elements not only add more detail, they also affect the pace of the sentence. The parentheses and dashes slow us down and speed us up, and sometimes they change the voice we hear in our heads (the italics do this too, but that's a discussion for another day).

The passage also uses the three different nonessential markers to imitate the discursive style of an actual person. In this case, our narrator is Alex Portnoy, a young man ostensibly speaking to a psychiatrist. In the cited passage, Alex uses dashes to further comment on the setting in the first line: "Just standing nice and calm — nothing trembling, everything serene — standing there in the sunshine . . ." He uses nonessential commas to put comic emphasis on his love for Duke Snider in the phrase "like my king of kings, the Lord my God, the Duke himself." And he uses parentheses to set aside a fantasized voice of a radio announcer: "the third out of the inning (*and Alex gathers it for out number three, and folks, here's old C.D. for P. Lorillard and Company*) . . ." These techniques would seem too subjective for a third-person narrator, but they match perfectly with Alex's neurotic, digressive persona. Thus the punctuation markers and their attendant phrasing help to characterize him as much as the content of his speech.

But why, you may ask, do we have all three of them? If they do the same thing, couldn't we have gotten rid of one or two by now? Well, no, because they don't do the *exact* same thing. Understanding how their functions differ, and putting those differences to use, involves wrangling with some nuance and ambiguity. But in general, when you're wondering whether you should use commas, parentheses, or dashes to set apart a nonessential phrase, an important consideration is the level of formality you want to create.

Dashes, parentheses, and nonessential commas can all be seen as informal to some extent, because they surround phrases that are technically frivolous. They throw in an added bonus, the way the guy behind the counter at Home Depot might throw in an extra tape measure if he likes the cut of your jib. Giving a reader nonessential information seems like a gesture of kindness and confession, an act that brings us closer to the narrative voice. Consider the following example from Harold Brodkey's "The State of Grace": "I was smart and virtuous (no one knew that I occasionally stole from the dime store) and fairly attractive, maybe even very attractive." The essential parts of the sentence give us a type of confession. But it's a confession that withholds a little, it's something the narrator might say to a lot of people. Only the parentheses contain the revelation of a secret the narrator will not share with anyone but you, the reader, his best and only friend.

Or consider how much we cherish the parenthetical information offered to us in the following sentence from Vladimir Nabokov's *Lolita*: "My very photogenic mother died in a freak accident (picnic, lighting) when I was three." Humbert Humbert, our protagonist, has inserted a truly remarkable aside here. In the course of giving a factual account of his mother's death, he throws in a pair of words that clarifies what he means by "freak accident." The nonessential information is by far the most interesting part of the sentence, and it opens up the protagonist's personality to us. We see all of Humbert's insouciance and callousness represented in the parenthetical phrase.

Even when the nonessential phrase isn't as directly revealing as this, it still retains a sense that it privileges the reader in some way. Look at this line from Flannery O'Connor's "A Late Encounter with the Enemy": "She had bought a new dress for the occasion—a long black crepe dinner dress with a rhinestone buckle and a bolero—and a pair of silver slippers to wear with it." The aside within the dashes doesn't spill a big secret or give details of a horrific death. Yet it does bestow something on us that we're happy to get. The details help us to see the dress better, and they give us an improved sense of the character; think about how bland the sentence would be without the words within the dashes. The reader takes the nonessential phrase as a sort of blessing, a freebie offered up by a benevolent narrator who cares about our enriched understanding of the story.

If we accept the point that nonessential punctuation is a way of calling a small time out to give some bonus information, and of thereby creating a kind of informality, then the natural question is, which one does it best? Which one creates more of a sense of informality, and which is more formal—more impersonal, but also perhaps more dignified or authoritative?

I think the answer is pretty simple. Others may disagree, and it may not hold for all kinds of writing, but in regard to fiction, I believe the parentheses is the most informal, the nonessential comma is the most formal, and the dash is somewhere in the middle.

PARENTHESES

Parentheses are visually obtrusive. They take up a lot of vertical space and physically wall off the phrase within them. A sentence from Humbert Humbert that read, "My very photogenic mother died in a freak accident—picnic, lightning—when I was three" wouldn't have as powerful an effect, because the phrase "picnic, lightning" would not be as segregated. More than any other mark, parentheses have the effect of sequestering the words within them, and therefore the parenthetical words don't have to conform to the rules of the rest of the sentence.

Often this means that the parentheses' interior differs stylistically from the rest of the sentence. An extreme example would be the way magazines and newspapers sometimes use parentheses to involve an entirely different voice, in sentences like "That cockroach Parker would make a lousy governor (*editor's note*: this magazine does not endorse the opinions of the writer)." This kind of shift can happen in fiction—in the Roth example, italics and parentheses team up to introduce a new voice in the line *"and Alex gathers it for out number three"* —but usually the parentheses allow for a less overt, but still significant, change in voice or tone.

Another example from *Portnoy's Complaint* provides a useful example of a parenthetical shift in tone. In the following passage, Alex describes the books in his childhood home, which his parents received as gifts for various hospitalizations. Note that in the essential part of the sentence, Alex has adopted a flat, non-ironical descriptive tone; he simply tells us what's on the shelves. The parenthetical sections, however, allow him to expand beyond this tone, they allow him to comment on what the books symbolize to his parents, and also to comically mention what surgical procedures he associates the books with:

> One third of our library consists of *Dragon Seed* (her hysterectomy) (moral: nothing is never ironic, there's always a laugh lurking somewhere) and the other two thirds are *Argentine Diary* by William L. Shirer and (same moral) *The Memoirs of Casanova* (his appendectomy).

Portnoy maintains a very informal tone throughout the novel. Yet even he gets trapped at times by sentences that can only do certain things in terms of tone and purpose. He uses parentheses to escape from such dictatorial sentences, to add irony or subjectivity or humor to sentences whose essential elements don't quite welcome it.

NONESSENTIAL COMMAS

The nonessential comma is the most formal of the nonessential markers, the least likely to induce chumminess without help from content or word choice. For one thing, nonessential commas look exactly like other commas, so the reader doesn't get a visual clue that an aside is coming, the way he does when a parentheses or dash appears.

Commas themselves are unobtrusive. They slow down the pace, but they don't change the rules or the tone of the sentence altogether. Thus, when they separate nonessential elements, the separation isn't as total as it is with the other marks; commas don't sequester the phrase as absolutely. Let's look back at that example from Ron Hansen, using just two of the variations:

> Even in his editorial notes in the collected *Poems* of 1918 (which he titled identically to his own first book) Bridges could not forgive his friend's licenses.

> Even in his editorial notes in the collected *Poems* of 1918, which he titled identically to his own first book, Bridges could not forgive his friend's licenses.

I said before that both versions would work grammatically, and I stand by that. But an attentive reader will notice the connotative differences in these sentences. The first one calls a pretty big time-out to give us the nonessential phrase. It wants us to see the fact that Bridges stole his friend's title as somehow outside the rest of the sentence, and thus it comments on it; it treats the titling of the book in a gossipy way. If we read the sentence out loud, we probably change our voices when we get to the parenthetical part, either lowering our pitch or rushing through the phrase.

In the second version, the line about the book title should be read with the same tone and pace as everything else. We perceive it as just another element of the sentence. We pause a little after the first comma simply because it's a comma, not because we know that nonessential information is coming. It's only after we've received the information and the final nonessential comma that we understand the unnecessary nature of the phrase.

And it's not just a visual or aural matter. Under the rules of grammar, nonessential commas don't give their interior phrases as much freedom as the other markers do. That is to say, they are not just integrated into the rest of the sentence visually, but also by their obligations to the sentence's grammar and syntax. Again, consider Nabokov's line "My very photogenic mother died of a freak accident (picnic, lighting) when I was three." Because we give such license to words within parentheses, we aren't bothered by the fact that "picnic, lighting" doesn't fit grammatically into the rest. The parenthetical phrase gets its own grammar, it basically exists as a separate entity. But look at what would happen if Nabokov had used nonessential commas instead: "My very photogenic mother died of a freak accident, picnic, lighting, when I was three." This doesn't make sense, because we don't know how to read the commas. We don't know that the first one is a nonessential marker, while the last one (after "lighting") indicates a return to the rest of the sentence, because these commas look exactly like the other one in the sentence (the one between "picnic" and "lightning"). How are we supposed to sort through all that while keeping our attention on the story?

Commas have many different functions. Yet no matter what they do, they all look the same. We can only tell that commas are nonessential based on how they are integrated into the sentence. Thus they have to play by the rules, grammatically speaking. And like anything or anyone who plays by the rules, they come off as more formal, more authoritative, basically on the right side of the law.

DASHES

The dash sits somewhere in the middle of all this. Unlike with a comma, when we see a dash we pretty much know a nonessential phrase will follow (although there are exceptions). But unlike the parentheses, the dash does not look or act like a total separation from the sentence, and it's more beholden to the grammar and voice of the sentence than the words within parentheses are. One indicator of this is that phrases within dashes tend to be kept short, while it's not unusual to find a parenthetical phrase that goes on for an entire paragraph. We're meant to read the parenthetical insert as its own animal, while the dash is partially integrated into the rest.

The dash also stands somewhere in the middle because of its repertoire of functions. While any given comma may serve one of a dozen purposes, and any given parenthesis can only do one thing, the dash has a small handful of roles. In addition to setting off nonessential elements, a dash can set off and call attention to an essential concluding phrase, as Melville does in this passage from "Bartleby, the Scrivener": "I must be permitted to be rash here, and declare that I consider the sudden and violent abrogation of the office of Master of Chancery, by the new Constitution, as a—premature act." Melville's mild-mannered narrator works himself into a frenzy, and just when he's about to deliver the promised castigation, he lets us down by calling the move not criminal or idiotic, but "premature." The dash stresses the climactic, or anticlimactic, nature of the word.

The dash can also serve as a sound and rhythm signifier in dialogue or first-person narration. The following is from Joseph Conrad's "Youth":

> But you here — you all had something out of life: money, love — whatever one gets on shore — and tell me, wasn't that the best time, that time when we were young at sea, young and had nothing, on the sea that gives nothing except hard knocks — and sometimes — a chance to feel your strength — that only — that you all regret?

The dashes give a sense of the catches and stutterings of this narrator's speech, his hesitancy and his haste. Hard to imagine how Conrad would have captured the same effect without the *je ne sais quoi* added by the punctuation.

CAUTIONARY NOTES

I said before that my own style involves using dashes quite often, and this is also true of parentheses (as you may have noticed). I also said they should be used for good rather than evil, by which I mean that these markers are tempting to use and, like all temptations, should be approached with suspicion. It's true that dashes, parentheses, and nonessential commas are versatile little markers, useful weapons in the writer's arsenal. But using them too much can distract the reader.

Remember that these are physically obtrusive marks, especially the parenthesis and dash. Unlike when we see a period or apostrophe, our brains notice in a conscious way when they appear; we adjust for the small time-out the writer asks us to take. We can make this adjustment easily enough for the occasional one, but too many in a cluster will make us think about the writer's addiction to them. We may consider the writing mannered, which is to say that we think the writer is more concerned with sounding clever or funny or whimsical than he is about getting the story and characters across. Or we may suppose that the writer doesn't know what to focus on, so he's riffing and digressing until he latches onto something of interest.

Fiction writers continually confront the problem of narrative balance: How much should we move the story along at a speedy clip, and how much should we linger and digress in order to enrich the fictional world? In the short story "Click," John Barth dramatizes this dilemma using characters named Valerie and Mark. After putting their natures into conflict — Valerie lingers, Mark advances — Barth arrives at this conclusion:

> A satisfyingly told story requires enough "Valerie" — that is, enough detail, amplification, and analysis — to give it clarity, texture, solidity, verisimilitude, and empathetic effect. It requires equally enough "Mark" — that is, efficiently directed forward motion, "profluence," on-with-the-storyness — for coherence, anti-tedium, and dramatic effect. In successful instances a right balance is found for the purpose (and adjusted for alternative purposes).

As a metafictional joke, Barth overloads his story with parentheses, dashes, nonessential commas, and other digressive techniques, including foot-notes. It gets a bit Postmodern, but the point is clear: nonessential punc-tuation markers give the writer a welcome opportunity to augment and enhance, but they must be used judiciously, so that the story doesn't get lost in digression.

fourteen

Exclamation Points and Italics

A quick note: even though this chapter appears in the "Nuances of Punctuation" part of the book, italics are not punctuation marks. Punctuating involves inserting a symbol that shows how a reader should interpret the words around it, while italics change the typography of the words themselves. But I really think they belong in this discussion, so please forgive the fudging.

In the last chapter, we looked at three methods of setting things apart. Parentheses, dashes, and nonrestrictive commas physically enclose the words within them, and thereby act as safe havens in which those words behave differently from the other words in the sentence to varying degrees. The two elements we'll look at in this chapter—exclamation points and italics—also differentiate words and word groups, but they do not put barriers around those things. An even more significant difference is that these two elements emphasize words, whereas the punctuation marks from the last chapter de-emphasize words by showing that they're nonessential.

Of course, putting in exclamation marks and italics are not the only ways to add emphasis. Writers often get creative when they want to stress an element of their prose, especially in our era, when these two methods can seem a little sentimental or hyperactive. One interesting example occurs in the poet Seamus Heaney's translation of *Beowulf*. Because the poem was written before the regulated use of punctuation, its translators have to add their own, which has led to lots of scholarly bickering over the years (then again, what hasn't?). However, there has been consensus on a few points, one of which is that a line on the first page—"þæt wæs god cyning!," meaning "that was a good king!"—is so emphatic that it deserves an exclamation point. Virtually every translator for two centuries has included one.

But Heaney dissents, and translates the line as "That was one good king." That is, he inserts the idiomatic use of the word "one" as an emphasizer, the way we use it in phrases like "that was one big sandwich" or "that was one heck of game." Indeed, this phrasing adds more emphasis than "that was a good king"; "*one* good king" shows us the writer really means it.

Heaney's version adds a jolt of chumminess to the tone, but its main advantage is that it's about as unobtrusive as you can be when you're trying to stress something. Other methods will stand out more. I've had students add emphasis and differentiation by typing phrases in alternative fonts and sizes, while others have used boldface. A colleague once told me of a student who used different color ink to differentiate the speech of his characters, similar to the way some publishers in the early twentieth century called attention to Jesus's words in the New Testament by printing them in red.

That last example encouraged John Irving, author of *A Prayer for Owen Meany*, to differentiate and emphasize the speech of his book's Christ-like protagonist by using all-caps, as in: " 'IT'S A GREAT PART FOR A GREAT ACTOR,' Owen said stubbornly." This method not only shows the awkward, grating nature of his voice — "to be heard at all, Owen had to shout through his nose," the narrator tells us — but it also makes his dialogue physically exceptional, just like Christ's words in the "red-letter" bibles. In an introduction to a later edition of his novel, Irving admits to the influence of those works. One reason he didn't imitate them directly, he says, is that "to have Owen speak in red letters would have been too expensive for my publishers." Later he adds, "I also thought the capitals would be more irritating than red letters. Owen's voice is irritating, not only because of how he sounds but because of how *right* he is."

That last point is important. As a realist, Irving must have preferred using a technique of emphasis that made realistic sense in the context of the work, and that the reader would be somewhat used to, rather than one that would come off as highly unusual and symbolic. The all-caps dialogue allows us to hear Owen's speech with precision and clarity, and it doesn't distract us as much as a different color would have. Green ink for a jealous character, large font for a character who shouts — these are clever tactics, but ones that ask the readers to think about the nature of language and type. Italics and exclamation points can also call attention to themselves, depending on how you use them, but at least we recognize them as the conventional ways of adding emphasis.

EXCLAMATION POINTS

Exclamation points, like adverbs, often receive criticism from writing pundits. But unlike adverbs, they're not going to get a rigorous defense from me. Although I'll argue that they can be used to good effect in certain situations, I personally find it hard to respect exclamation points, in part because they're too easily adopted by discourse communities that don't care about the elegant use of language. That's right, I'm talking to you, text messagers and Twitterites. The added emphasis in phrases like "Goin 2 the beach 2-day!!!!" or "Can u buleeve Kim did that!!?!!!?!" makes this a good time to be an exclamation point—there's lots of work to go around—but a bad time to be a language purist. I'm not saying everyone writes like this when they use digital media. I'm merely suggesting that digital formats encourage the cavalier use of grammar and punctuation, and often that informality involves exclamation points. (The NFL lineman Ndamukong Suh once used 108 of them in a Twitter post. I think that's a record.)

But perhaps this is not entirely the exclamation point's fault—in such cases, it's guilty of aiding and abetting rather than perpetrating the language crimes. However, we can blame it for the function inherent in its nature: it differentiates a statement or sentence by adding an extreme, sometimes hysterical degree of emphasis to it.

In the most famous comment made about the issue, F. Scott Fitzgerald said "an exclamation point is like laughing at your own joke," by which he meant that the mark communicates something about a thing that should already have been communicated by the thing itself. If you tell a joke well enough, you will not have to laugh to indicate to others that you have been funny. If you write a sentence that is dramatic or emphatic or vigorous, presumably the reader will understand that you've done so without learning it via punctuation. The exclamation point can thus be seen as a typographical sign that says, "In case you didn't notice, the preceding information is exciting."

The charge relates to the one made against adverbs: if the writer has been clear enough, they're redundant. We saw in the adverb chapter that the critique doesn't always hold true, and to a lesser degree you can say the same thing about exclamation points. Sure, they often don't need to be there, but you can defend their use when the other elements of the passage don't show the required emphasis, or when the over-the-top nature of exclamation suits your aesthetic purposes, or for various other reasons.

The most forgivable use of them is when you're writing dialogue. If you put one at the end of a character's "What an enormous pigeon!," you're not judging the assertion, you're describing the pitch or volume with which it was spoken. I wouldn't throw them in automatically whenever a character gets excited or angry, though. John Grady's commands to the captain at the end of *All the Pretty Horses* are all the more menacing for their lack of emphasis; "Get back over there and set down!" or "Get on that horse!" would have made it seem like he was trying too hard to be fearsome.

The issue becomes more complicated when we consider the exclamation points in narrative sections, especially in our era. Many of us don't like them in prose fiction because they seem excessively earnest, which is to say a little too nineteenth century. And sure enough, nineteenth-century writers were not afraid to use them. Sarah Orne Jewett's "A White Heron," for example, ends with the lines "Whatever treasures were lost to her, woodlands and summer-time, remember! Bring your gifts and graces and tell your secrets to this lonely country child!" Because it's a third-person narrative, we have to attribute the emphatic sincerity to Jewett herself. And even when writers of that era use first-person narrators to deliver exclamation points, we often get the sense that the authors endorse the emphasis. When Jane Eyre says, "Reader! I forgave him at the moment," I don't think Bronte wants us to see Jane's emotion as excessive or embarrassing. Nor is Melville making fun of the passion and earnestness of his narrator's "Ah Bartleby! Ah humanity!"

These works are admired by millions for good reason. Yet when we admire some elements of their prose, we do so out of a kind of nostalgia. We find it quaint and endearing that they could be so unsnarky in their use of exclamations. That usage is pretty much off limits today, because it seems melodramatic. As we saw in chapter 11, melodrama ensues when readers sense that the writer is too eager to make them feel certain emotions, and what is an exclamation point but an overt signal that we should feel emotion? Contemporary writers—who guard against sentimentality and melodrama above all things—almost always use exclamation points with irony. Either a first-person narrator uses them while the author sits back and winks at us, or a third-person narrator uses them with hyper-self-awareness.

It's worth asking why we abandoned the earnest, literal use of exclamation points, as well as other methods of emphasis like capitalization. In part it happened because writers and readers gravitated toward a specific type of irony and understatement, for a number of cultural / political / economic reasons that your neighborhood sociologist would be happy to explain. But another factor was the publication of Gustave Flaubert's *Madame Bovary* in 1856. That novel presents a third-person narrator who offers no guidance about how we should judge the dreadful people and events it describes. The objective narrative style doesn't seem radical now, but before Flaubert, novels with third-person narrators boldly displayed the opinions and personalities of their authors. Here, for example, Harriet Beecher Stowe discusses her narrative methods in *Dred*: "We would like to linger here over many curious scenes and histories of those old plantation days, but we must not make our story too long." In this passage from *Père Goriot*, Balzac defensively predicts how his work will be received: "You will read the story of Old Goriot's secret woes, and, dining thereafter with an unspoiled appetite, will lay the blame of your insensibility upon the writer, and accuse him of exaggeration, of writing romances." But under the influence of Flaubert and his inheritors, anything that indicated a third-person narrator's subjectivity or personhood went out of style within a few decades.

Postmodernism in the sixties and seventies disrupted this trend, in that many of its practitioners sought to call attention to the personality of the writer; that's what "metafiction" is all about. But by then the ship had sailed in terms of being able to do so without distracting the reader from the story. In post-Flaubert fiction, writers either avoid calling attention to the authorial presence by invoking a "pay no attention to that man behind the curtain" attitude, or they do so with an ironic, Postmodern flair. It won't help to look at examples in the former category, because what we'll find is a lack of exclamation points. Most realists have agreed with Elmore Leonard that "you are allowed no more than two or three per hundred thousand words of prose."

But writers in the second category—the Postmodernists—have made ecstatic use of the exclamation point and all its baggage. "Postmodern" is, as I've said before, a slippery term, so I should explain that here I'm using it to refer to writers whose language is meant to be about their use of language in some significant sense. They may have great characters and plots, but readers are also meant to notice and think about the language with which they render them. You can see why the exclamation point, with its ability to radically adjust tone and meaning—not to mention its "look at me" quality—might appeal to such writers.

The first example we'll look at doesn't come from a work of fiction, but from an essay by David Foster Wallace. In his "A Supposedly Fun Thing

I'll Never Do Again," Wallace describes a man who "has not only his own earmuffs, plus his own shotgun in a special crushed-velvet-lined case, but also his own skeetshooting range[130] in his backyard in North Carolina." What's odd (and Postmodern) about the sentence is the superscripted "130" after the word "range." The number directs us to a footnote at the bottom of the page that reads "!" and nothing else.

The technique works well, I think. It's funny and original and comprehensible. By using a footnote, Wallace calls a brief time-out and meets us at the bottom of the page, where he acknowledges the outrageous nature of what he describes. In effect, the single exclamation point says, "The guy has a skeetshooting range in his backyard—can you believe that?!" He also asks us to rethink our expectations of footnotes, which generally contain more information. And he accomplishes all this with a single punctuation mark.

It is, however, a disruptive punctuation mark, because of where it's placed. The more conventional and less physically distracting method would be to write "but also his own skeetshooting range in his backyard in North Carolina!" Anyone who's read much of Wallace knows he would never write such a thing, but it may be instructive to explore specifically why he didn't do it in this case.

One of the reasons is technical, and it shows the inherent limitation of the exclamation point: when placed at the end of a sentence, it emphasizes the entire sentence. In this instance, that would be a lot, because the sentence contains over seventy words. By putting the footnote after the word "range," Wallace isolates a phrase and makes the exclamation point apply to it exclusively. The narrative enthusiasm gets placed only on the point he finds truly outlandish.

It's an ingenious technique, but Wallace didn't really have to do it; he could have used a more traditional method of emphasizing one specific aspect of a sentence, like italics (as we'll see). So we may suspect that his reasons had more to do with the irony and distance created by the use of the exclamation point, and with avoiding the knee-slapping quality that traditional exclamation points lend to prose. To finish with "his own skeetshooting range in his backyard in North Carolina!" would be, in Fitzgerald's terms, to laugh at one's own joke. The writer would be calling blatant attention to the odd fact of the shooting range, as well as to his own amazement. Wallace's footnoted exclamation is so removed, so muted and tangential, that it doesn't take its enthusiasm very seriously.

I'd be remiss if I finished a section on exclamation points without referring to Tom Wolfe. It may seem odd to place him in our discussion of Postmodernism, since he wrote an article in the late eighties denouncing the movement, but that had to do with subject matter rather than prose style (he didn't think Postmodernists wrote enough about the Big Issues of the time). If we think of Postmodernists as being writers who call overt attention to their manner of writing (or their personalities), then Wolfe qualifies. Ask people on the street what they know about him, and you'll most often hear "he wears white suits" and "he uses a lot of exclamation points."

Does he ever. Here's a passage from his novel *Bonfire of the Vanities*:

> He stared at her. It wasn't a trick! She was sincere! And yet *zip zip zip zip zip zip zip* with a few strokes, a few little sentences, she had . . . *tied him in knots!*—*thongs of guilt and logic!* Without even trying!

Although this particular passage explores the thoughts of the character Sherman McCoy, Wolfe uses the style no matter whom he's describing, and in virtually all of his books. Therefore, we attribute the language to him, rather than to a character, just as we do with nineteenth-century authors. The clear difference between them and Wolfe, however, is that they applied the exclamation point literally; they wanted to emphasize a sentence because they considered it worthy of emphasis, and for no other reason. Wolfe uses the marks ironically. Even if we couldn't tell this by his tone, we'd know from his excess. He not only gives exclamation to five sentences out of six in this passage, he also places the redundant stress of italics on some words. In phrases like "*tied him in knots!*" and "*thongs of guilt and logic!*" he does everything but put the words in neon type. This would be a silly thing to do if he actually wanted the emphasis to stick in a literal, non-distracting way. So what's his point?

A few answers to that question present themselves. You could say, for example, that the marks actually do add a sense of zest and urgency to the prose, even if we know they're tongue in cheek. But the more likely possibility, I think, has to do with the distance the exclamation points create between the writer and his characters. In Wolfe's case that distance is useful, because he so often deals with people who deserve the reader's scorn or condescension. Wolfe gives exclamation points not only to the portraits of adulterous investment bankers but also bullying mayors ("He can handle hecklers! Only five-seven, but he's even better at it than Koch used to be! He's the mayor of the greatest city on earth—New York! Him!"), unscrupulous journalists ("What admiring British faces all around him! How they beamed!"), and many others. In each case, these self-aggrandizing characters would believe that their thoughts deserve the utmost emphasis. But neither the writer nor the reader agrees. In using the language of exclamation and exaltation to portray his characters' petty, hypocritical concerns, Wolfe makes a subtextual judgment, and invites the reader to join in.

That's the limit of my ability to justify Wolfe's style. To be honest, I can only read so much of his fiction without having to turn to something that doesn't contain all the linguistic fireworks. In this, and in other opinions, my sensibility leans closer to the traditionalists, so please consider that if your tastes run to the experimental or Postmodern.

ITALICS FOR EMPHASIS

In some circumstances, italics create the same effect as exclamation points. "Tied him in knots!" and "*tied him in knots*" both give a sense of giddy enthusiasm to Wolfe's phrase (presumably Wolfe thinks that using both methods doubles the giddiness). But in significant ways, italics can add a different kind of emphasis. When you see an exclamation point, you know immediately what's going on: someone's telling you to get worked up. Not so with italics. They can serve a variety of functions, so they don't signal their intentions as directly. We're not sure what kind of italics we're getting until we've digested the context and content, which grants them a relative degree of subtlety.

And even when they add emphasis, italics don't automatically invoke the extreme stress that exclamation points do. The latter mark lays a qualitative emphasis on the sentence — it's meant to show or provoke excitement ("Land ho!) or surprise ("The pastor was the culprit all along!") or outrage ("Their offer was twenty grand below asking price!") or some other extremity of emotion. But italics often tell us to receive the stressed information in a more neutral tone. When Frederick Exley uses the italics in the following passage from *A Fan's Notes*, he's emphasizing the words, but he doesn't want you to get excited about them:

> "I don't understand," she said. "Don't laugh at me." Then she started to weep again. At that moment, I *did understand*, and when I did, the room started going round and round.

Exley highlights the words so that we'll see how they contrast with the words in the dialogue. If he'd written the unitalicized "At that moment, I understood," we would have seen that as an awkward, unintentional echo of what the woman had said. Pointing out that "I *did understand*" contrasts with the speaker's "I don't understand" allows him to get away with the repetition. If he'd used the other traditional method of emphasis—"At that moment, I did understand!"—he would have sounded weirdly exuberant. Exley uses italics because he wants to underscore his words for contextual purposes, not emotive ones.

In cases like this, italics imitate the stress we place on certain words when we speak. When writers visually differentiate a phrase, they imply that it would carry an aural differentiation if it were spoken. It's understandable, then, that italics commonly appear in dialogue—"Why, you couldn't *pay* me to leave this place!," "the figure was *not* that of a goat"—where they basically function as indicators of phonetics, not boosters of emotion. The first sample sentence (from Ken Kesey's *One Flew Over the Cuckoo's Nest*) contains emotion, but it's provided by the exclamation point. The italics merely tell us how to hear McMurphy's pronunciation of the word "pay." The second example (from Poe's "The Gold Bug") doesn't contain any noticeable extremity of excitement or anger—it just shows that the speaker vocally stresses "not."

The role of italics in underscoring or differentiating a sentence element makes sense when we consider that it's virtually the same thing as underlining. Italicizing has been used for hundreds of years, but for most of that time only printers and publishers could actually do it. When ordinary folk using quills or pencils or Smith-Corona typewriters wanted to add the effect of italics, they had to underline the phrase instead. Once we all gained the power to create our own italic text via word processors, underlining became mostly unnecessary. But we still have a vestigial sense of underlining as a way of saying we *really* mean something, perhaps because we still do underline when we handwrite, and sometimes the act of slashing that line under a phrase makes us feel the emphasis physically. So it could be handy to think of italics as a more stylistically acceptable method of putting a line beneath a phrase.

ITALICS FOR EVERYTHING ELSE

Italics can serve other purposes, all of which may be useful to fiction writers to varying degrees. Here they are, in no particular order:

1) You should italicize the titles of most creative or literary works. This is a broad category, which includes visual art (*Guernica* and *Dogs Playing Poker*); novels, long poems, and plays (*Emma* and *Paradise Lost* and *Macbeth*); dramatic performances (the musical *Grease* and the opera *Otello*); newspapers and magazines (the *New York Times* and the *Atlantic Monthly* — you never italicize or capitalize the "the"); and films and television series.

The main exception to the rule concerns written works that are short, like stories and pop songs and essays and poems; with those you use quotation marks. Another exception has to do with works of such religious/historical significance that they are treated as proper nouns, not titles: the Declaration of Independence, the Bible (and works within the Bible, like Exodus and the Book of Mark), the Upanishads, the Emancipation Proclamation, etc.

2) Some style guides advise italicizing the names of websites and databases, and some don't. I think fiction writers should follow the latter advice. "Jenny logged onto *Facebook* before deciding to contact him on *Twitter* instead" presents an example of how italics can pull a reader out of the scene. You can get away with it, I suppose, but the reader of such a sentence might start thinking about the writer's fastidiousness, or even worse, she might go to the Internet to see if his usage is correct. At the very least, you should know where you stand on the issue. Not so long ago, the most advanced technology I'd included in a book was an automatic transmission, but nowadays it's hard to avoid referencing YouTube and Facebook unless you write historical fiction.

3) The names of vehicles. You sail on the *Oasis of the Seas*, christen your Dodge Caravan the *Hellfire*, see *Apollo 11* at the Smithsonian. For some reason, this rule always makes me think we're supposed to italicize the name of bands as well (perhaps because of the Cars. But seriously, folks . . .). That's not the case. Band names get capitalized, nothing else.

4) You should italicize foreign words or terms, but only if they haven't fully made their way into English, as J. M. Coetzee does in *Disgrace*: "In the desert of the week Thursday has become an oasis of *luxe et volupté*." Be careful with this one. As we saw in chapter 10, English is largely composed of words that were considered foreign at one point, so the language eagerly

consumes such things. You'll look silly if you italicize *kayak* or *sauerkraut* or *guru*.

5) You should use italics when you refer to a particular word itself, rather than using the word as part of the sentence's meaning. When Twain writes "*Hadleyburg*, synonym for *incorruptible*," both italicized items are meant to be considered as physical entities, not the objects or ideas represented by the words. Sure, we know that the phrase equates the town with a virtue, but technically the italics turn these content-loaded sets of letters into factors in an equation: word X (*Hadleyburg*) = word Y (*incorruptible*).

You may notice that, whenever I've referred to particular words in this book, I haven't followed my own advice and italicized them. Instead I've put them in quotation marks, as when I wrote, " 'fire' isn't any cruder than 'conflagration' " in chapter 10. In referring to words as entities, you can italicize them *or* put them in quotes. It's up to you. I had my reasons for using quotation marks, the main one having to do with the frequency of italics in this book. I've used them a fair amount to stress words, to give the titles of novels, and for a few other purposes. So for the sake of clarity, I tried to avoid throwing another one into the mix.

Let's clarify the problem by imagining a sentence in which italics identify a word as an object, show the foreign nature of a phrase, stress a word, and identify a title:

> The name *England* began to be used by the *hoi polloi*, but this was
> *before* the great poem *Beowulf* was composed.

Four different sets of italics, each one carrying a different kind of emphasis — *quel dommage* and *que lastima*! The reader can only figure out what the italics mean based on content, which is bound to divert some of her attention from the narrative. The writer of the above passage would be better off putting "England" in quotes, and he could probably get away with leaving the italics off "hoi polloi," a Greek phrase that's been thoroughly incorporated into English.

Quotation marks can be used in a few different ways, too, of course. They can portray a quotation from a work or person, and they can indicate the titles of short works like stories and poems. These are both functions I ask them to serve throughout this book, but I don't think many situations come up where we see different quotation mark functions used in close proximity.

As twenty-first-century readers know all too well, there's a third function of quotation marks: they can imply an ironic or delegitimizing usage: "The so-called 'experts' say I shouldn't drink so much," or "My 'friend' Petra stole all my credit cards." But I'd avoid this usage as much as you can, even if you're writing in first-person. It's inherently defensive and bitter, and too many ironic quotation marks are just annoying.

6) Sometimes writers use italics to indicate thought or speech. We already saw this in chapters 2 and 5, so I don't want to dwell on it here. However, I do want to point out that it's sometimes the most appropriate or convenient method for quoting speech that doesn't belong to one particular character—when it's a phrase uttered by a group of people, or in a generalized way. You can see this technique in Carol Shields's *The Stone Diaries*: "Always, one or two of these young people will break into a run. *First man there is a starving bear.*" The second sentence is spoken aloud, but not by any particular character. The point is that the words are spoken, it doesn't matter who says them. The italics indicate the generalized nature of the words, whereas quotation marks might have made them too specific—we would have wondered where the dialogue tag was.

7) All kinds of other reasons. Many editions of the Bible italicize words to show that they're not direct translations from the original Hebrew. Sometimes publishers italicize the entire first line of every chapter in a book (I've never figured out why, even though my own publisher did this with my second novel). Writers sometimes italicize text at the beginning or end of a chapter or story to indicate a shift in narrative point of view. I've even seen entire stories written in italics, though I wouldn't recommend doing it—italics are hard to read for more than a page. On a fundamental level, italic type differentiates words, and there are innumerable reasons why a writer might want to do that.

part four

Common
Errors

fifteen

Verb Tense Shifting

In outlining this book, I had to make some difficult decisions about which elements of grammar, convention, and style a fiction writer most needs to master. While I feel strongly about the topics ultimately included, I'm sure I've failed to address a few important issues, and probably some of the chapters won't be helpful for everyone. But throughout the project, this chapter and its subject shone as a beacon in my dark night of uncertainty. From the moment I conceived of the idea for the book, I knew it would need a chapter on verb tense shifting, and no one was going to talk me out of it.

I need to clarify what I mean by "verb tense shifting," because any written work will contain a multitude of verb tenses, depending on the situation and intent. The error we're talking about here occurs when a writer moves from the past tense to the present tense, or vice versa, with no grammatical, contextual, or aesthetic reason for doing so. That is, he makes the shift arbitrarily ("arbitrary verb tense shifting" — A.V.T.S. — might be a better name for it, but it's a bit inelegant). Here are two examples:

> Jacoby turns and begins to strike a match. He lit the cigar and smiled at Henrietta.

> It was cold, so she and Dennis stay in and listen to Gershwin albums.

This may not be the most common error made by writing students — some would argue spelling problems or comma misuse takes the prize — but it's certainly in the top five. Furthermore, it needs to be addressed more stringently than the others because it's the most insidious.

I have two reasons for saying this. The first is that writers tend to make the mistake even when they've been warned about it; like a radon leak, it's wickedly difficult to detect in your own house. The second reason I consider verb tense shifting so dastardly is that it will break a reader out of the fictive dream like no other language error.

At this point, we seem to have arrived at a dead end. I've pointed out the error, shown examples of it, and explained that it's one of the most significant and common mistakes made by writers on all levels (and I mean it—I've read manuscripts submitted for fiction contests and grad school applications that were clean of virtually every language error except for A.V.T.S.). I've also asserted that it does more damage to the reader's suspension of disbelief than any other linguistic mistake. So now you know to watch out for it. What else is there to say?

By now you know me well enough to guess that the answer is "Lots." I'm weirdly fascinated by verb tense shifting, and I have a few theories about why it's so common, why it's so distracting, and how even this travesty may be used for artistic effect. So I encourage you to engage with the ideas in the sections that follow.

You should know, however, that I've already said the most important thing I can say about this topic: arbitrary verb tense shifting is extremely common and extremely damaging. As I tell my students the day before they hand in an assignment, "In spite of my warnings, at least one of you will turn in a work that arbitrarily shifts verb tense. Do everything in your power not to be that person."

THE SOURCE OF THE DISTRACTION

In the climactic scene of the fourteenth-century narrative poem *Sir Gawain and the Green Knight*, the reader encounters the following passage (italics mine):

> When he *came* to the stream he refused to wade:
> He *hopped* over on his axe, and forcefully *strides*
> Fiercely grim on a clearing . . .

It's a stirring scene, but what should stand out to you is the way the author shifts verb tense. (NB: although the passage has been translated from Middle English, the shift also occurs in the original.) He tells us that the green knight "came" to the stream, "hopped" over it, and "strides" to a clearing. One of those things, as they say, is not like the other.

According to George Sanderlin, "seemingly random shifts from present to past, and from past to present, are common in early literature." Dr. Sanderlin is being polite with the "seemingly"—these shifts *are* random, not based on any grammatical or contextual logic. Scholars offer various explanations for why they occur, one of which has to do with the works' oral origins. When people tell stories out loud, they can shift verb tenses without anyone noticing or caring (listen for this the next time someone tells you a long story). The theory, then, is that the scribes who wrote down certain works of early literature simply incorporated the speech inconsistencies. Another theory posits that medieval authors sought to imitate classical Latin, which allows for tense shifting as a rhetorical flourish.

Interesting stuff for medievalists to chew on, perhaps, but we're more interested in the effect of shifting—as I said, it distracts the reader quite a lot. This is no knock on Middle English writers, because by "reader" I mean the modern reader, a person who, unlike his medieval counterpart, carries certain baggage that makes arbitrary shifting detrimental.

Our baggage becomes obvious when we read *Gawain* and encounter elements that remind us we're out of our context. The poet's avoidance of modern-style realism is one such element. In the course of the poem, Gawain finds a girdle that protects its wearer from axe blows, meets a green-skinned knight who does not die when his head gets chopped off, and has sundry other adventures so wonderful that "it would be hard to recount a tenth part of them," and none of these events are narrated with the imagery and detail that a modern writer would feel obliged to include. Sophisticated readers recognize that the writer's responsibility to describe events with verisimilitude—the way he "argues the reader into acceptance," as John Gardner puts it—is a contemporary notion, not one the Gawain poet felt bound by. So we forgive him, for the same reason we forgive Stowe for using all those adverbs: our rules were not theirs.

However, it's hard to be so forgiving of the verb tense shifts. We can tell ourselves to consider historical context all we want, but still it's tough to accept that the knight "vaulted" across the river in one line and "strides" to the clearing in the next. Sometimes you can't think your way out of your culture, and in this instance, I can't find a way to make that shift not bother me. And apparently, neither can other readers—most translations of *Gawain* correct the tense shifts. More than the giants and monsters and indestructible knights, the shift reminds us we're reading a fictional work, and that disrupting reminder is anathema to the modern reader.

But not all disruptions are the same. In many cases, when we come to a minor linguistic slipup, we move on quickly. If the error is a typographical one, not much happens in the reader's mind to derail him, because the nature of the mistake is so clear. It's an infelicity, but that's all it is. We change "whn" to "when" or "posses" to "possess" on behalf of the writer and editor, and we congratulate ourselves on our generosity.

But when a writer tells readers that a character did something in the present ("Jacoby begins to strike a match"), and a moment later she tells them that a near-simultaneous event occurred in the past ("he lit the cigar"), she's done something else: she's been incoherent in aggregate, not in discrete units. Individually, one part of her sentence or paragraph makes sense, as does the other part. But they don't make sense when they're combined, so they invalidate a larger part of the text. When the shifting occurs throughout a story, it invalidates the whole work. We are not just momentarily bothered. We have begun to doubt the writer's command over something elementary and fundamental, and some part of us spends the rest of the story waiting for the next shift to occur. The work can never consume us as it did before the shift. Like a cheating spouse, it has lost a part of our trust forever.

POSSIBLE REASONS FOR ARBITRARY VERB TENSE SHIFTING, PART ONE

While scholarly explanations for the medieval and ancient use of verbs can be interesting, they don't offer much help for the modern creative writer or teacher. I suspect my sophomores in ENG 215 aren't shifting tenses as an homage to Seneca.

At the beginning of my teaching career, I assumed that students weren't proofreading their stories, and I started to warn them specifically about tense shifting. In fact, I added a section to my grading rubric that took a significant number of points off any work that shifted tenses. But students continued to make the error, among them some very good students, which told me something besides sloppiness was going on.

I then wondered if students were committing what John Gardner called the "sin of frigidity." Gardner said this happens when a writer doesn't believe in her characters as much as she should. If a writer fully imagines her work, I thought, then it will be impossible for her to shift verb tenses. If she sees Jacoby light a cigar with such immediacy and clarity that she relates it in the present tense, how can she say a moment later that the lighting took place a while ago? Such a writer, I decided, was merely putting words together, not truly imagining the scene.

Both of these causes — not proofreading enough and not imagining the scene vividly—certainly can and do lead to verb tense shifting. If you find yourself committing the error frequently, I'd suggest looking to these as causes. But there's more to it in some instances. I've had a number of students who imagined their characters vividly, and who proofread like New Yorker copy editors, yet who still shifted tense.

In chapter 1, I presented you with two choices for telling a story: you use the present tense or the past tense. I probably implied that once you made your decision, you didn't need to worry much. But the truth is, even once you've committed yourself to a verb tense, you must think about certain aspects of its nature that make it difficult to use consistently.

The present tense, I would say, contains the highest degree of difficulty, because it's non-standard and thus isn't as easily handled by our instincts. During the writing process, many of our faculties shift into autopilot, because there are so many other issues to deal with. Michael Agger, in summarizing a theory by psychologist Ronald Kellogg, tells us that "the writer's brain is juggling three things: the actual text, what you plan to say next, and—most crucially—theories of how your imagined readership will interpret what's being written." Given so many things popping around in your brain, you have to entrust certain areas of writing to your innate abilities. This is why it's so important to master language. Writers don't have time to recite the i-before-e rule, or to look up the uses of the semicolon, they just have to know these things in their bones.

But in lapsing into autopilot, a writer relies on traditions and conventions. Her framework for knowing what grammar and style to use has largely been constructed by her reading of other works. Since most of those works were written in the past tense, that is her default mode. Faced with a passage in which she has to construct a nuance of the hero's personality while underscoring a thematic point while throwing in some vivid setting details, the issue of verb tense takes a back seat, and her reptilian writer's brain may slip her into the traditional tense.

In short, when I begin reading a student's work and see that it uses the present tense, I wait to see when the shift to the past will occur. Invariably, it doesn't take long, and usually it's in a passage where the writer had a lot of other things to worry about. The writer's autopilot moved him to the past tense, and he wasn't focused enough on language to notice.

That's not to say that the past tense is smooth sailing. Many writers make the mistake seen in the second example from above: "It was cold, so she and Dennis stay inside and listen to Gershwin albums." One possible explanation for this type of shift is that the writer sees the action too vividly in his mind's eye. Perhaps the scene of the couple listening to music on a winter's night appears so clearly and precisely in his brain that it demands present tense narration; he sees it happening right there and then, so it's only logical to write that they "stay" and "listen." The writer might also be encouraged by the fact that he established the past tense narration with the bland verb "was."

Taking up on that point, we often see arbitrary shifts occurring after verbs that don't call much attention to themselves, verbs like "was" or "had" or "said," which we may not consider verbs so much as placeholders, indicators rather than actors. If you begin a sentence with "The cold *hammered* the city and *tortured* its citizens," you notice the forceful verbs you've used, so you'll be more likely to imitate their tense in the second clause. But when you begin with "It was cold," you won't think about the verb as much. Plus it's in an irregular form (no *-ed* at the end, which usually tips us off about the past tense), so it's easier to miss.

One also commonly sees shifts after a verb tense that is neither past nor present, as happens in "Jacoby turns and begins to strike a match. He lit the cigar." This writer may have been confused by the infinitive nature of "to strike," which stands between the mismatched "begins" and "lit." An infinitive verb by definition isn't conjugated — it can never be past tense or present tense or future tense, and that neutrality can cause you to lose your bearings. This may not be a good excuse — it wouldn't get the student out of the missed points in my class — but I think it's emblematic of why shifting happens in many cases. We have to use a number of different verbs and verb-like objects when we write, going from past or present tense verbs to infinitives and gerunds and participles, and in all that moving around we may get disoriented.

POSSIBLE REASONS FOR ARBITRARY VERB TENSE SHIFTING, PART TWO

Yet another simplification I made in chapter 1: I shortchanged the present tense somewhat. I said that it has a limited temporal span, in that it refers to events happening *at this very moment*, which is usually true if we consider how a writer uses the present as a primary tense in a fictional work. When Hilary Mantel writes, "King Henry pauses" in *Wolf Hall*, she means for us to see the action happening at one specific moment, not eternally. This form has been given the oxymoronic phrase "the historical present," because it treats an event from the past as if it's happening right now.

But the present tense can be used in other ways, which expand its scope. An argument can be made, in fact, that in some instances the present tense takes up even more space on a theoretical timeline than the past tense does. For example, when you write, "water is wet," the statement has always been true, and always will be; it will never make sense to say "water was wet" or "water will be wet." This form of present tense, called the factual case, applies to scientific or general facts that don't change ("ice melts," "garbage stinks," "power corrupts").

You can also imply the past and future with the habitual case, when you write, "I play basketball on Sunday" or "We spend our summers in Toulouse." You're not giving a general truth of the universe, but you're saying something that was true for at least some of the past, is currently true, and will be true for some of the future. Linguists divide present tense forms into even narrower categories, but these two are good enough for our purposes.

Often one or both of these present tense formations will sneak into a narrative. Look at this example from Brock Clarke's *An Arsonist's Guide to Writers' Homes in New England*:

> Anne Marie answered the phone. It was Wednesday afternoon, four
> o'clock or thereabouts. She smokes a cigarette in the morning, another
> before dinner, and a third last thing at night, and she must have just
> smoked one, because her voice came at me like a distant train . . .

This is technically a verb tense shift, because the narrator uses the past tense as the standard mode ("Anne Marie answered . . . ," "It was Wednesday . . ."), and shifts into the present with "She smokes." But the shift isn't arbitrary; Clarke has a grammatical reason to do so. The phrase "She smokes a cigarette in the morning" is habitual, because he's referring to an action Anne Marie performs every day, not one she does at a specific moment in the narrative.

One particular use of the factual case may explain why some writers, especially those who are in school or who are still trying to shed its influences, lapse into the present tense when they don't mean to. I'm referring to present tense usage when it applies to literary works.

As you may recall from tenth grade, when we're writing an essay for lit class and we refer to a historical event, we use the past tense: "Sylvia

Plath *wrote* the novel in 1962." But when we refer to something that happens inside a narrative, we use the present tense: "In Sylvia Plath's novel, Esther *moves* to New York." We do this because the fictional event—which comprises words, not actions—is still going on, for as long as a copy of the book exists. Your high school teacher might have punctuated the idea by opening a book and pointing vigorously at the literary "event" to prove its ongoingness, as mine did. We call this style the "literary case."

Many essays about literature address both biographical/historical details and assertions about the events taking place in the work, so the shifting between past and present tenses is hard to avoid. A student writing about *The Bell Jar*, for example, might compose a passage like this:

> In Sylvia Plath's novel, Esther *moves* to New York, where she *works* at a
> women's magazine. Plath herself *moved* to New York in 1953 and *worked*
> as an intern at *Mademoiselle*.

The shifting here is not arbitrary; there's a theoretical reason to use both "works" and "worked."

Be that as it may, a student who has written a number of papers that rationally shift tenses is susceptible to the true danger of the literary case, which I'll try to unpack here. Imagine a student has had the concept of the literary case engrained in her. For years she's written, "At the beginning of the story, Gabriel greets his Aunt Julia" and "In a pivotal scene, Bigger murders Mary," like a good little English major. Then, she goes to a creative writing class, and begins contributing to the enormous body of literature, rather than just writing about it. She now gets to come up with her own Gabriels and Aunt Julias, she gets to have her own Biggers murder her own Marys. And, as she's been taught to do with literary characters, she describes these events using the present tense. She does this because, following the logic of her English teachers, she recognizes that her characters will always be there, on that printed page or in that Microsoft file, greeting and murdering each other for all eternity.

So that explains why she might use the present tense—she just carries the idea of the literary case into her fiction. But other forces encourage her to use the past tense: almost every book she's ever read. Discipline and theoretical reasoning have led her to write, "Gabriel greets his Aunt Julia," but when she actually experienced this event (in Joyce's "The Dead"), it was rendered in the past tense. In the essay she wrote for her American Lit class, "Bigger murders Mary" worked fine, but when Richard Wright first showed her the scene in *Native Son*, he wrote, "Mary's body *surged* upward and he *pushed* downward upon the pillow with all his weight." Professor X has told the student about the literary case of the present tense, but a thousand writers have shown her that the past tense is standard.

I think some people get caught in the crossfire. They integrate the historical present into their work because it's been the preferred style when they've written about literary characters. But in the midst of composition, habit and imitation take over, and they revert back to the style they've seen in most of the works they've read. That's one explanation for it, anyway.

AESTHETIC USES OF THE SHIFT

Yes, it's true, sometimes writers shift verb tenses for no grammatical reason, while fully understanding that they're doing it. They shift because their artistic instinct tells them it works. Given all I've said about the disruptive nature of tense shifting, how could such a thing be possible? And when we write, how can we know when we should trust the instinct to shift?

Let's take these questions in reverse order. The short answer to "when should we trust the instinct to shift?" is "we shouldn't." If you're happy taking that as a rule, feel free. But of course we're avoiding dogma in this book. Many of you, I'm sure, have it in you to ungrammatically move from the present to the past and back again in a way that will aesthetically improve a passage. Say it with me: *I am a writer, nothing in language is off limits to me.*

But you should approach non-grammatical verb tense shifts very carefully, because the people reading your work—agents, editors, teachers—may not give you the benefit of the doubt. Instead they may take shifting as evidence of a writer without mastery, a writer who is frigid or distracted. This likely will happen even when you shift on purpose. It's unfair, but true.

If you still want to see how ungrammatical tense shifting can work, you should look at examples of writers who have used it effectively. Even if doing this does not reveal any specific rule or guideline, it can still be instructive to figure out, on a case-by-case basis, why these writers chose to violate standard tense usage. Let's do so by investigating the shifts of two unquestioned masters of language.

The first example comes from David Mitchell's *Black Swan Green* (I've italicized the relevant simple past tense verbs and underlined the simple present tense ones):

> So I *went* in, thinking of a bride going into Bluebeard's chamber after
> being told not to. (Bluebeard, mind, was waiting for that to happen.)
> Dad's office <u>smells</u> of pound notes, papery but metallic too. The blinds
> *were* down so it *felt* like evening, not ten in the morning. There<u>'s</u> a serious
> clock on the wall, exactly the same make as the serious clocks on the
> walls at school.

Here the novel's teenage narrator, Jason Taylor, describes sneaking into his
father's office, which is off-limits to him. He begins by portraying the event
in the past — "I *went* in" — which makes sense, as the narrator is describing
action that has already occurred.

But then he shifts to the present tense, with "Dad's office *smells* of pound
notes." The vividness of the memory, evoked by smell — the most associa-
tive of the senses — causes Jason to see the event so clearly in his mind's
eye that he has no choice but to use the immediate verb tense. The event
happened only a year before its narration, which makes the confusion of
past and present even more explicable. That confusion gets reinforced by
the rest of the passage, which shifts back to the past tense ("The blinds
were down") and then again to the present ("There [*is*] a serious clock on
the wall"). For much of the scene, Jason consciously narrates past action for
an audience, but the intensity of the memory overcomes him on occasion.

In this instance, the author gets away with the shift by attributing it
to a first-person narrator — the reader is meant to understand that Jason,
not David Mitchell, is responsible for the error. This point has many larger
implications, so we're going to veer into a digression. I'll try to keep it short,
or at least useful.

When we read a first-person work of fiction, we may be tempted to
attribute any linguistic quirks to the narrator rather than to the writer.
Indeed, we're often supposed to, as we just saw. In other chapters, we've
seen additional examples of writers misusing language to indicate something about the narrator's personality and background — Alice Munro and
Raymond Carver give their casual narrators lots of comma splices, Peter
Carey makes the outlaw Ned Kelly ignore the rules of punctuation. Picking
up on the benefits of this technique, sometimes one of my students will
claim the prerogative of the first-person when I point out a mistake in her
work: "Well of course the narrator misuses colons, he's a moron!" In other
words, the student will claim she made the error for the sake of realism.

There's an evil genius to this argument, because if you follow the logic it means that every linguistic mistake—and every non-linguistic one, too—can be attributed to the narrator's ignorance rather than the writer's. While the content and language of a third-person work should be held to the highest standards, a story told from the point of view of a child, a middle school dropout, or a golden retriever can be imbued with the errors that those narrators would likely make. In theory it means you never have to proofread, as long as you choose a narrator who's inarticulate enough. Right?

Of course not (being reasonable people, my students don't really make the argument that often). It's true that many of the people we choose as first-person narrators would not have mastery of a fiction writer's language—they would dangle modifiers and mishandle commas and screw up dialogue formatting like crazy. But the fiction writer must carefully manage the way such a character misuses her language, because the concept of verisimilitude actually tells us that we *don't* want a first-person story to be similar to what such a person might write in real life. We can see how this works in Emma Donoghue's *Room*, which is narrated by a five-year-old boy:

> Ma sounds all wobbly, she says, "What, what? Did you have a bad dream?"
>
> I'm biting Blanket, soft like gray bread in my mouth.
>
> "Did you try something? Did you?" His voice goes downer. "Because I told you before, it's on your head if—"
>
> "I was asleep." Ma's talking in a squashed tiny voice. "Please—look, look, it was the stupid jeep that rolled off the shelf."
>
> Jeep's not a stupid.

Donoghue gives the narrator simplistic diction, childish locutions like "his voice goes downer" and "sounds all wobbly," and other tics of an unsophisticated voice. This helps create verisimilitude, the sense that a child, rather than a professional writer, relates the scene.

But of course no child could have written this passage, and not only because no five-year-old could spell this accurately. There are also stylistic elements—the subtle presentation of dialogue, the consistency of the present tense, the use of the dash to indicate interruption—that are hard for a lot of adults to get right. To create true realism, in the sense of imitation rather than verisimilitude, Donoghue would have had to misspell almost everything, avoid dialogue tags and punctuation, write in crayon—basically make it incomprehensible.

This is an obvious point about first-person narratives, although we don't think about it much; suspension of disbelief encourages us not to. As I mentioned earlier, some of the narrators of Faulkner's *As I Lay Dying* probably can't even read. Mark Haddon's *The Curious Incident of the Dog in the Nighttime* is narrated by an autistic teenager, a figure who would be unlikely to recount his experiences. You could argue that most first-person narrators—almost all the ones who are not professional writers—could not have written the works attributed to them. But where would we be as readers if we constantly reminded ourselves of that fact, or if the writer, through carelessness or mischievousness, kept pointing it out to us?

The issue reminds me of the cartoon trope in which an animal writes some kind of sign. Invariably, the animal spells poorly—a dog in a *Far Side* cartoon traps a cat by writing "CAT FUD" on a washing machine door; a cow on the Chick-fil-A billboards tells us to "EAT MOR CHIKIN." If we think about it too much, we may suspect that even if these animals were literate, their handwriting would be much worse than it appears in the cartoons and billboards, or their syntax would be incomprehensible, or the words would be spelled even more poorly (or maybe not—if a dog could learn how to spell "cat," why couldn't he learn how to spell "food"?). But the creators of the scenarios need the words to communicate, so they can only bow to realism so much. Yes, a certain kind of narrator may be prone to grammar mistakes, but you need to be careful in selecting those mistakes. You need to give him the ones that will provide a sense of his character without disrupting the reader's experience.

The matter of intentional grammar quirks in general, and arbitrary verb tense shifting in particular, becomes more straightforward when we look at third-person narrators. If they shift tense for no grammatical reason, we unhesitatingly attribute the decision to the author, not the character. For an example, let's look at a passage from Philip Roth's *Sabbath's Theater:*

> When Sabbath reached his car, he walked beyond it some twenty feet
> along the hiking trail into the woods and there he hurled the bouquet
> into the dark mass of the trees. Then he did something strange, strange
> even for a strange man like him, who believed himself inured to the
> limitless contradictions that enshroud us in life . . . Something horrible
> is happening to Sabbath.

In this paragraph, the novel's protagonist, Mickey Sabbath, visits the grave of his mistress. The scene culminates in Sabbath doing "something strange, strange even for a strange man like him," which indeed is so disturbing I don't feel comfortable quoting it here (sorry to be so squeamish). The act is the final one in a chapter that has seen Mickey's life disrupted by grief and despair, a disruption that causes the baroque descent portrayed in the rest of the novel. Roth gives us all of these things in the past tense.

But in the chapter's final line, Roth moves to the present: "Something horrible is happening to Sabbath." I'm fascinated by how the shift of verb tense changes the function and attitude of the third-person narrator. Where it had been a traditional, past tense describer of action, it's now a bemused, horrified observer. When the narrator delivers this line in the present tense, it doesn't give a Godlike judgment of the character, or provide a profound insight into Sabbath (it's fairly obvious that something horrible is happening to him). Instead, the narrator provides the kind of comment the reader might make after witnessing this grotesque scene. It's what we whisper to ourselves, in awe and disgust, at the end of this chapter: something horrible is happening to this man, right before our eyes, that is, in the present tense.

So if you feel up to it—if you're encouraged by the examples from Mitchell or Roth or other authors who include aesthetically pleasing, if ungrammatical, shifts of verb tense—then you should try it out. Just keep in mind that editors, agents, and teachers will generally assume you didn't do it on purpose, not because they have a low opinion of you, but because they've seen it done accidentally too many times to count.

sixteen

Commas

A discussion on commas could have gone in any one of the parts of this book, but I filed it under "Common Errors" because, well, the misuse of commas is a very common error. It stands to reason that the comma should trouble people more than something like the period, because it has more functions than any other punctuation mark. Its versatility can make it seem random and subjective; some people think you should just scatter commas around whenever your sentences don't have enough, the way you add garlic salt to chili.

In fact, there are specific principles that govern the way commas should be applied—between eight and twelve of them, depending on whom you ask. I certainly encourage you to educate yourself on as many of these rules as possible, because to some extent a fiction writer is in the same boat as everyone else when it comes to comma usage: screwing up any of the rules will damage your work. But an analysis of all twelve (or eight) of these rules would be long and tedious, plus you can easily find other books or websites that explain such matters. As with most things we've discussed, some aspects of comma usage apply to fiction writing more directly than others, so we'll look at just four of those eight (or twelve) rules, the ones that in my opinion give creative writers the most trouble. In the final section, we'll go through three particular problems of comma usage that tend to crop up in creative work, and that don't have much to do with the four rules.

I apologize in advance if this reads more like a chapter from a standard grammar manual. It's hard to differentiate the points without getting a bit technical, and I may have to overexplain some things. But it really is important to keep these rules straight; a lack of appropriate comma usage will mark your fiction as amateurish. I've even numbered the sections this time, so you know I'm serious.

THE DO'S

1. *Use a Comma Before a Conjunction That Unites Independent Clauses* I almost lost a job because I misunderstood this rule, so it can conceivably have practical effects on your life. But it's also one whose violation most readers won't notice, and therefore fiction writers often ignore it for rhythmic effect.

Here's the story of the nearly lost job. I had applied to teach a freshman-level writing class at a university whose curriculum was relatively grammar-heavy. Although I like to think my cover letter and CV were mostly clean, my boss later confessed that she'd almost dismissed my application because I kept putting commas before the conjunction in sentences with compound predicates. She told me this in a voice full of empathetic shame, as if she were saying I had toilet paper on my shoe.

Indeed, it was an oversight; if you're applying to be an English teacher at an elite university (an expensive one, anyway), the standard for your grammar is going to be a bit higher than anywhere else. But I honestly didn't know I was making a mistake. No one ever told me about it, and making the error didn't make my prose look or sound odd.

To understand this rule, we have to establish the difference between compound sentences and simple sentences that have compound predicates. "I went to the game, and I bought a hot dog" is compound, meaning it consists of two independent clauses ("I went to the game" and "I bought a hot dog") that have been joined with a coordinating conjunction ("and," "for," "but," "or," etc.). A comma should come before that conjunction.

In considering the nature of simple sentences, don't be fooled by the name—the term doesn't apply just to things like "Fire burns" or "Spot bit Jane." The "simple" part refers to the fact that these sentences contain a subject/verb combo that completes a thought; simple sentences achieve the minimum requirement for sentencehood. But there's a twist: they can contain more than one of those core elements. A simple sentence might have two or more subjects, as in "Yale, Park, and Baylor are private universities." They also can have more than one verb: "Bart wheezed, coughed, and died." When they do have multiple verbs, we refer to them as simple sentences with compound predicates, because "predicate" is the word for a verb and its entourage—direct objects and prepositions and so on. The sentence "I went to the game and bought a hot dog," though similar to the example we used for compound sentences ("I went to the game, and I bought a hot dog") is a simple sentence with a compound predicate. Only one subject is given — "I" — and the two predicates after it ("went to the game" and "bought a hot dog") both belong to that subject.

So here's the other part of that above-stated rule: when a conjunction joins two predicates in a simple sentence, you should *not* place a comma before the conjunction. That's why there's no comma before "and" in "I went to the game and bought a hot dog." Again, in a compound sentence, you *should* put a comma before the conjunction, which is why there's one before the "and" in "I went to the game, and I bought a hot dog."

While I didn't keep the cover letter that nearly scuttled my career, I imagine the mistake I kept making as I pleaded for employment looked something like this:

> I have not enclosed references, but can provide them upon request.
> I would be pleased to teach at such a fine institution, and would work
> diligently if hired. I hope you give me this job, and will sink even
> deeper into poverty if you do not.

According to the rule, I could have fixed the sentences with one of two methods. If I wanted them to be read as simple sentences with compound predicates, I should have dropped the commas ("I have not enclosed references but can provide them . . ."). If I wanted them to be read as compound sentences, I should have put an additional "I" before each of the verb combinations ("I hope you will give me this job, and I will sink even deeper into poverty if you do not.").

You can see how adhering to the rule can make sense. While commas have various functions, they all have one thing in common: they tell the reader to pause. And that pause, in the case of compound sentences, lets us know that the two entities are meant to be read a bit separately ("Vegas appeared out my window, and I gave a prayer of thanks"). In simple sentences with compound predicates, we want the reader to move more quickly, because the second verb needs to be attached to the subject ("Dave grabbed the money and got the hell out of there"), and if the reader waits too long he might forget that.

However, there's no reason to be dogmatic about this rule. In "Neighbor Rosicky," Willa Cather violates it with "She had known him when he was a poor country boy, and was boastfully proud of his success." Because "was boastfully proud" is a second predicate that shares a subject ("She") with the first one, a comma shouldn't precede it. But fixing the error might be a rhythmic mistake: "She had known him when he was a poor country boy and was boastfully proud of his success." The first predicate is somewhat lengthy, so if you don't pause before the second one the sentence becomes too rushed and hurried, especially when compared with the rest of Cather's leisurely prose. The ungrammatical pause in this long simple sentence gives it a welcome caesura.

On the other side of the rule, writers sometimes omit the commas from compound sentences in order to create a sense of thrust and speed. Mona Simpson creates this effect in a passage from "Lawns": "I see him and right away I know it's him and I have this urge to tiptoe away and he'll never see me." The sentence contains four independent clauses, and each one is connected to the next one with a conjunction ("and"), rather than the more grammatical comma-plus-conjunction. This is the kind of sentence people often refer to as a "run-on." It's not a run-on (see chapter 12), but you can see the temptation of that term. The lack of pauses where we would normally expect them gives the sense that the sentence is running on like a stampeding cow. And of course that's what the writer of such a sentence wants.

Omitting the coordinating comma can lead to confusion at times, however. When you read, "Jerry whacked the baseball and his father grinned with pride," you momentarily get the image of Jerry doing violence to both his father and the ball, before the rest of the sentence makes you go back and revise the image. It's not a process any writer wants his reader to go through.

But often when a writer leaves out the coordinating comma, or when she includes one in a simple sentence with compound predicates, there's neither a big distraction nor a significant rhythmic payoff. "The door opened, and I left" and "The door opened and I left" contain subtle differences, but neither one will to stop a reader in his tracks. If we give them the benefit of the doubt, we can imagine that the writers who violate these comma rules have considered the aesthetic implications of their decision to prioritize style over grammar. If we don't give them the benefit of the doubt, we may assume they didn't know the rule. It's certainly possible. I wrote my first novel without knowing it (I don't have the heart to look through *The Cuban Prospect* to see how often I messed it up). But I'm not sure how much it matters. Whether a writer knows a usage rule or not, she's often led by her sense of pace and rhythm. While I stand by the accepted wisdom that writers should master a rule before they're allowed to violate it, I suspect that in this one case the violation occasionally comes before the mastery, and somehow we all survive.

2. *Use Commas to Separate Items in a List* The following sentence, surprisingly enough, comes from Hemingway:

> Could you say she did first what no one has ever done better and mention plump brown legs, flat belly, hard little breasts, well holding arms, quick searching tongue, the flat eyes, the good taste of mouth, then uncomfortably, tightly, sweetly, moistly, lovely, tightly, achingly, fully, finally, unendingly, never-endingly, never-to-endingly, suddenly ended, the great bird flown like an owl in the twilight, only in daylight in the woods and hemlock needles stuck against your belly.

The passage contains many commas used in different ways, which means it will also come in handy when we discuss the next section. But first things first: the rule of comma usage that we'll look at now states that you should use commas to separate items in a list.

That would be what happens in the first part, as the narrator identifies all these delightful parts of Trudy. He basically lists a series of nouns: legs, belly, breasts, arms, tongue, eyes, taste. But many of these items are modified with adjectives and compounds, so it's actually a list of word groups, rather than a series of single words ("plump brown legs," "hard little breasts," "flat belly," etc.). In order to keep everything straight, commas are used. You learned this lesson in grade school, probably when your teacher showed you what havoc would ensue if your mom didn't use any commas when she gave you a shopping list that read, "ice cream cheese bread and milk." Do I get ice cream or cream cheese? Or ice and cream and cheese bread? And why am I doing the shopping when I'm only in third grade?

As cherry-picked as the ice-cream-cheese example is, failure to separate listed items with commas truly does get confusing once the list goes beyond two or three words. If I write, "The landscape teemed with goats, cacti, dried dung, tumbleweed, cattle bones, and snakes," I'm not using the commas because I'm worried you'll consider "goats cacti" or "dung tumbleweed" compound nouns. I just know that leaving out the commas would make you have to slow down a lot. Not many writers are going to violate this basic rule.

The only controversial part of it has to do with the serial comma, also called the Oxford comma, which is the comma you put before the "and" when you finish a list, as in "red, white, and blue." The other method is to consider that last comma redundant, because the "and" shows we're coming up on the last item, as in "red, white and blue." Both the pro- and anti-Oxford comma factions have their arguments, and these arguments get boring very quickly. The upshot to all the bickering is that there's no standard convention, so it's up to you how to handle it.

Stylistically, there are two ways in which authors might fiddle with the standard comma usage in a list of nouns. Both of the alternative methods can be seen in a passage from Tim O'Brien's "The Things They Carried." The story requires O'Brien to make many lists, so he pulls out all the stops to make them interesting. In the following passage, we need to consider all the sentences, but I've italicized the two that are more germane in terms of how he lists items.

> They carried infections. *They carried chess sets, basketballs, Vietnamese-English dictionaries, insignia of rank, Bronze Stars and Purple Hearts, plastic cards imprinted with the Code of Conduct.* They carried diseases, among them malaria and dysentery. *They carried lice and ringworm and leeches and paddy algae and various rots and molds.*

In the first italicized sentence, O'Brien lists things in a fairly standard way, except that he doesn't include an "and" before the final item, "plastic cards," which he would be obliged to do in most formal writing. Eschewing the "and" in such situations can serve a few functions. We already saw in chapter 12 why you might remove the conjunction for rhythmic purposes: when the units separated by commas are phonetically or contextually simi-lar—as in Strunk and White's example "The gates swung apart, the bridge fell, the portcullis was drawn up"—the "and" is not included because it would disrupt the balance. (That sentence gives us a list of clauses rather than items, but the principle's the same.)

Also, ending a list without the standard conjunction can make it seem truncated or stark. The reader doesn't get the warning that the sentence is about to close, so the last item sneaks up on him. Hence the abrupt power of this sentence from Dorothy Allison's "River of Names": "Somehow it was always made to seem they killed themselves: car wrecks, shotguns, dusty ropes, screaming, falling out of windows, things inside them." Again, this works especially well if the content of the sentence itself is somewhat chaotic and/or stark.

Whatever O'Brien's motives, it's indisputable that the non-standard style also allows him to mix things up a bit. The passage's first sentence, "They carried infections," is not a list at all, but it resembles the others in asserting what the men carried. Then O'Brien includes a long list with no conjunctions, only commas. Then comes another one-item assertion, and then another long list, but this one contains no commas, only conjunctions—the opposite of the style used in the second sentence. In short, I think he's trying to alter the listing sentences so that they don't become repetitive, which is a good enough reason.

The method of non-standard listing that appears in the second highlighted sentence—using "and" repeatedly instead of commas—achieves a different effect. Repeated conjunctions exaggerate the extent or intensity of the list, as in the famed example "lions and tigers and bears, oh my!," a phrase that underscores the bounty and richness of the scene more than "lions, tigers, and bears." Or, to stick with the animals theme, we can see the effect in Cormac McCarthy's *Blood Meridian*: "and the stiff bodies of deer and javelina and ducks and quail and parrots . . ." By physically adding to the sentence—"and" uses more characters than a comma—and by not allowing the reader to pause, the method gives a sense of sprawl and abundance and plenty.

3. Use Commas to Separate Coordinate Modifiers The rule discussed in the last section works best when applied to nouns and verbs. When a writer strings together of series of modifiers—meaning, usually, adjectives or adverbs—she has to put a bit more consideration into where the comma goes. In the Hemingway excerpt we just looked at, he lists a great many adverbs:

> then uncomfortably, tightly, sweetly, moistly, lovely, tightly,
> achingly, fully, finally, unendingly, never-endingly, never-to-endingly,
> suddenly ended

It's not a list in the way that the run-down of Trudy's body parts is, because it's not self-contained. The words need something to complete their meaning, which in this case is the verb "ended." Because all the adverbs have the same purpose (modifying that verb), we call them coordinate adverbs—the "coordinate" implies they push at the same wheel, tug at the same rope, etc.

To sum up the rule, then: when a series of adverbs or adjectives modifies the same word, they are coordinate modifiers, and they need to be separated with commas. We see such a series in Hemingway's "uncomfortably, tightly, sweetly . . ." phrase. One key point is that the commas signify an equality among the items in the series; they imply that the words are functionally equivalent and thus interchangeable. You could write "tightly, sweetly, uncomfortably" or "sweetly, tightly, uncomfortably" and the meaning would remain intact.

Non-coordinate modifiers, on the other hand, are not such paragons of egalitarianism. If not placed in a specific order, they lose their intended meaning. Those commas that indicated equality among the items in a list, therefore, are no longer necessary. So don't separate non-coordinate modifiers with commas. That's easy for me to say, but of course the trick is to figure out when your modifiers are non-coordinate. In general, that involves asking if they act in the same way on the same word. It will help, naturally, to look at some examples.

Consider the sentence "Gordon is the fat German Shepherd, while Mitch is the spastic, gray poodle." Each clause has one word being modified, "Shepherd" and "poodle," respectively. In the first clause, the adjectives don't modify the same thing. "German" modifies "Shepherd," and when it does it creates its own noun phrase, "German Shepherd." That noun phrase, rather than just the single word "shepherd," is what "fat" modifies. So "fat" and "German" modify slightly different elements, ergo they're not coordinate. In the second clause, both "spastic" and "gray" modify "poodle," so they are coordinate.

One trick to figuring out if you need the commas is to stick a theoretical "and" in between the modifiers. "Gordon is the fat *and* German Shepherd" sounds questionable, while "Mitch is the spastic *and* gray poodle" works. Another method is to reverse the order of the modifiers. "Mitch is the gray, spastic poodle" means the same thing as the first version, so you need commas between the coordinate adjectives. But if you write "Gordon is the German, fat shepherd," the sentence changes a bit (the capitalization of "Shepherd" also factors in, but ignore that for now). Any number of examples can illustrate this method—changing "he's a pretty stupid guy" into "he's a stupid pretty guy" turns the adverb "pretty" into the adjective "pretty," while altering "a lovely spring day" to "a spring lovely day" just doesn't make sense. In both cases, the irreversibility of the modifiers means they shouldn't be separated with commas.

We've now hit upon another rule that is sometimes violated for effect. Occasionally, fiction writers will omit the commas from a series of coordinate modifiers. Hemingway did it in the previously discussed list of body parts, when he referred to Trudy's "plump brown legs." The word "legs" is being modified, while the words "plump" and "brown" are adjectives that do the modifying. And they're clearly coordinate: "plump and brown legs" and "brown, plump legs" have the same meaning as "plump, brown legs." So a comma technically should separate the adjectives. But he got away with not including them because the coordinate adjectives are short, staccato words—we don't trip over "plump brown legs" or "quick searching tongue" the way we might over "elongated luxurious legs" or "vivacious inquisitive tongue."

Hemingway could also eschew conventional punctuation for reasons of clarity: the list already contains a great many commas, the ones that are used to separate Trudy's body parts, so if he had used commas to separate coordinate adjectives as well, things would have gotten messy. He might have had to call in semicolons to separate the actual nouns in the list (to serve as "Special Policemen," remember?), the way Don DeLillo does in this list from *White Noise*:

> The roofs of the station wagons were loaded down with carefully secured suitcases full of light and heavy clothing; with boxes of blankets, boots, and shoes, stationery and books, sheets, pillows, quilts; with rolled-up rugs and sleeping bags; with bicycles, skis, rucksacks, English and Western saddles, inflated rafts.

While it seems consistent with DeLillo's narrator—a bemused, expansive university professor—the punctuation-heavy style won't work for every narrative situation.

In general, writers might exclude commas between coordinate modifiers when they want the words to come out in a rush. In "The Red Bow," George Saunders writes, "He might be just a fat little unemployed guy," a phrase in which the three adjectives ("fat," "little," and "unemployed") are coordinate because they all refer to the word "guy." But doing the grammatically correct thing and turning it into "He might be just a fat, little, unemployed guy" would put too many pauses in a casual phrase that's meant to be dashed off in an instant.

4. *Use Commas after Introductory Sentence Elements* Often our sentences don't get to the heart of the matter right away. Before giving the reader our subject and verb—the core components—we like to start things off with phrases or individual words that the sentences don't technically need. When you begin with such an introductory feature, you should put a comma at the end of it.

Many times these introductory elements will modify. As we saw in chapters 8 and 9, modifiers come in all shapes and sizes. The example sentences below all include openers that alter or mitigate or further describe something that follows. Each introductory element is italicized, and the technical name for the phrase follows the sentence in parentheses.

In the summer of 1968, Ron was working as a cabana boy. (prepositional phrase)

Begrudgingly, Greta got to work on the casserole. (adverb)

To truly get a sense of Fellini's work, one must see *Amarcord.* (infinitive phrase)

There are others, but the point is simple. If a sentence opens with an introductory element—be it a prepositional phrase, an adverb, whatever—the element must have a comma after it.

An important and useful exception: you don't have to put a comma after an introductory element that is short. By "short" I don't just mean one word, because often we do put commas after one-word intros, particularly when that word is a polysyllabic adverb: "Ideally, the Royals wouldn't be so terrible," or "Unfortunately, I had to cancel the masseuse." But it depends on the way you want your sentence to be read. "Ideally the Royals wouldn't be so terrible" and "Unfortunately I had to cancel the masseuse" work just fine, at least from a punctuation standpoint.

You also can keep out the introductory comma after a phrase that is short in terms of words or syllables: "In Rome you can get good potato chips," "With her I'm a different person." This exception also allows you some leeway. If you don't like the way commas look, or the way they ask a reader to pause, you can stretch the limits of the exception, as Jean Toomer does in "Blood-Burning Moon": "Up from the deep dusk of a cleared spot on the edge of the forest a mellow glow arose and spread fan-wise into the low-hanging heavens." Everything from "Up" to "forest" is a prepositional phrase. Normally a comma would separate such a long introductory element from the sentence's subject ("a mellow glow"). But that opener, which is composed of hard monosyllables, creates a powerful thrust that Toomer apparently wanted to keep going; no time to pause for grammatical convention.

Writers won't push this too much, especially when clarity is at stake. We can follow along when prepositional or participial phrases begin a sentence, but if the opener looks like an independent clause—that is, if the reader might think the core sentence has begun—the comma lets us know that it's just an introduction, that the real stuff has yet to appear.

THE DON'TS

The problem with these rules is that they're positive in nature. Overall we like to be positive about grammar, but at times we have to turn negative, and talk about what *not* to do. This is because many errors involving commas don't overtly violate a specific rule, they're just random errors. If I write, "I hate, airports so, much," I haven't ignored any of the aforementioned principles, but I sure have screwed up. Yes, you could read through the eight-to-twelve rules every time you're tempted to use a comma, to see if it's specifically called for. But a more practical approach is to familiarize yourself with some of the more common ways in which they get abused.

1. *Don't Put a Single Comma Between a Subject and a Verb* If a comma separates these elements, it has to be joined by another one, because that indicates you've put in a nonrestrictive phrase. Here's how commas can come between subjects and verbs: "*Boyd*, who often gets mistaken for Pavarotti, *refuses* to travel to Florence." Here's how it can't come between the subject and verb: *Boyd*, *refuses* to travel to Florence.

2. *Along the Same Lines, Don't Put a Single Comma Between a Verb and the Direct Object* The direct object is the thing that receives the action of the subject-verb combo: "Paula (s.) ate (v.) a sandwich (d.o.)." Here's how not to do it: "Paula ate, a sandwich."

It's rarely advisable to separate a verb and a direct object, even with a pair of nonrestrictive commas. This is because the verb and the object that the verb acts upon depend on their close proximity to each other. "Paula ate, bewildered and hungry, a sandwich" is a tough sell.

3. *Don't Use Too Many Commas in One Sentence* Yes, this is subjective. And in fact, it's not just subjective for any particular writer, but for any particular literary era. Readers of the nineteenth century preferred a sentence overpopulated by commas to a series of shorter sentences separated by periods, as we saw in that long excerpt from George Eliot's *Silas Marner* in

chapter 12. Here's another doozy from the same book, which was published in 1861:

> His life, before he came to Raveloe, had been filled with the movement, the mental activity, and the close fellowship, which, in that day as in this, marked the life of an artisan early incorporated in a narrow religious sect, where the poorest layman has the chance of distinguishing himself by gifts of speech, and has, at the very least, the weight of a silent voter in the government of his community.

Eliot's style was encouraged by a readership that was better than we are at handling long complex-compound constructions (blame the Internet, or maybe MTV).

But we presumably write for contemporary readers, to whom such a comma-packed sentence will be unpalatable. Eliot may have employed all her commas correctly, according to the dictates of usage, but commas don't function as theoretical objects, markers that can earn you a perfect score on a grammar test. They do something to the way readers hear and see a sentence. Specifically, they slow us down, which means that the space after a comma speeds us up—it makes us push off the blocks. In a sentence with as many commas as the Eliot example, this results in a lot of stopping and starting, which leads to a herky-jerky effect that is the aural and visual equivalent of driving in a diesel truck that's been filled with unleaded gas. The sentence has trouble gaining fluidity and rhythm.

I now feel the way I do at the end of my first class period of the semester, after I've spoken for eighty-five minutes about the various policies and requirements that are desperately important for my students to know, and which they have zero chance of remembering. That is, I've handed out lots of information that isn't retained easily, while repeatedly mentioning how important it is to retain it. Fortunately, no one will expect you to know comma rules off the top of your head. Instead—and this is still good news—they'll merely expect you to put them into practice. I'd recommend keeping a list of the rules somewhere, whether you've jotted them down or photocopied a page from a manual. The one thing you don't want to do is assume that, since commas are notoriously difficult, no one will care if you misuse them. True, many people don't have mastery of commas, including people who write good fiction in other respects. But the goal shouldn't be to hide your ignorance by blending in with this crowd; it should be to differentiate yourself by displaying care and precision.

seventeen

Betrayals of Language

My students sometimes get confused when I use the phrase "the betrayal of language." They don't understand how something like language can betray a person, and in general they think I take the whole matter too personally. So let me explain.

Most of the time when you make a mistake with grammar or style, you're betraying yourself and your vision. When you shift verb tenses, dangle a modifier, or make any of the other missteps we've talked about, it's a case of you not having mastered language to the extent you need to have, and this lack of mastery prevents you from fulfilling your artistic mission.

You shouldn't be too hard on yourself, though. Mastery is tough to achieve, and even if you have it, you can't apply it all the time. The most diligent student of grammar and the most accomplished author will occasionally slip up. Remember that Hemingway accused himself of being a bad speller, which was his way of acknowledging that making fiction is too complex an endeavor, and the writer too fallible a creature, for him to use language perfectly.

This makes it all the more painful when you're betrayed by something other than yourself. When you spell a word wrong, you know whom to blame, and the experience encourages you to watch out for such mistakes in the future. But when you're doing everything right—applying your mastery and considering your reader and regularly consulting *The Language of Fiction*—and *still* your language fails in some crucial way, it's tempting to shake your fist skyward and shout "Cruel fates! Why do you mock me?"

In short, these moments occur when something inherent in the language, rather than your own failings, distracts the reader or muddles up the meaning. At that point, all you can do is clean up a mess that you didn't even make.

Actually, not all the mistakes we're looking at in this chapter are pure betrayals of language. Often the writer has something to do with them as well, and if you let one of these things stand in your final drafts, you've committed the self-betrayal of not editing enough. Still, most of the problems we're talking about here arise out of the structure or character of the English language. Specifically, most of the issues have to do with various forms of repetition, which I believe is the most common type of linguistic betrayal.

Repetition also serves as a technique for creating lyricism. This is especially true in poetry, where key devices include alliteration (the repetition of initial consonant sounds), assonance (the repetition of vowel sounds), anaphora (the repetition of initial phrases in a series of lines), and that's just the *a*'s. Rhyme itself, a staple of formal verse, is a type of repetition.

Because sound devices in poetry also get used in prose, it's important to think about how various forms of repetition can contribute to a fiction writer's language. Here's how Marilynne Robinson uses word and phrase repetition ("grass," "black leaves," "fallen braches," "our") to underscore not just a thematic point, but also to invoke an incantatory rhythm:

> A narrow pond would form in the orchard, water clear as air covering grass and black leaves and fallen branches, all around it black leaves and drenched grass and fallen branches, and on it, slight as the image in an eye, sky, clouds, trees, our hovering faces and our cold hands.

It's just lovely, isn't it? I'd also point out that Robinson serves up the repetition in exactly the right dose—one more iteration of the refrain might have been too much.

Another form of repetition that rewards restraint is alliteration. When you repeat initial consonant sounds, it doesn't take long for your prose to turn into a series of tongue twisters. In the opening of *Lonesome Dove*, Larry McMurtry uses alliteration with subtlety:

> Evening took a long time getting to Lonesome Dove, but when it came it was a comfort. For most of the hours of the day—and most of the months of the year—the sun had the town trapped deep in dust . . .

The passage contains many repeated sounds—"came/comfort," "most/months," "town/trapped," "deep/dust"—but it doesn't overdo any of them, so they work on the ear with a light touch.

These examples, obviously, concern intentional repetition. McMurtry didn't repeat those consonants on accident, and Robinson didn't keep using "fallen branches" because she couldn't think of a better phrase. For aesthetic and thematic reasons, writers go out of their way to repeat certain elements of language, whether it's a word or a syllable or a letter or a sentence (as we saw in chapter 11 with Vonnegut's "So it goes"). The success of aesthetic repetition is a matter of taste, but the judgment process begins with the notion that the writer did it on purpose.

Unintentional repetition is a different animal. It's often awkward or ugly, and weeding it out of your prose requires reading for sound as well as content. In the next four sections, we'll look at different ways it can seep into your work. Then, in the chapter's final section, we'll shift gears and deal with a miscellany of other betrayals of language.

UNINTENTIONAL WORD REPETITION

There are two ways unintentional word repetition bothers editors, teachers, and readers: the repeated use of an unusual or obscure word throughout a work, and the excessive recurrence of a single word within a sentence or paragraph.

We all have words and phrases that we favor, consciously or not. Literature scholars depend on this fact when they try to identify the authors of anonymous works; often they use computer software to look for diction tendencies in the text. And you may have noticed yourself that certain authors or books favor certain words — I haven't read *Lord of the Flies* in twelve years, but I remember noticing how often it uses "ululate." To some degree our habits of word choice and grammatical arrangement are good things, because they give each of us a unique style.

But while you shouldn't mind if computer programmers or English professors can catch on to your linguistic habits, you don't want the average reader to pick up on them in the course of your novel, lest they become distractions (*How many times is this guy going to use the word "indefatigable"?* the exasperated reader asks). This is all about knowing thyself. No one has read as much of your fiction as you have, so you should be able to spot your tendencies. Take an honest look at your fiction, note the words and phrases you invoke too often, and when it comes time to revise, make use of Microsoft's Find tool. As soon as I'm done with this manuscript, I'm going to go through and replace the words I've overused in the past ("dearth," "enormously," "sanguine"), and look for new ones I've grown too fond of. In revision, you should be able to identify some of your problematic favorites. If you can't, that doesn't mean you don't habitually repeat certain words, it means you don't know which ones they are. Your readers will.

Unintentional repetition on a smaller scale occurs when a writer repeats a particular word in a sentence or a paragraph in a clumsy and distracting way. This happens not just when we overuse a word because of laziness or inattention, but when we use a word that may later be used as a root of another word, or one that, because of the nature of the subject, will appear in different guises. Consider this paragraph:

> He sat on the workbench, and in his peripheral vision he saw samples of the previous owner's handiwork. A birdhouse, a spice rack — nothing too ambitious, but the workmanship was exquisite. No matter how hard he worked — and working long hours didn't bother him — his own pieces didn't measure up. Things just didn't work out for him, in woodworking as in everything else.

Sure, the writer has to take some ownership of the awkward repetition of "work," but notice how the language works (there it is again!) against him. Words like "workbench," "handiwork," "workmanship" are hard to avoid given the scene's subject matter. And in other places, the word slips in through idiom ("work out") and participial phrasing ("working long hours"). The writer has expressed himself clearly and honestly, but the nature of language has conspired against him.

Repetition doesn't only register awkwardly when a word is excessively used — sometimes just one repetition is too much. Look at this passage from Elizabeth Bowen's "The Demon Lover," in which Mrs. Drover receives some mail:

> . . . so his negligence in the matter of this letter, leaving it to wait in the dusk and dust, annoyed her. Annoyed, she picked up the letter, which bore no stamp.

I think this is obviously unintentional, because the repetition of "annoyed" is so graceless. We've just been told that the postman's negligence annoyed Mrs. Drover, so why state that she was annoyed when she performed the next action? Even if the redundancy of the sentiment doesn't bother you, it's still strange that Bowen chose to use the exact same word when so many synonyms — "irritated," "peeved," "irked," "aggravated" — present themselves. We have to chalk this up to a moment of carelessness on Bowen's part. It's not a mortal sin, perhaps, but it's truly distracting. I last read this story during my junior year in college, but it bothered me so much that, when I needed an example of awkward repetition sixteen years later, I knew to go looking for it. That's an error with staying power.

All right, so the Bowen repetition may not be an instance of language betraying an author. In that case, the language did its best to provide a synonym, and the writer dropped the ball. It happens. But the next example of word repetition truly is the fault of the language rather than the writer, and I'm not just saying that because the writer is me. Basically, I was forced—*forced*, I tell you—to repeat a word through no fault of my own during the drafting of this very chapter.

It happened when I composed a sentence that began with the clause "The line employs an exact rhyme." I knew that, in the second half of the sentence, I wanted to indicate that the writer used the rhyme for no apparent purpose. I also wanted to do something with tone—up until then, the paragraph had been austere and technical, so it needed a dose of informality. One way of making prose more casual is to invoke a cliché (as we'll see in chapter 18) and the only appropriate cliché that came to mind was "for no rhyme or reason." So I put that in, and the result was "The line employs an exact rhyme, but for no rhyme or reason."

We can all see the problem here, right? The relatively short sentence uses "rhyme" twice, and it uses the word in two different ways, which makes the reader's job even tougher. In the first clause I'm using "rhyme" in its literal sense, but in the second the word slips in as part of an idiomatic phrase. The "rhyme" part of "rhyme or reason," a centuries-old cliché, originally referred to poetry in general, while "reason" referred to the logical faculties. But as is the case with all idiomatic speech, the actual meaning of the words doesn't matter. When you say, "It's raining cats and dogs," you don't want your listener to think about each word, you want her to understand an idea that our culture has imposed on this otherwise meaningless verbiage. In my case, the actual words in the cliché, rather than the phrase's figurative meaning, did me in.

I was in good company, at least. Raymond Chandler has a similar thing happen to him in this passage from *The Long Goodbye*:

> From here on it didn't quite add up. You'd expect her to look for him and find him and make sure he wasn't hurt. It wouldn't hurt him to lie out on the ground on a warm summer night for a while.

The first use of "hurt" is literal, a synonym for "injured." But the second one is figurative and colloquial; Chandler's "it wouldn't hurt him" carries the same meaning as it does in "it wouldn't hurt him to lose a few pounds," or "it wouldn't hurt you to say thank you to your grandmother." Finding a way out of this one presents difficulties. It wouldn't be like Marlowe, Chandler's tough guy narrator, to use the Latinate "injured," and the second sentence expresses the point exactly as we would expect him to. Maybe Chandler just decided to live with the awkwardness.

So there's a lot to worry about in terms of word repetition. As we'll see in a while, however, sometimes the cure for it can be worse than the disease — that is, attempts to avoid repetition carry with them risks of their own, and the writer might find himself damned if he does, damned if he doesn't.

REPETITION OF SOUNDS

Another problematic form of repetition involves the unintentional use of alliteration. Purposeful alliteration can be lyrical and striking, as we can see in the above McMurtry example, or in many passages of John Dos Passos's "Great Lady on a White Horse" ("The place was full of smokewriting slants of sunlight . . .") or in Nabokov's gaudy riff at the beginning of Lolita ("Lolita, light of my life, fire of my loins. My sin, my soul. Lo-lee-ta: the tip of the tongue taking a trip . . ."). But overall, many writers would sacrifice the ability to create such resonant moments if it meant we no longer had to deal with the curse of alliteration, which is that sometimes phrases come together with perfect rhythm and meaning and lyricism, and then we realize every word starts with an *f*. You can get away with a few accidentally alliterative words, but no reader's going to make it through "Frederick fought the ferocious Finn with frantic fists" without wondering what's wrong with you.

Another form of sound repetition is assonance, the repetition of vowel sounds within words, which doesn't get as much press as it should. It's often used in music, because it lets a vocalist force rhymes that don't really exist. The first two lines of Eminem's "Lose Yourself" contain the words "sweaty," "heavy," "sweater," "already," and "spaghetti," few of which rhyme in the technical sense. But when Eminem sings them, they all sound like they do, because he stresses the similar vowel sounds within them.

While assonance is especially helpful for musicians who can't find an exact rhyming word (it allowed the Beatles to somehow rhyme "loner" and "Arizona"), it's also useful in poetry, and even prose writers employ it effectively at times. That previously quoted sentence from "The Dead" contains the assonant phrase "like the descent of their last end," and in

"The Way to Rainy Mountain" N. Scott Momaday describes foliage that "seems almost to writhe in fire." But those instances appear in the midst of highly lyrical prose, writing that is already close to poetry. In most circumstances, prose writers find that the poetic nature of assonance clashes with their purpose or tone. Again I have to provide my own experience as an illustration. I apologize if this seems self-indulgent, but the fact is it's hard to find examples of this, because good writers and editors try to weed it out before it gets published.

In any case, this one happened as I was drafting chapter 15. At one point I finished a sentence with the phrase "that a modern writer would feel obliged to provide." It seemed okay at the time, but when I went back and read the chapter out loud to my dogs, I noticed that "writer would feel obliged to provide" gives three long i sounds. Of course, you can't get rid of every repeated vowel—there are too many for that, and most vowel repetitions are harmless. But in this case the repetition jars the ear, because the vowel sound, that long i, gets the stress in all three words (WRI-ter, ob-LIGED, pro-VIDE). So I changed it to "obliged to include." This is the kind of thing writers spend much of their time doing—cleaning up small messes that may seem trivial to normal people, but that will distract the reader either momentarily or cumulatively.

THE LIMITS OF VOCABULARY

"Nature's first green is gold / her hardest hue to hold," Robert Frost wrote in 1923, and as far as I'm concerned that was the last time "hue" was used to good effect. There's nothing intrinsically wrong with the word, it's just that it almost always functions as a bench warmer; it doesn't get into the game unless the starter—the word "color"—is too injured to play.

In case my sports metaphor doesn't quite illuminate the point, let's look at an example from Stephen Crane's "The Open Boat."

> None of them knew the color of the sky. Their eyes glanced level, and
> were fastened upon the waves that swept toward them. These waves were
> of the hue of slate, save for the tops, which were of foaming white, and
> all of the men knew the colors of the sea.

"Hue" doesn't quite work here, since it doesn't have the exact same meaning as "color"—it means more of a gradation or a shade, yet the sentence doesn't call for that differentiation. Crane basically wants to say the waves were the color of slate. But he can't do that, because he uses the word "color" two other times in this brief passage, and a third invocation would have distracted.

Crane gets something of a pass because he lived in a time when "hue" sounded less archaic than it does now. In any case, this section isn't just a warning about the temptations of one specific word. The point is, in our attempts to avoid repetition, we sometimes stumble upon a worse sin, which is the use of a word that calls attention to the fact that we're trying to avoid repetition. When that happens, you've replaced one kind of awkwardness with another.

You might think this wouldn't be too big a problem, based on a fact we explored in chapter 10: the English language is so enormous and varied that we usually have many options when looking for synonyms. True, much of the time you can find an adequate replacement. Your sentence leads you to a repetition of, say, "tiredness"? No problem, just find Anglo-Saxon synonyms like "weariness" and "sloth," or Latinate/Norman ones like "lassitude" and "indolence" and "inertia," or Greek ones like "lethargy" and "apathy," or . . . you get the idea.

More often than you'd think, however, English fails us by offering synonyms that come off as second-stringers. We've already seen how this works with "color/hue," and other examples that come to mind are "face/countenance/visage" (has anyone in this century ever used the word "visage" when they didn't have to?), "finger/digit," "sleep/slumber," "eye/orb" (yuck), and so on.

In such instances, the reader will be more forgiving if the writer bites the bullet and repeats a word, instead of subjecting us to an awkward synonym. To see how this works, we should take another look at that previously cited passage from "The Demon Lover":

> . . . so his negligence in the matter of this letter, leaving it to wait in the dusk and dust, annoyed her. Annoyed, she picked up the letter, which bore no stamp.

We've already dealt with the problem of "annoyed," but you may notice that the passage repeats the word "letter" as well, and indeed that word appears several more times in the paragraph this excerpt comes from. "Letter" is a noun, no less prominent than the verb/participle "annoyed," so why doesn't that one bother us? To some degree, it's because the repeated words stand farther apart from each other than the two instances of "annoyed." But more significantly it's because the available synonyms for "letter" — "missive," "dispatch," "correspondence," "epistle" — are obscure and archaic. If Bowen had written, "Annoyed, she picked up the epistle," we would have seen what she was up to. Thus we forgive her the extra uses of the word because we know she's chosen the minor evil of repetition over the major one of awkward diction.

Not that these are the only two options. A writer in this situation will usually want to rearrange the prose so that he can avoid the second word altogether.

UNINTENTIONAL RHYME

Let's transition to our next subject by looking at an instance in which "hue" usage isn't the biggest problem, and not just because the text comes from the nineteenth century:

> . . . the spicy gales wafted from Arabia's fragrant coast, flowers of every hue, opening to the rising sun and glittering with the dew, charmed his senses, an eternal spring reigned in this paradise.

"Hue" by itself actually works okay here, because the definition of the word seems appropriately matched with the content, plus we don't see any instances of "color" nearby, so it doesn't look like the author made the choice out of necessity. Or perhaps we don't mind "hue" because we focus all our aggravation on a larger error, the awkward way it rhymes with "dew." When we read this, the childish part of us wants to tell the writer, "You're a poet and you don't know it."

However, the real problem isn't the use of "hue" and "dew," it's their location in the sentence. The words both come at the end of complete phrases, before commas. Those commas make us pause, and during that pause the most recent words we've read hover in the air. Thus we notice their rhyming nature. A rearrangement of the sentence solves the problem: "flowers of every hue, opening to the rising sun that causes the dew to glitter." You still have the rhyming words, but because "dew" is sped over as we rush on toward the period, the rhyme doesn't demand attention. This is the good news about unintentional rhyme: it doesn't necessitate the scrapping of both words, it merely requires you to put one of them in a new syntactical position.

It's an odd cruelty of the universe that unintentional rhyme is very difficult to catch when you're the writer. This is because the words are more visual or imaginary in the composition process than they are in the reading process. As you type, your mind teems with characters and settings and actions and thematic points, and your brain translates those images and ideas into words via the magic of your keyboard. Often, sound gets left out of that process, at least until the revision phase (for those diligent few who read their words out loud).

GENERAL PROBLEMS

Now let's turn to those betrayals of language that don't involve repetition, but that are nevertheless frustrating, damaging, and fairly common. If you're a disciplined fiction writer, you put down about a thousand words a day, and in that outpouring of prose, you're bound to discover some interesting ways in which language can monkey with your process.

One such linguistic perfidy arises out of the selection of proper names in your work, specifically the names of major characters. Naturally, a work of fiction will invoke these names quite often. So when one of those names runs up against prose tendencies or necessities, the results are not just awkward, they have the potential to be awkward over and over again.

The most obvious way this can affect your prose concerns dialogue tags. Regardless of the stance you take on the issues addressed in chapter 3, most of the tags you use in fiction will be "he/she said," or the character's name followed by "said." In a novel, you'll probably invoke these phrases hundreds of times, and even short stories can have a lot of them. Remember, the goal of the style is to be inconspicuous. We don't want the reader to think about the writing, so we make the tag as subtle as possible.

One way to ruin the subtlety is to build in a mechanism that ensures many of your dialogue tags will rhyme (okay, so we're still talking about repetition, but this is a bit different). That is, by choosing a character name that rhymes with "said." While literature contains Edmunds (*Chronicles of Narnia*) and Edgars (*Wuthering Heights*) and Fredericks (*The Collector*), I can't think of any main characters named Ed or Fred (or Ned or Ted). No doubt some readers will contact me with suggestions, but I maintain that there aren't many of them, and it's because the rhyming tags "Ed said" and "Fred said" sound awkward. At least that's true for third-person works. First-person narrators can be called almost anything, because they rarely have to invoke their names. Stephen King got to call his narrator "Red" in "Rita

Hayworth and the Shawshank Redemption" because whenever he speaks the tag reads, "I said," not "Red said."

Another bit of oft-invoked advice is that writers should avoid main characters whose names end with *s*, for the simple reason that it looks strange when you have to turn an *s*-ending word into a possessive: "The Joneses's dog," "Cass's nose," etc. As these examples show, the standard is to add an apostrophe and an *s* in the possessive form of names that end in *s*, although you can get away with adding just an apostrophe if you're consistent with it: "The Joneses' dog," "Cass' nose." (Strunk and White assert that you should use the apostrophe-*s* style with contemporary names and the apostrophe-only style with ancient ones, as in "Achilles' heel." I've always wondered how this would apply to NBA legend Moses Malone).

There are pros and cons for both methods, I suppose. The punctuation in the title of Denis Johnson's short story collection *Jesus' Son* encourages us to pronounce "Jesus" with just one *s* at the end, which is helpful — "Jesus's" would force us to cram three *s* sounds into a very short space. Then again, the apostrophe and *s* method is more common, because it avoids giving us words that end with an apostrophe, a construction we don't see often in Standard English. But both methods can be visually and aurally distracting.

So I have to concur that you should avoid character names that put you in this position, unfair as it may be to all those Les Joneses and Bess Rosses who will never get a character named after them. In some situations, however, you won't have a choice. When Robert Graves wrote about ancient Rome in *I, Claudius*, he had to use many names that end with *s* (he went with "Tiberius's" and "Julius's" and so on). And some novelists have done it successfully when they didn't have to, the most obvious example being Thomas Hardy, who used "Tess's" ninety-two times in *Tess of the d'Urbervilles*. Still, I don't know why you'd want to give yourself another thing to worry about. And frankly, all those "Tess's" begin to look strange after a while.

In your writing lives, you'll certainly stumble upon other betrayals of language — you might choose a phrase that sounds fine but looks weird because of typography, for example, or you might use a perfectly harmless word that accidentally forms a pun when placed next to another. I hope it doesn't happen too often. But when it does, the best tactic is usually to rearrange the syntax or phrasing or even the entire scene. The linguistic awkwardness may not be your fault, but that's not going to matter to the reader.

eighteen

Cliché

A poster that hangs on the walls of high school classrooms across the nation tells us to "Avoid clichés like the plague." Although I dislike the device of cheekily committing a grammatical sin in the very sentence that warns against it (it's kind of a cliché itself), the lesson has merit. In most cases, clichés will damage your fiction, especially if they're used thoughtlessly, the way we use them in speech. Most editors and creative writing teachers would agree that the use of cliché phrasing is one of the biggest problems with the fiction put before them. So let's get that straight before we go any further: it's usually a bad idea to write "it seemed like an eternity," or "she had a heart of stone," or "he was stubborn as a mule," or any of the innumerable dead phrases that clutter our language.

But even this issue gets more complex the closer you get to mastery. To truly grapple with the issue of clichéd expression, I believe the fiction writer should understand three things: 1) what exactly a cliché is, 2) why you're told to avoid them, and 3) why they may not be as deadly as advertised.

WHAT IS A CLICHÉ?

The term "cliché" doesn't only refer to a linguistic problem, of course. We often apply it to acts or concepts that we find unoriginal, as in "Darla's opening a cupcake shop; geez, what a cliché." In fiction, we have to worry about clichés in that sense as well. We don't want to portray actions, characters, or themes that are trite, stereotypical, hackneyed. It's a significant matter, and you may find comfort in how other writing guides deal with it. But we won't address any of that stuff in this book, because those aren't linguistic issues. Here we'll use "cliché" only to mean a phrase or expression that has become so overused it is no longer vivid or interesting. If you want examples, watch an interview with a professional athlete.

Clichés often appear as figurative language, which is an umbrella term for phrasing that indicates something other than what it technically means.

It's the opposite of "literal language," which refers to words that mean exactly what they signify in a denotative sense. The distinction matters. Someone who says "I am going to kill my husband" figuratively has different emotional and legal needs than someone who says it literally. Clichés often take the figurative form because it can be more interesting and colorful than literal language, and thus is more likely to get passed along and overused. Many of the more dastardly clichés in sloppy fiction involve figurative devices like metaphor ("That day was a roller-coaster ride of emotion"), simile ("the seconds passed like hours"), hyperbole ("he would give you the shirt off his back"), and so on.

One type of figurative language that requires more consideration is idiom. An idiom is a phrase whose meaning is separate from the actual words it contains. Consider a robot that has been programmed to know every word in the dictionary and every rule of syntax and grammar. If you give this robot a simile like "Her little girl's as pretty as a peach," it will understand what you're saying—that the girl is pretty in the way that a peach is pretty. But if you give the robot an idiom like "I've got butterflies in my stomach," it will think you have actual Lepidoptera in your abdomen, not that you're nervous.

Robots aren't the only ones who have trouble with idioms—they're also difficult for anyone who's learning a language. Imagine knowing the basic vocabulary and syntax of English, then hearing someone say "I make no bones about my past" or "you can sit shotgun." The difficulty arises from the fact that idioms are language- and culture-specific. They work only when our listeners share with us a cultural or linguistic experience, whether that experience is national (Australians use "up a gum tree" to mean "in trouble") or regional (for American Southerners, "losing my religion" means "running out of patience"), ephemeral ("Where's the beef?" will probably die out with Generation X) or enduring ("give the devil his due," and dozens of others, come from Shakespeare).

Before we finish with definitions, we should acknowledge that not all clichés are idioms, while all idioms are clichés. The phrase "as far as the eye can see" is certainly a cliché, but it's not an idiom because the words mean what they say; the aforementioned robot would comprehend the phrase. The second point is more controversial, but the logic isn't hard to follow. If an idiom is a phrase that doesn't mean what it actually says, then how on earth can it communicate? The answer is that it communicates only if the reader has encountered the phrase before, and thus knows what meaning to attach to it. My two-year-old son has a fairly good grasp of English, but if I told him "it's raining cats and dogs" he would look outside for cats and dogs, because he hasn't encountered that idiomatic phrase before. When someone is unfamiliar with an idiom, it doesn't work. And if someone can understand a phrase of such strangeness that its meaning has nothing to do with its actual words, then she must have heard it quite a few times — ergo, it must be a cliché.

In spite of that argument (which, I should say, not everyone buys), the term "idiom" has a more positive connotation than "cliché" — no one tells you to avoid idioms like the plague. But this could be a product of self-delusion. We may not want to associate with something as bland and unoriginal as cliché, but in truth most writers, even the great ones, use them quite a lot.

WHY SHOULDN'T WE USE CLICHÉS?

If the first function of language in fiction is to communicate, as I've argued, then clichés may not seem problematic. They communicate just fine. The very definition of a cliché means that it's overly familiar, so most English-speaking adults will comprehend most of them.

But of course language isn't just meant to communicate. If that's priority #1, then priority #1a is to communicate with elegance and vividness. So the short answer to the question posed by the section heading is, we shouldn't use clichés because they're inert and boring, whereas we want to write prose that will keep the reader engaged. If a writer tells us, "Susie was happy as a clam," this is somehow worse than if he'd written, "Susie was happy." It's worth pausing to think about why this is the case. After all, we've also heard the phrase "she was happy" before; in fact, we've probably heard it more than we've heard "happy as a clam."

The reason we don't consider "she was happy" a cliché, or get annoyed with the writer for using it, is that we recognize the phrase as a functional assertion. The writer has signified that, in his aesthetic opinion, only priority #1 matters at that point in the story. The prose is not meant to achieve heights of elegance, but to serve its primary purpose of communicating. With "happy as a clam," the writer indicates something else: that the moment calls for emphasis or clarification or vividness. In addition to priority #1, he believes priority #1a should be invoked. But the writer has taken an extremely lazy route to achieving #1a. He's chosen to underscore his point by asking us to refer to a phrase that someone else came up with, and which we've heard so many times we don't even think about it (if we did, we'd be in trouble—"happy as a clam" is idiomatic, thus it doesn't make sense). Bring-your-own-intensifier, so to speak.

Furthermore, the use of clichés can disrupt readers' full immersion in the fictive experience. It encourages them to skate on the surface rather than to plunge into the depths of the narrative. In her novel *Housekeeping*, Marilynne Robinson writes, "She was an old woman, but she managed to look like a young woman with a ravaging disease." I find this to be a startlingly effective and original description. It allows me to see precise details of the woman (poorly dyed hair; inappropriate wardrobe choices; gauche makeup), to apply certain personality traits to her (vanity, delusion), and to understand the authorial attitude toward her (the word "managed" implies that it's something of a triumph for the woman to look this way). The language of the sentence plunges me into the reality of the character's existence, it deepens my understanding of the fictional world.

Compare this to what would have happened to my experience if Robinson had written "she was an old woman, and she looked like something the cat dragged in," or "she looked rode hard and put away wet," both of which communicate the same point as the first version. I would understand the idea clearly, but it would be a somewhat theoretical understanding—I would know what the writer wanted me to know, but I wouldn't *know* it.

On top of all this, the avoidance of cliché may be a defining characteristic of literary fiction, not just a nice bonus quality. To see how this is true, we need to think about the origins of written literature. Ancient and medieval works, as we discussed in chapter 15, were often composed and passed on orally. Poets and bards would memorize the basic structures of long narratives and recite them at parties and banquets. Because it's hard to memorize something like the *Iliad*, the bards used certain tricks, one of which was the utilization of formulaic phrases (this also helped them stick to the prescribed meter and alliterative patterns). Such phrases include "dawn with her fingertips of rose" (meaning "morning") in the *Odyssey*, and "swan of blood" in *Beowulf* (meaning "raven"). If you've read these works, you surely noticed they repeat stock phrases. No one calls them clichés—they're known as epithets or kennings—but that's what they are: phrases that communicate through familiarity.

To figure out if a work was composed in the oral tradition, or whether a specific author sat down on a specific day and wrote it, scholars sometimes calibrate a work's formulaic density. They count up what percentage of a work consists of original language, and what percentage consists of formulaic phrases. If a work has a high degree of formulaic density, it's likelier to have been composed orally. I say "likelier," because a high rate of cliché by itself doesn't prove such matters — if it did, we'd have to assume that most modern romance novels are composed orally (with "heaving bosom" and "trembling lips" as their kennings). Still, the fact that an excess of familiar phrasing can support a case for a work's orality indicates something fundamental about prose composition: when writers have the time and leisure to compose a work in writing, they make their language as innovative as possible. Formulaic phrases may help when you need to keep the meter consistent in front of the King of Thrace, but when it's just you and a quill or a typewriter or a laptop, you strive for originality.

SO WHAT'S THE CATCH?

We now have to delve a little deeper into this idiom business. Two sections ago, I declared that all idioms are clichés, while hinting that not everyone agrees with me. Well, I stand by my logic, but I don't want to be obtuse about the point. While idioms are clichés, we shouldn't consider the terms interchangeable. Idioms tend to be a specific type of cliché, in particular a type that a writer can feel more comfortable using. The reason no one says, "avoid idioms like the plague" is that the majority of idioms do less damage to one's prose than other kinds of clichés, plus they're much harder to avoid.

To sort through this, let's look at a sentence from George MacDonald Fraser's *Flashman and the Redskins*. In this passage, the narrator, Harry Flashman, discusses his facility with languages, and his curious inability to learn Apache.

> Still, it's odd that I never got my tongue round it, for apart from fleeing and fornication, slinging the bat is my strongest suit; well, I speak nine languages better than the natives, and can rub along in another dozen or so.

Flashman invokes five phrases that depend on the reader's familiarity with them: "I never got my tongue round it," "slinging the bat," "my strongest suit," "rub along," and "or so."

Let's start with an easy one. "My strongest suit" is clearly idiomatic; though it's widely understood to mean "my best trait," someone not imbued in Anglo-American culture might not understand it, because it makes an oblique reference to a card game. "I never got my tongue round it" also invokes a familiar phrase, albeit with a twist. The actual idiomatic expression is "got my head around it," used to connote that you understand something. Flashman has replaced "head" with "tongue" because he's talking about languages. It freshens up the cliché a bit, but even that version has been used quite a few times.

"Slinging the bat" is, I think, the best evidence for my point about successful idioms being clichés, because it shows what happens when an idiom is not familiar. In the novel, the phrase comes with an editorial note telling us that "slinging the bat" is British Army slang for speaking languages. It's an idiom because it depends on the reader's prior understanding of its meaning, but it fails to communicate to a general readership because it's not a cliché in a broad sense — it's only a cliché to British soldiers. If an idiom has not been heard numerous times by its listeners, it will fail the first job of language, as this one does (that's why we need the editorial note). The next idiom, "rub along" may also be somewhat culture-specific, being more British in tone, but most English-speaking readers will have heard it enough times to get the point.

That brings us to the one that provides the key for how we can use idioms without causing the negative effects clichés usually entail. The phrase "or so" is an idiom; nothing about the dictionary definition of its words would indicate that, when put together, they should mean "approximately," but that's indisputably what Flashman wants them to mean. Yet there's nothing distracting about the phrase "or so," nothing that makes us pause and accuse the author of laziness or triteness.

These are the kind of idioms that work, the ones that don't stand out to readers as figurative language at all. In a way, they're so overly familiar we don't recognize the separation between words and meaning, even if we read them over a few times (they're so cliché they're not cliché anymore!). Identifying such phrases is a subjective process, although on one end of the spectrum we have easy calls like "or so" — idioms that most people will agree don't affect us the way other clichés do. Such phrases tend to be short, and they tend not to contain strong nouns. They tend not to be noticeably metaphorical, and they tend not to use poetic sound devices like alliteration. They include phrases like "to push for," "to live up to," "to call on," "to cut a deal," "to go back on," etc. Such phrases are common in all forms of prose — I took these examples from an article chosen at random from the *New York Times*. They're clichés, but they're not what the poster means when it says "avoid clichés like the plague."

Many readers and writers will also accept idioms that are a little more vivid or metaphorical than these. I'm thinking of phrases like "clear the air," "not cut out for," "it's a gray area," "flesh and blood," "a losing battle," "by the book," "a close call." Here are some idioms in this category from the first page of the novel *Disgrace*: "to his mind" (meaning "in his opinion"), "he has been on her books" (meaning he has been a client of hers), "rounded up" (meaning gathered), and "make love" (which has only carried its current meaning for a few decades). The author is the Nobel Prize winner J. M. Coetzee, and the narrative style is third-person, so we can't write off any clichés or idioms as an amateur's slipups or the quirks of a first-person voice. These clichéd idioms, being not too poetic, not too imagistic, avoid calling attention to the borrowed nature of the language.

As the phrases move toward the longer and more ostentatious, readers will have less patience with idiom. I'm fairly confident that Coetzee would never make his narrator say something like "David Lurie was an eager beaver who kept his nose to the grindstone" or "they shot the breeze for a while, until it was time to hit the hay." These metaphorical idiomatic constructions are cliché in a distracting, attention-grabbing sense. At some point in history they probably seemed powerful and vivid, in the way that less ambitious idioms like "all right" or "get used to" never did. But if we read them in a work of fiction, their usage strikes us as cynical, because we think the writer was too lazy to look beyond the closest available phrase. Or even worse, we assume that he tried and failed to come up with a better one.

My overall point is that we actually don't avoid all clichés when we write, especially if we consider that idioms happen to be clichés, and idiomatic speech is virtually impossible to avoid. It would be weirdly dogmatic to tell a writer never to use the phrases "once in a while," "lose track of," "now and then," or any of the hundreds of others that readers won't even notice.

When we accept this point, though, the advice to avoid cliché reveals itself to be highly contingent. Clichés are dangerous, yes, but we have to use them, so they're dangerous in terms of degree, not kind. The old saw "avoid clichés like the plague" pretends that the matter is simple: never employ a phrase that has been overused and you'll be fine, it tells us. But it's not honest advice, because it's not possible to follow — or if you did follow it, undesirable things would happen to your prose. Consider this passage from Ann Patchett's *Bel Canto* (italics mine):

As far as Mr. Hosokawa *was concerned*, his trip was not for the purposes of business, diplomacy, or a friendship with the President . . . Mr. Hosokawa disliked travel and did not know the President. *He had made his intentions, or lack of intentions, abundantly clear.* He did not plan to build a plant . . . *He was not much for* celebrating his birthday with people he did not know . . . And if she was the present, who would decline? *No matter how* far away, how inappropriate, how misleading *it might prove to be*, who would say no?

The italicized parts are clichés. Some are idioms ("he was not much for") and some are not ("he had made his intentions abundantly clear"). Some are obviously familiar phrases ("As far as X was concerned") while some are barely noticeable as figurative ("no matter how"). But the passage contains quite a few of them. If you forced Patchett to follow the anti-cliché advice, she could have replaced "He had made his intentions . . . abundantly clear" with the non-cliché assertion "He had told them clearly," and "it might prove to be" with "it might be." The difference does not seem so dramatic, but there would be a cumulative effect.

Some clichés and idioms can be useful when you want to add a casual, informal tone to your prose. They imply a familiarity with the reader, a sense that we've all let our guard down, that we're sharing things on a level pitched below that of a grad school thesis or a business letter. Because fiction is, to some degree, about the conveying and sharing of emotion, most writers don't want to craft an overly stringent or austere tone. Cliché and idiom can be a way of instilling a sense of ease and comfort. And I'm not even talking about first-person fiction, in which an author might create a narrator with a tendency toward cliché. I mean that in third-person narratives, even those that, like Patchett's, are not rigidly aligned with a single character, cliché and idiom can lessen the psychic distance between reader and narrator. There, I said it.

I'm not just trying to be contrarian with this suggestion, which is in effect a refutation of the standard *for God's sake don't ever use clichés* advice one generally hears in creative writing books and classrooms. I myself pass that advice along to my students, but only because I don't have the time to explain in class everything I've explained here. Besides, knowing that there's a time and place for cliché doesn't solve everything. It still takes a good deal of practice to utilize it in a way that works tonally. Patchett is an absolute master of tone, and she uses the technique with extreme care and effectiveness. If I hadn't used the italics, you may not have noticed the clichés, although you would have sensed the intimate quality of her language. But it's easy to see how any slight misstep in the above passage could have wrecked things. If she'd written, "He did not plan to build a plant, not in a month of Sundays," or "to celebrate his birthday with people he did not know from a hole in the ground," any gains in tonal informality would have been outweighed by the reader's disdain for the prose. To say that clichés and idioms, if used with sensitivity, can add a certain element to your fiction is not to say that you should fire at will.

But for those writers who want to exploit every possible aspect of language, now's the time to stop pretending that clichés don't exist in quality fiction. A young writer who's heard that falsehood will wonder why Jim Crace starts one of his best novels with the cliché "For old times' sake" or why the exquisite stylist Mark Helprin describes a father and daughter as being "the picture of strength"; why virtuosos like David Foster Wallace and John Updike use cliché expressions with as much fervor as they use original ones; why even omniscient authoritarians like Henry James and A. S. Byatt can be found slumming in idiomland from time to time. It's because God did not engrave on one of the tablets "thou shalt not use clichés." Instead, that advice has been adopted as a useful way of encouraging novice writers to sharpen and vivify their prose. An excellent intention, to be sure, but it may remind you of a certain cliché concerning what the road to hell is paved with.

THE REAL CHALLENGE

I hope I've given you some different ways to think about cliché without muddying the water too much. If you like, you can stick with the "avoid clichés like the plague" dogma, and do your best to find sparkling, vivid phrases instead of settling on idioms like "it never came up" and "come to grips with." Or you can decide where you personally draw the line between distracting clichés and acceptable figures of speech.

The more troubling element of clichés is that you can't recognize them if you haven't been exposed to them enough. When I re-read the stories I wrote in high school, I'm amazed by the cliché phrases (and plotlines and characters) I invoked with enthusiasm — I actually titled one of my stories "No Day at the Beach," and I wasn't being ironic. In some instances, I hadn't thought enough about what clichés were or what they did to my fiction. But often, I just didn't know I was using them.

A writer can be forgiven if he's too young to have experienced enough of life and literature to know when something is a cliché. And the process of familiarizing oneself with language never ends — I still hear people refer to phrases as being cliché when they strike me as perfectly original (my wife tells me, for example, that "epic fail" has become a common phrase. Did everyone else know this?). But even if it's not your fault, the fact remains that your prose will be damaged in a significant way until you can recognize as many linguistic clichés as possible. The ability to do that comes with reading and time. Time you can't do anything about, but you certainly can get to work on reading. If you don't, and if you don't carefully consider the way people use formulaic language in television and movies and pop music, on Facebook and Twitter and blogs, you'll have difficulty crafting original prose that either avoids or makes intelligent use of cliché.

Afterword

Our language is full of secrets and wonders, many of which are revealed to us when we read. In "The Wives of the Dead" Nathaniel Hawthorne challenges our interpretation of an entire story with the ambiguous use of a pronoun. In *Bleak House* Charles Dickens uses a grammatical mistake thirty times in a row as he delivers a vivid portrait of London. Toni Morrison proves in *Song of Solomon* that one sentence can contain the thematic promise of a whole novel. What is there to do in the face of such extraordinary discoveries but be grateful, and keep on reading?

We discover language's darker secrets, however, when we write. We find hidden perils and paradoxes that snap shut, like the teeth of a bear trap, just as we think we've written the perfect phrase. We also learn about the insufficiency of language, how it often can't meet the challenge of true expression. "Language, it seems, has only been invented for the average, the middling," Nietzsche says, and all writers have moments when we mournfully shake our heads and respond, "Ain't it the truth, brother."

In such moments, we may come to see language antagonistically, as a problem to be solved or an enemy to defeat. If so, then it makes sense to engage in this struggle by mastering language, to make sure we don't give it the opportunity to befuddle us with its lack of a personal third-person pronoun or its tendency to make us repeat things or its complex rules of comma usage. I hope I've shown that achieving at least a degree of such mastery can be a manageable and even enjoyable task.

I also believe that task can provide a good deal of psychological comfort—it certainly did for me as I began my career. Once I put away my romantic notions about what a writer was, I pursued mastery of language with the zeal of the convert, largely because it made me feel better. I compared myself to a mediocre baseball player who mastered fundamentals like bunting and baserunning in order to compensate for his lack of God-given talents like speed and power. I may not have had the innate intelligence of

A. S. Byatt, or the instinctive feel for dialogue of Scott Spencer, but at least I could know everything there was to know about language.

That framework is sustainable and useful, I think. Lots of writers get by on a sense of underdogness, the belief that they'll win the day with hard work and integrity. Indeed, they're right. Trite though it may sound, working hard and accepting rejection is much, much likelier to lead to success than relying on your inherent gifts is. So use that perspective if you like. Consider language, the most manageably mastered of fiction's mysteries, to be your way of seizing an advantage that other writers may not take.

But I also believe there's a grander and more precise way to think of it. The fact is, the baseball analogy doesn't hold up in a couple of ways. For one thing, the necessity of mastering the fundamentals applies to all aspects of writing, not just language; almost none of it comes to you except through work. I no longer believe there are any equivalents of Manny Ramirez or Josh Hamilton in fiction writing. Surely some writers have natural abilities, but innate talent doesn't play nearly as significant a role in fiction as it does in something like baseball.

And here's another reason the analogy is flawed: mastery of language isn't merely something that keeps you from screwing up, or that can compensate for the fact that you're screwing up in other areas. Employing a nuanced verb tense, splicing commas to rhythmic effect, presenting interiors in a forceful way, avoiding common errors that distract readers—these are ways to ennoble and expand your fiction, not simply to make it functional.

How exactly it does that ennobling is difficult to say. Perhaps a mastery of language allows you to shift into your prose autopilot so thoroughly that you can focus more of your attention on the other elements. Perhaps a control of diction, punctuation, and syntax gives you so many more options for how to say things that you gain access to otherwise inaccessible perceptions. Or perhaps, as Keats's urn tells us, beauty is truth, and so to create beautiful prose—language that is not just lyrical but also efficient, flawless, precise—is to necessarily achieve profundity. It doesn't really matter how it works, just that it does. That's my theory, and I'm sticking to it.

Even if that sounds a bit romantic and dubious to you, the fact remains that all writers will have to accept a greater responsibility to master language as the methods and manners of publication change. No one knows how the digital publishing movement will play out, but it seems likely to lead to a world in which fiction does not get the same amount of editorial treatment it once did. While the old model of publishing depended on editors and copyeditors to address language issues, in the digital age nothing stands between the writer and his audience except a few clicks of the keyboard.

This reality will lead to the publication of many works that don't use language well. As we've seen in so many other forms of digital media, that's the result of democratization. The primary—and often the only—goal of a writer on Facebook and Twitter is to communicate. Writing that communicates with elegance and lyricism is not just de-emphasized in those venues, it's practically discouraged. In the digital future, some fiction writers will care only about what they say, not how they say it, and some people will buy and possibly even celebrate these works.

But in the end, readers will demand linguistic mastery from their literature, no matter how it's delivered, because clarity and grace of expression are necessary features of literature. A writer who thinks his audience will overlook comma problems and verb tense shifts just because his story is exciting or his sex scenes are vivid will soon learn that all readerships have certain linguistic expectations. It's true that tastes and tolerances change based on genre and era: some audiences don't mind clichés as much as others, some expect casual diction, some won't put up with too many metaphors. But all of them will reject prose that distracts through error, that does not exhibit respect for the material, or that fails to recognize convention. Audiences will also find and celebrate works that use language in extraordinary ways, or at least they will do so with as much justice as they did in the old model. These are the only things I know for sure about the future of publication.

So there are your reasons. Master your language because it provides you the comfort of knowing that at least one aspect of this mysterious art is under your control (to some degree). Master your language because it can enhance and ennoble other aspects of your fiction. Master your language because audiences want you to, whether you're planning to publish in the digital world or in print (or, for that matter, if you're handing in a story for your Intro to Fiction class). Or you may want to master your language simply because you're a writer, and you love words and sentences, and you want to treat them with respect.

If you need another way to think about the whole thing, I'd recommend looking at Richard Wilbur's poem "The Writer," in which Wilbur describes hearing his young daughter tap out a story on a keyboard as he pauses outside her door. Blithely comparing the writing process to a sea journey, he wishes her "a lucky passage," but then he reconsiders the analogy. He recalls a time when a starling that was trapped in his daughter's room spent an hour banging itself against the windowpane in an effort to escape, before finally "clearing the sill of the world." Wilbur realizes that this is the more appropriate metaphor for writing—not the smooth sailing of an ocean voyage, but the painful, frantic attempt of an animal to free itself from a prison. In the final stanza Wilbur tells his daughter, "It is always a matter, my darling / Of life and death, as I had forgotten. I wish / What I wished you before, but harder."

I find this to be an achingly wise and apt image of artistic creation in all its glory and its pain. The opening in the window is tiny relative to the size of the wall, and the bird must crash over and over in its attempts to make it through. That's what writing is.

But this is no tragedy of fate; a writer has agency. Not only can she keep crashing and gathering her wits so that she can crash again, she can also do certain things to edge up the windowpane a little higher. The moving of the sash, the widening of the aperture, that's what mastering language is. And that's all it is—I don't want to overpromise on its behalf; fiction is too messy and complex and magnificent a problem to be solved with one strategy. But if you're the starling, even the slightest nudging of the window matters quite a lot.

Glossary of Terms

Adjective a word that modifies a noun or pronoun.

The lean, mysterious stranger ordered a tall glass of hard liquor.

Adverb a word that modifies a verb, adjective, clause, or even another adverb.

Unfortunately, the client shuddered violently and gave a quite emphatic grimace.

Alliteration the repetition of consonant sounds at the beginning of words.

Beowulf was bent upon battle.

Anglo-Saxon technically, the language spoken in the British Isles before the Norman invasion of 1066. Generally refers to a style of diction that is characterized by short, common words.

His grim face showed no pity as he swung the mace.

Antecedent the word that a pronoun replaces.

Maybelline informed the waiter that she is allergic to shrimp.

Appositive a word or phrase that renames or re-identifies a noun or noun phrase.

Paul, my brother-in-law, lives on a farm.

Assonance the repetition of vowel sounds within words.

I strive to find the right type of hang glider.

Clause a grammatical unit that contains at least one subject and one verb.

Margo smiled.

Comma splice the mechanical error that ensues when a writer attempts to connect two independent clauses using only a comma as the connective element.

Donkeys sink in quicksand, mules do not.

Complex sentence a sentence construction that involves an independent clause joined with at least one dependent clause.

After a great deal of bickering, we decided to share the fudge.

Compound predicate a sentence element that gives two or more pieces of information about what the subject is doing.

Jules *drove the stake into the vampire's chest and howled in triumph.*

Compound sentence a sentence construction that involves two or more independent clauses.

Jimmy cracked corn, and I don't care.

Compound-complex sentence a sentence construction that involves two or more independent clauses and at least one dependent clause.

Although I like Wham, I never saw them live, and now I've missed my chance.

Conjunction a word that serves as a connecting element between words, phrases, and clauses.

The Beer and Bowl is fine for casual dates, but for formal occasions I recommend a more elegant place, or at least one with napkins.

Consonance the repetition of consonant sounds within words.

The pack of hawks cackled in the dark.

Coordinate modifiers a series of modifiers that all apply to the same noun, and thus should be separated with commas.

The meaty, rich, aromatic dish made me forget that I'd given up pasta for Lent.

Dangling participle an error that occurs when a writer uses a modifying participle but does not provide a noun for the participle to attach to.

Gazing intently at the red flow, the volcano looked amazing.

Dash a punctuation mark that comprises two hyphens. A pair of dashes sets off a nonrestrictive element, while a single dash calls attention to whatever follows.

Flying a large plane—flying any plane—requires a great deal of effort. I should know—I've crashed twice.

Demonstrative adjective a word that modifies a noun by referring to its distance in time or place. Demonstrative adjectives will be always paired with a noun.

That movie is disgusting.

Demonstrative pronoun a pronoun that replaces a noun and refers to the noun's relative location in time or place. Demonstrative pronouns stand alone, not attached to a noun.

That is disgusting.

Dependent clause a clause that cannot stand alone as a sentence.

After a few minutes the tingling stops, <u>because you've become numb.</u>

Dialect speech that is particular to a region, nation, culture, ethnicity, etc.

I reckon we done et enuff biscuits n' gravy fer now.

Dialogue tag a phrase that indicates who has spoken a line of dialogue, and sometimes how that dialogue is spoken.

"Hop on in," <u>the driver said.</u>

Dialogue supplement any sentence that is not technically a tag, yet which is meant to comment on the speech or speaker.

"Hop on in." <u>The driver smelled like petunias.</u>

Diction refers generally to the writer's choice of words. See entries for "Anglo-Saxon" and "Latinate" for examples.

Factual case a mode of present tense that implies something is true eternally.

The sun burns with great heat.

Figurative language language that is meant to indicate something other than what its words actually state.

The <u>car was a lemon</u>, but I needed to <u>get out of Dodge</u>, so I <u>forked over</u> the <u>dough</u>.

First-person narration a method of narration in which the storyteller is a character in the story; the first-person pronoun forms ("I," "me," "my," "mine") are used in the narration.

Call me Ishmael.

Formulaic density the ratio between original content and idiomatic/formulaic content in a work of literature, helpful in determining how a work was composed.

Free indirect style a method of third-person narration in which the voice of a character occasionally seeps into the narrative prose.

She considered the proposition dispassionately. <u>Garbage, probably.</u> Her sense of objectivity gradually left her. <u>Absolute rubbish. Pure crap.</u>

Gerund a word that was once a verb, yet which has taken on the role of a noun by having an –ing added to it.

<u>Going</u> to the cabin is important to Victoria, because of her love of <u>hunting</u> and <u>fishing</u>.

Habitual case a mode of present tense that implies something is presently true, has been true for some of the past, and will be true for some of the future.

Dave goes curling on Thursdays.

Hyperbole a figure of speech that uses exaggeration to make a point or create an effect.

I've seen a million bad movies in my day, but that one truly astounded me.

Hyphen a punctuation mark that uses a horizontal line to connect two words.

The writer-director completed the project in thirty-eight days.

Hypotaxis a sentence construction that indicates one element of a sentence is prioritized over another; its opposite is "parataxis."

The blue army marched to the west, while the gray army marched to the east.

Idiom a phrase whose words do not mean what they denote. An idiom depends on its reader/listener having heard it before.

He was out of there in a New York minute.

Independent clause a phrase that can stand alone as a complete sentence; it contains a subject and verb, and it completes a thought.

You don't bring me flowers anymore.

Infinitive phrase the basic form of a verb, consisting of the core verb and "to."

To strive, to seek, to find, and not to yield.

Interiority the portrait of a character's inner thoughts and emotions.

Jennifer looked at the ticket, not believing her good fortune. She thought of her parents and wondered how they would try to get their hands on the money.

Interrogative pronoun a pronoun that is involved in the asking of a question.

I ask you, sir, who is cheating whom?

Ironic quotation the use of quotation marks to delegitimize a word or phrase.

The "geniuses" in the state house keep telling us that there's a "plan." Yeah right!

Latinate a form of diction involving words that are more complex in meaning and sound than those used in Anglo-Saxon diction.

A feasibility investigation of the proposal reveals an incompatibility between the corporation's logistical aspirations and its fiduciary responsibilities.

Literary case a mode of present tense that indicates the events within a literary text are eternal.

Hawthorne portrays the novel's heroine as a complex and inscrutable figure.

Lyricism the quality of being mellifluous, pleasant sounding.

*In your rocking chair, by your window dreaming, shall you long, alone. In your rocking chair, by your window, shall you dream such happiness as you may never feel.
(From Theodore Dreiser's Sister Carrie)*

Melodrama the quality of something that is overtly and aggressively dramatic, and which tries to manipulate the audience into feeling strong emotion.

Horror! Calamity! Outrage! Dear reader, dost not thy heart break for the poor child!

Metafiction a postmodern style that calls attention to the fictional nature of a work of fiction.

Metaphor the figurative comparison of two unlike objects.

Steve is a big fat pig.

Misplaced modifier the grammatical mistake that arises when a writer places a modifier in close proximity to a word that it is not meant to modify.

Soaring obliviously over the lake, <u>Nora</u> took aim at the goose.

Modernism a literary movement of the 1910s, 20s, and 30s, characterized by experimentalism in language, form, and content.

Modifier a word or phrase that is meant to further describe, qualify, specify, or clarify another sentence element.

Mrs. Dalton, <u>in a stroke of genius</u>, paired the <u>rich</u> entrée with a <u>mellow</u> cabernet.

Modifying participial phrase a participial phrase that describes, qualifies, specifies, or clarifies another sentence element.

<u>Shouting like a maniac</u>, Rodney drew the attention of local authorities.

Non-coordinate modifiers a series of modifiers that do not modify the same object, and thus should not be separated with commas.

The <u>fluffy mashed</u> potatoes left a stain on my <u>favorite blue</u> jeans.

Nonrestrictive/nonessential commas a set of commas surrounding a phrase that is nonrestrictive/nonessential. (See the commas in the example sentence for "nonrestrictive phrase.")

Suriname<u>,</u> a nation one rarely thinks about<u>,</u> is well worth a visit.

Nonrestrictive/nonessential phrase a phrase that is not necessary for a sentence to achieve its basic meaning, yet which offers some additional—and presumably helpful—information.

Suriname, <u>a nation one rarely thinks about</u>, is well worth a visit.

Objective pronoun a pronoun that acts as an object in a sentence.

The coyote chased <u>them</u> until Marco charmed <u>it</u> with his lute.

Onomatopoeia the quality of a word that sounds somewhat like the thing it denotes.

To amuse the boy, Grandpapa <u>quacked</u> like a mallard.

Parataxis a sentence construction in which an equality of the clauses is implied.

The blue army marched to the west, and the gray army marched to the east.

Participle a word that acts as either a verb or adjective. It's usually created when an *–ed* or *–ing* is added to a basic verb form.

<u>Exhausted</u> and <u>starving</u>, the survivors had <u>staggered</u> onto the beach and were <u>waving</u> their hands wildly.

Past participle a participle that is usually created when an *–ed* is added to a basic verb form, although there are many irregular cases, like "done" and "rung."

Exhausted, staggered

Past perfect a verb tense created when "had" is combined with a past participle. It implies that the action took place in a time that preceded another past tense action.

Rupert <u>had hoped</u> for the best, but Melissa bought him a paperweight.

Past perfect progressive a verb tense that implies an action took place for an ongoing period of time, prior to another action the reader is aware of. It is constructed by using "had been" with a present participle (I know, this gets complicated).

Because I <u>had been running</u> a marathon all day, I didn't hear the news until that night.

Past progressive a verb tense that refers to an action that was ongoing for a prolonged period in the past. It is constructed by using a past tense form of "to be" with a present participle.

Poppy <u>was riding</u> her bike when the thunderstorm hit.

Pastiche an artistic device, often associated with Postmodernism, in which the writer overtly borrows elements from another work and integrates them into his/her own.

Phonetic spelling spelling that seeks to represent the actual sound of speech, and thus usually violates the prescribed dictionary spelling of a word.

"<u>Fer sher</u>," replied Starbeam. "I mean, <u>tohhhhtully</u>."

Possessive pronoun a pronoun that indicates ownership.

<u>His</u> repeated jokes about <u>her</u> haircut finally ruined <u>their</u> relationship.

Postmodernism a literary movement generally associated with the post–WWII era, whose authors used experimental devices and forms to react against previous literary conventions.

Predicate the part of the sentence that says something about the subject. It usually gives information about what the subject is doing or what is happening to it.

The Chiefs <u>are not having a successful season.</u>

Preposition a word that locates in time or space the object/phrase that follows it.

<u>In</u> the time <u>of</u> the plague, <u>around</u> the city <u>of</u> Kiev, a rumor spread <u>about</u> the pope.

Prepositional phrase a phrase that begins with a preposition.

<u>On top of</u> Old Smokey, all covered <u>with cheese</u>

Present participle a participle that is created when an –ing is added to a basic verb form.

Starving, waving

Present progressive a present tense form that indicates continuous or ongoing action. It is constructed with a present tense form of "to be" and a present participle.

We <u>are willing</u> to negotiate, but that music <u>is driving</u> us crazy.

Prose minimalism a style that limits unnecessary verbiage, seeking to communicate directly and simply. It's often associated (sometimes inaccurately) with Anglo-Saxon diction.

The wind was cold and the men marched through the fields to the town.

Psychic distance refers to the emotional space between the reader and the narrator, a distance that is carefully controlled by the writer.

Relative pronoun a word that connects a noun or noun phrase to a modifying element—these words are usually "that," "which," "who," and "whom."

The man <u>who</u> knew too much wandered into the town <u>that</u> time forgot.

Run-on sentence the error that ensues when a writer tries to connect two independent clauses without using any connective element such as a comma, semicolon, or conjunction.

It's around here somewhere it can't just have disappeared.

Sentence fragment a word group that is treated as a sentence by the writer—in the sense that she has ended it with a period—but that does not contain the requisite subject-verb combination, or that does not complete a thought. (See also "dependent clause.")

<u>Computers</u>. They drive me nuts. <u>Because I just don't need the hassle.</u>

Simile a metaphorical comparison that uses the words "like" or "as."

Steve is as greedy as a big fat pig.

Simple past tense a past tense construction that consists of a subject and a past participle.

The couch <u>tumbled</u> down the stairs.

Simple present tense a present tense construction that indicates an action that is true in the present. In the first and second person, it is constructed by using a base form of the verb (the one you see in the infinitive) with no auxiliary; in third person singular, an *s* is added to the base form.

I <u>like</u> holidays, but Santa Claus <u>scares</u> me.

Simple sentence a sentence that contains just one subject or group of subjects, and one verb or group of verbs. (See also "compound predicate.")

Joanie and Chachi loved each other.

Stream of consciousness a method of portraying a character's interior that seeks to capture in words the fragmented, chaotic, often incomprehensible nature of thought.

Guitar music playing. Redbone, was it? Too much G chord. Not discordant enough. Discordant. Like corduroy, those scratchy-scratch pants. Only on Sundays, mind. Spring Sundays. Too hot in June. Those soccer matches in June. Ref tweeting, ball thumping. Win it for the old school!

Subjective pronoun a pronoun that acts as the subject in a sentence.

Lily and Graham came in second place. <u>She</u> will never forgive him for losing the passports.

Subordinate clause a clause that contains a subject and verb but that does not complete a thought, usually because it begins with a subordinate conjunction or relative pronoun.

I meant what I said. <u>That you should not touch the stove.</u>

Subordinating conjunction a conjunction that implies the ensuing clause will depend on another one to complete its meaning.

<u>Because</u> you've been bratty, you don't get any cheese.

Subtext literally "below the text," it refers to ideas or concepts that are not explicitly stated by the narrator or characters, but which become clear through careful reading and interpretation.

Suspension of disbelief the concept that a reader of fiction should try not to think about the fact that the people and events portrayed in the work did not actually exist/occur.

Syntax this has a few technical definitions, but it generally refers to the arrangement of grammatical units in a sentence.

Yoda uses some odd syntax when he says, "Agree with you the council does."

Third-person narration a method of narration in which a disembodied voice, rather than a character, tells the story.

Mr. Edwards climbed the stairs, wondering what he might find in the attic.

Thought tag a tag that implies the character is thinking certain words, rather than speaking them.

Wow, <u>the barista thought</u>, I've never seen so much foam.

Verb tense shift one of the deadliest of the stylistic errors, this ensues when a writer shifts from the past tense to the present tense, or vice versa, for no grammatical or aesthetic reason.

Dr. Underwood asked her why she'd come in. Her stomach, she says.

Verisimilitude literally "truth-seeming," it refers to a realistic or mimetic quality in fictional events or characters.

Exercises

The best way to master a subject is not merely to read about it (easy for me to say, after I've just asked you to read about it for 230-plus pages), but also to practice it. So to help you put into use some of the rules and conventions we've examined, I've included the following exercises, which are organized based on the concepts we tried to master—or at least to understand—in the various chapters or groups of chapters.

1. Making Verb Tense Decisions (Chapter 1)

Find a passage from a novel or story that you particularly admire, then rewrite that passage by changing its primary verb tense. You might change a work written in the past tense to the present ("It is the best of times, it is the worst of times . . .") or one written in the present to the past ("A screaming came across the sky . . ."). What is lost by changing the fundamental verb tense? Is anything gained? How is the effect on the reader's experience going to be different?

2. Punctuating and Presenting Dialogue (Chapters 2 and 3)

A. Find a dialogue exchange in a play or screenplay and convert it into fiction using the standard double quotation mark convention. As you do this, you'll have to make decisions about how to translate the stage directions into dialogue tags or supplements. For some clues as to how this works, it can help to look at a play that has been turned into a story by its author, such as Susan Glaspell's "Trifles," which Glaspell rewrote in story form as "A Jury of Her Peers."

B. Write a scene with more than two characters in which no dialogue tags are used. Try to make it clear who is speaking without resorting to forced or unnatural usage of characters' names. Keep it going for as long as you can—it will be a challenge to get past the first page.

3. Representing Non-standard Speech (Chapter 4)

A. One of the real difficulties of portraying accents is that most of us are only personally familiar with one or two of them. When we think about the speech of Cajuns, or nineteenth-century aristocrats, or Gloucester fishermen, we probably rely on the portraits we've seen in film or on television, which are prone to stereotype. Therefore, the best way to try out representations of accents is to listen to the ones you hear every day. No matter where you live, the people around you will likely have some eccentricity of speech that is particular to your area. Begin to analyze the speech of people you know in terms of its sound, grammar, syntax, volume, tone—take notes if you have to (this may confuse your friends, but we must suffer for our art). Then, write a lengthy dialogue that seeks to capture, with any of the three styles mentioned in chapter 4, how the people of your region speak.

B. Choose a method of speaking that does not have to do with accent, but instead with some other condition or situation that changes a person's voice—in chapter 4, I discussed speech impediments and drunkenness, but there are many other things that affect how we speak (age, social class, emotional state, etc.). Write a dialogue that does not overtly refer to this condition/situation, but that makes it clear one of the participants speaks in a non-standard way. Try to represent this manner of speaking without using stereotype or exaggeration.

4. Dealing with the Past Perfect Tense (Chapter 6)

Begin writing a scene that uses the simple past as its primary verb tense, then transition into a flashback (the flashback part should be fairly lengthy). You should use the past perfect tense for transitioning purposes, but at some point in the flashback, abandon the past perfect and narrate the rest of it using the simple past tense. The goal is to stop using "had" and "had been" at some point, but to not do it so early in the scene that the reader will be distracted or confused. Use the example from John Casey's *Spartina* as a model (p. 67).

5. Mastering Pronouns (Chapter 7)

A. In the following sentences, fill in the blank with "who" or "whom" or "whoever" or "whomever." Try not to just go by your ear and instinct—be able to explain your reasoning.

Do you know _____ the letter is addressed to?

_____ invented Easy Cheese is a genius in my book.

The best candidate for the job will be the one _____ manages not to offend Edna.

To _____ should I address my complaint?

_____ is going to tell Scotty about his Jeep?

B. In the following paragraph, fill in the blanks with the relative pronoun "that," "who," or "which." As with the previous exercise, don't just go by your ear or instinct—be able to explain why you've selected the particular relative pronoun.

The road _____ goes into Pittsdale, a town _____ has seen better days, is rough and bumpy. The town's mayor, _____ used to play fullback on the team _____ won the state championship, has promised to repave it someday. Pittsdale, _____ once called itself the aluminum capital of the region, has seen its mines depleted in recent decades, and the factory _____ once employed half of town has moved to Cedar Grove, _____ has no local tax, and _____ is closer to the turnpike.

6. Manipulating Diction (Chapter 10)

A. Rewrite the following passage from Walter Scott's *Ivanhoe* by turning as much of it as you can into Anglo-Saxon diction. That is, try to replace the longer, more Latinate words with shorter, more guttural-sounding ones. Does doing this have any real effect on how a reader might interpret the scene, or is it pretty much the same as the previous version? Does the "translated" version come off as ridiculous, or is it the kind of thing one might actually write?

Notwithstanding the occasional exhortation and chiding of his companion, the noise of the horsemen's feet continuing to approach,

Wamba could not be prevented from lingering occasionally on the road, upon every pretence which occurred . . . The horsemen, therefore, soon overtook them on the road. Their numbers amounted to ten men, of whom the two who rode foremost seemed to be persons of considerable importance, and the others their attendants. It was not difficult to ascertain the condition and character of one of these personages.

B. Now, rewrite the following passage from Raymond Carver's "Cathedral" by turning as much of it as you can into Latinate diction. Respond to the same questions from above.

That summer in Seattle she had needed a job. She didn't have any money. The man she was going to marry at the end of the summer was in officers' training school. He didn't have any money, either. But she was in love with the guy, and he was in love with her, etc. She'd seen something in the paper: HELP WANTED—Reading to Blind Man, and a telephone number. She phoned and went over, was hired on the spot. She worked with this blind man all summer. She read stuff to him, case studies, reports, that sort of thing. She helped him organize his little office in the county social-service department. They'd become good friends, my wife and the blind man.

7. Controlling Fragments (Chapter 11)

A. Imitate Charles Dickens (p. 127) by writing the first paragraph of a novel without using any complete sentences. The goal is to mix up the types of fragments and incomplete sentences you use, so that the reader doesn't necessarily notice you're doing it.

B. Have a conversation with someone in which you make a concerted effort not to use any complete sentences—everything should be a fragment (as in, "Yep." "You kidding?" "Because I said so." "For real?" and so on). Did the person notice? What was the effect on what you were talking about, or how you came across as a conversant?

8. Dealing with Commas and Semicolons (Chapter 12)

A. Use semicolons to act as "comma police"—that is, to keep order when many different types of commas are used—in the following long sentence. What organizing principle will you use in determining where the semicolons go?

> When I crashed my car into a lamppost, I discovered certain unpleasant truths about several people in my life, namely my insurance representative, who had woefully misrepresented her company's policy to me, back when I was signing up for the plan, my mother, who was apparently too busy with her bridge game to come pick me up, or indeed to even ask if I was okay, and my new girlfriend, who was similarly unwilling to rescue me, although she did ask if I'd broken anything.

B. Write a passage of your own that includes the following: at least two sentences that use comma splices for artistic purposes; one sentence that is technically a run-on but which, again, works for aesthetic reasons; and at least three grammatically necessary semicolons.

9. Handling the Nuances of Dashes, Parentheses, and Nonrestrictive Commas (Chapter 13)

Below you'll see part of the excerpt from Philip Roth's *Portnoy's Complaint* that we discussed in regard to its use of dashes, parentheses, and nonrestrictive commas. In this version, I've replaced many of these punctuation marks with blanks. It's your job to fill in which mark you think belongs in each blank. Don't just choose arbitrarily—think about what effect the writer might be going for, and which of the three markers is more likely to achieve that effect. It goes without saying that you shouldn't flip back to see which ones Roth actually used.

> Or just standing nice and calm____nothing trembling, everything serene____standing there in the sunshine____as though in the middle of an empty field, or passing the time on the street corner____standing without a care in the world in the sunshine, like my king of kings____ the Lord my God____The Duke Himself____Snider, Doctor, the name may come up again____standing there as loose and as easy, as happy as I will ever be, just waiting by myself under a high fly ball____ *a towering fly ball*, I heard Red Barber say, as he watches from behind his microphone____*hit out toward Portnoy; Alex under it, under it*____just waiting there for the ball to fall into the glove I raise to it, and yup, there it is____*plock*____the third out of the inning____*and Alex gathers it in for*

*out number three, and folks, here's old C.D. for P. Lorillard and Company*____and
in one motion____while old Connie brings us a message from Old
Golds____I start in toward the bench . . .

10. Avoiding the Dreaded Verb Tense Shift (Chapter 15)

This one may not be all that fun, but arbitrary verb tense shifting is a
serious problem that requires serious solutions—no time for games. Here's
what you should do: take a few pages from something you've written that
you think has some verb tense shifts. With the aid of a technical grammar guide like *Allyn and Bacon*, or a website like Purdue's online writing
lab (http://owl.english.purdue.edu/owl/), underline every single verb and
identify that verb's tense in the margin. Get as specific as you can—show
whether it's the simple past tense, the past perfect tense, the progressive
present tense, etc. When you've finished, determine whether the use of
shifts has been consistent or arbitrary.

11. Practicing Commas (Chapter 16)

A. Begin reading a novel or story that uses long, complex sentence structures—something by Faulkner or Henry James is a good candidate. As you
read, identify the function/purpose of each comma—that is, figure out
which ones are meant to set off an introductory clause, which ones connect independent clauses, et cetera. Keep going until you've found at least
one comma that represents each of the four different functions discussed
in chapter 16.

B. In the style of Tim O'Brien (p. 189), write a paragraph that includes
several lists. Use various comma techniques to avoid making the lists sound
repetitive or monotonous.

C. In the style of Jean Toomer (p. 193), write a sentence that uses a long
introductory element but does not include a comma after the element. The
goal is to make the introductory part as long as you can without making
the lack of a comma seem strange or confusing.

12. Watching Out for Betrayals of Language (Chapter 17)

A. Chapter 17 just scratches the surface in terms of explaining ways in which the English language can upset your plans. Think of your own betrayals of language (or jot them down as you experience them), and try to come up with techniques for avoiding or repairing them.

B. Write a paragraph that uses repetition in some form to pleasing effect. You might use rhyme, or assonance, or alliteration, or any other technique; the goal is to make the repetition aesthetically pleasing. When you've finished, write a paragraph that intentionally uses awkward or disharmonious repetition. What is the difference between the two paragraphs—why does one of them work and one of them fail, even though they're using the same rhetorical device?

13. Controlling Cliché (Chapter 18)

A. Write a paragraph that uses at least five clichés with elegance and fluidity—the reader shouldn't even notice that you're using overly familiar language, let alone become annoyed or distracted by the clichés. As we saw in the Ann Patchett example (p. 214), this can be done. The trick is using less colorful or metaphorical clichés.

B. Choose several different types of prose or poetry—the lyrics of a pop song, a poem in the *New Yorker*, a passage from a romance novel, the lead paragraph from a *People* magazine article, etc. Then, go through and calculate the formulaic density (p. 210) of each one. You don't have to be too precise, just get a general sense of the proportions between original and formulaic phrasing. What did you notice? Why might some of the works use a higher formulaic density than others? What does it say about the audience and purpose of the works?

Index

exclamation marks and italics, 159, 163–64, 167

dialogue, representation of: general types of dialogue portrayal, 37; mixture of various methods, 44–46; phonetic portrait of accent, 38–42; portrait of speech impediments and verbal tics, 42–44; use of dialogue supplements, 38

dialogue tags, 49, 50; avoidance of, 30–33; general ideas about, 25–26; repetition and, 205; supplements instead of, 33–36; verb usage in, 26–30

Diaz, Junot, 119

Dickens, Charles, 7, 30, 42, 127–28, 217

Dickinson, Emily, 146

diction, 20, 45, 54, 56, 93, 181, 198, 204, 219

diction, Anglo-Saxon, 115, 203; contemporary preference for, 111–13; definition and background of, 108–11 ; general nature of, 116–18; lyricism and, 113–14; moderate use of, 119

diction, Latinate, 201, 203; definition and background of, 108–11; general nature of, 114–18; and lyricism, 112–14; moderate use of, 119

Donoghue, Emma, 181

Dos Passos, John, 201

Doyle, Roddy, 22, 40

Ecclesiastes (quoted by George Orwell), 117

Elkin, Stanley, 50, 54

Eliot, George, 84, 142–43, 194–95

Eliot, T. S., 47

Ellison, Ralph, 106

exclamation points, 28, 53, 130; emphatic nature of, 156–57; general problems with, 158; nineteenth-century writers and, 159–60; postmodernist writers and, 160–63; used in characters' speech, 159; used to punctuate dialogue, 15, 18

Exley, Frederick, 163–64

Faulkner, William, 8–9, 12, 50–51, 52, 56–57, 112, 131, 182

Fitzgerald, F. Scott, vii–viii, 44, 158, 161

Flaubert, Gustav, 160

Ford, Richard, 7, 66

Franzen, Jonathan, 114–17

Fraser, George MacDonald, 211–12

Frost, Robert, 202

Gaddis, William, 30–31, 59, 141

Gardner, John, 131–32, 173, 174

gerunds, 45, 98, 176

Glaspell, Susan, 32–33

Gordimer, Nadine, 23

Graves, Robert, 206

Grisham, John, 78–81

Hannah, Barry, 5, 45–46

Hansen, Ron, 147, 152

Harding, Paul, 74

Hardy, Thomas, 81, 206

Harrison, Colin, 126

Haslett, Adam, 92

Hazzard, Shirley, 144

Heaney, Seamus, 156–57

Helprin, Mark, 215

Hemingway, Ernest, vii–ix, 19, 31–32, 52–53, 92–93, 112–13, 188, 190–92, 196

Henry, O., 115

Hurston, Zora Neale, 39–40, 44

idioms. See clichés

independent clauses, 35, 82, 194; and commas, 185, 187; and comma splices, 136–39; and modifying participial phrases, 100, 102–3; and run-ons, 139–40; and semicolons, 141, 143; and sentence fragments, 124–25

Irving, John, 157

Ishiguro, Kazuo, 74, 77, 84

italics, 43, 130, 149, 151, 161, 162, 215; for emphasis, 163–64; general nature of, 156–57; other functions of, 164–67; used in dialogue, 23–24; used to indicate thought, 50–51, 52, 54, 56

James, Henry, 55, 57, 92

Jewett, Sarah Orne, 114, 159

Johnson, Denis, 206

Jones, Edward P., 45

Joyce, James, 22, 53–54, 57, 80, 95, 140–41, 178

Kesey, Ken, 164

King, Stephen, 77, 87–88, 89, 96, 205–6

Krauss, Nicole, 23–24

Lahiri, Jhumpa, 5–6, 10

Latinate. See diction, Latinate

Lawrence, T. E., 145

Leonard, Elmore, 27, 29–30, 87, 89, 160

Lethem, Jonathan, 43

Lipsyte, Sam, 97

Lodge, David, 31

Mansfield, Katherine, 55
Mantel, Hilary, 7, 176
McCarthy, Cormac, 20–22, 159, 190
McMurtry, Larry, 197, 201
Melville, Herman, 9, 42, 153, 159
Messud, Claire, 75
Mitchell, David, 179–80, 183
modifiers, 25, 34, 111, 116–17, 126, 128,
    181, 196; coordinate and non-coordinate,
    190–92; definition and functions,
    85–86; introductory elements as, 192–93;
    misplaced, 102, 104. *See also* adverbs;
    participial phrases
Momaday, N. Scott, 202
Morrison, Toni, xi, 123–24, 217
Mukherjee, Bharati, 5–6, 9, 10
Munro, Alice, 18, 138, 180
Murray, Bill, 125

Nabokov, Vladimir, 9, 150, 152–53, 201
Nelson, Antonya, 84
Nietzsche, Friedrich, 217

Oates, Joyce Carol, 17–18
O'Brien, Tim, 189–90
O'Connor, Flannery, 150
Odyssey, The, 210
O'Neill, Joseph, 97
Ong, Walter, ix
Orwell, George, 117–18

paragraph fragments, 131–34
parentheses, 146, 152, 153, 156; cautionary
    note concerning, 154–55; general nature of,
    148–50; specific effect of, 150–51
participial phrases, 85, 193, 199; definition
    and function of, 98–99; illogical modifying,
    99–101; misplaced, 101–4; repetition of,
    104–6
past perfect, x, 3; definition and function of,
    63–66; methods for limiting use of, 66–68;
    and problems of excessive flashbacks,
    69–71; used to affect tone, 68
past perfect progressive, 3, 69; definition and
    function of, 64–65; methods for limiting
    use of, 66; and problems of excessive
    flashbacks, 70; used to affect tone, 68
past tense: illogical use of, 9, 11; in relation
    to past perfect, 63, 65–67, 69; as primary
    tense, 3–5; rhythm of, 13; and verb tense
    shifting, 175–76, 177–79, 180, 183
Patchett, Ann, 213–15
Patterson, James, 132

Poe, Edgar Allan, 164
present progressive, 7
present tense, 3, 24; in relation to past perfect,
    65–66, 69; reasons to use as primary tense,
    5–13; used in stories and anecdotes, 5; and
    verb tense shifting, 171, 174–81, 183
pronouns, 21, 102, 117, 129; demonstrative, ix,
    79, 123; interrogative, 72, 83–84; relative,
    72, 79–84, 144; simple, 72, 83; singular
    non-gendered third person personal, 73–78
Proulx, Annie, 54
Pynchon, Thomas, 13

Reed, Ishmael, 13
Robinson, Marilynne, 114, 197, 210
Roth, Philip, 148–49, 151, 182–83
run-on sentences, 17, 136; aesthetic uses of,
    140–41; definition of, 139; misidentification
    of, 187

Sanderlin, George, 172
Saunders, George, 192
Seferis, Giorgos, xi
semicolons, 136–40, 175; conceptual nature
    of, 143–44; formal nature of, 144–45; used
    to avoid confusion in complex lists, 142–43,
    192; used to join related independent
    clauses, 141–42
sentence fragments, 16, 67; dangers of,
    129–30; definition of, 124; used to imitate
    a journal or log, 129–30; various effects of,
    125–28
Shakespeare, William, 91–92
Shaw, George Bernard, 145
Shields, Carol, 167
Simpson, Mona, 187
Sir Gawain and the Green Knight, 172–73
Song of Roland, 109
Spencer, Scott, 65–66
Stegner, Wallace, 76
Stein, Gertrude, 57
Stockett, Kathryn, 41–42
Strout, Elizabeth, 15–16
Stowe, Harriet Beecher, 95–96, 160
Strunk and White, 87, 92, 96, 111, 117, 137–39,
    206

Terence, 97
Thackeray, William Makepeace, 4
Toomer, Jean, 193
Tremain, Rose, 132–33
Truss, Lynn, 142
Twain, Mark, 166